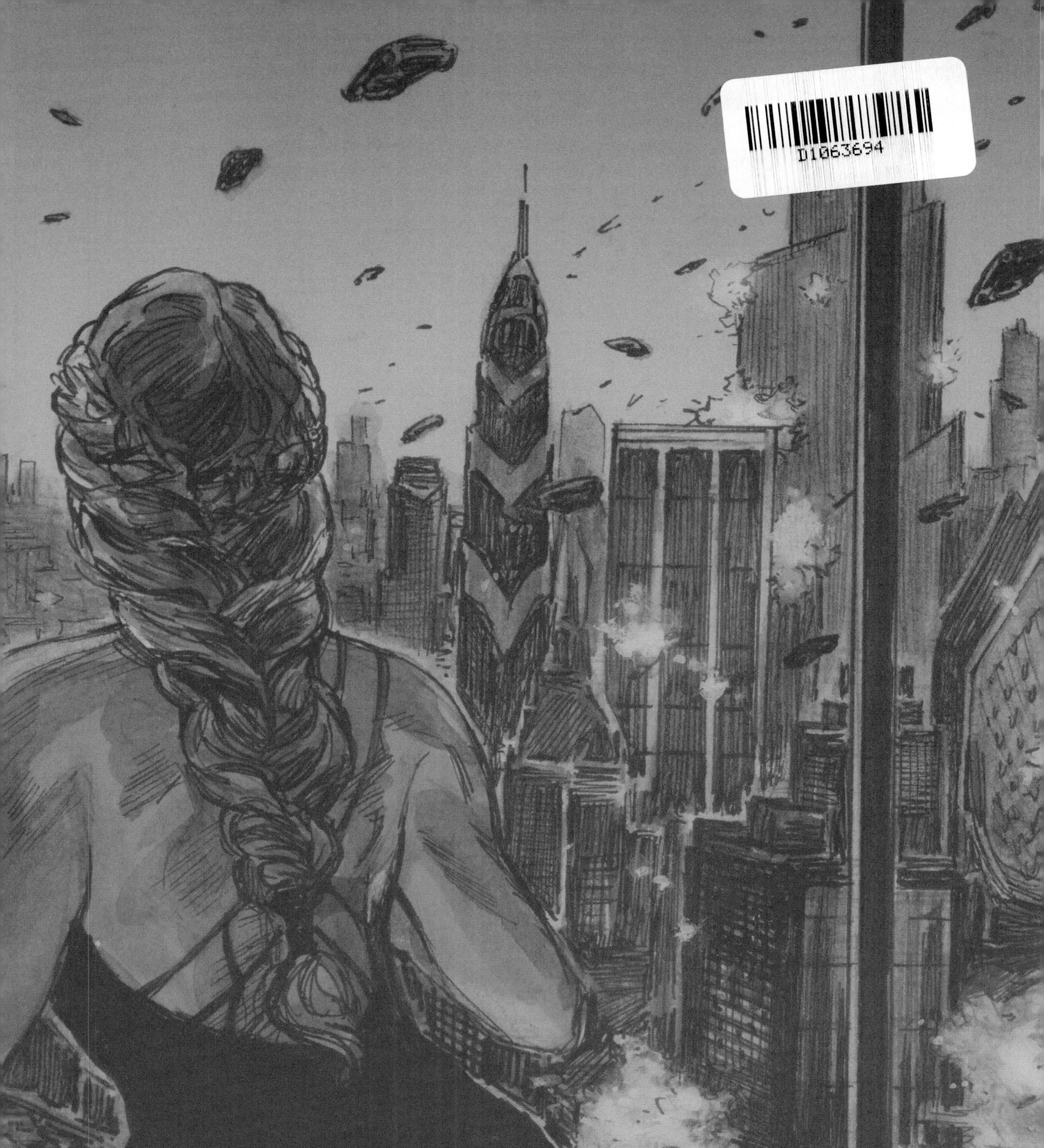

ASHES ASHES

MAGNETIC™

JD MORVAN
AUTHOR

REY MACUTAY
ARTIST

WALTER
COLORS

BASED ON THE NOVEL "RAVAGE" BY **RENÉ BARJAVEL**

Translation by Jeremy Melloul
Localization and Editing by Mike Kennedy
Layout and Lettering by Chris Northrop

MAGNETIC™

ISBN: 978-1-951719-12-8
Library of Congress Control Number: 2021909391

Ashes, Ashes by Morvan, Macutay, and Walter, Published 2021 by Magnetic Press, LLC.

Printed in China.

10 9 8 7 6 5 4 3 2 1

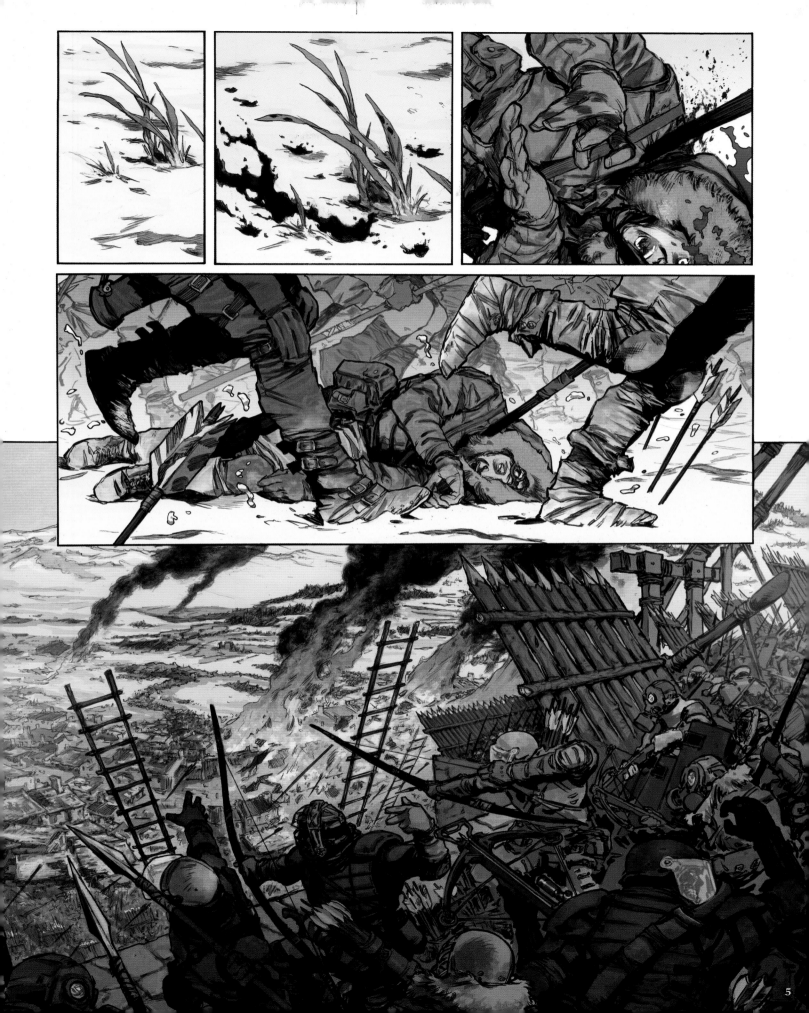

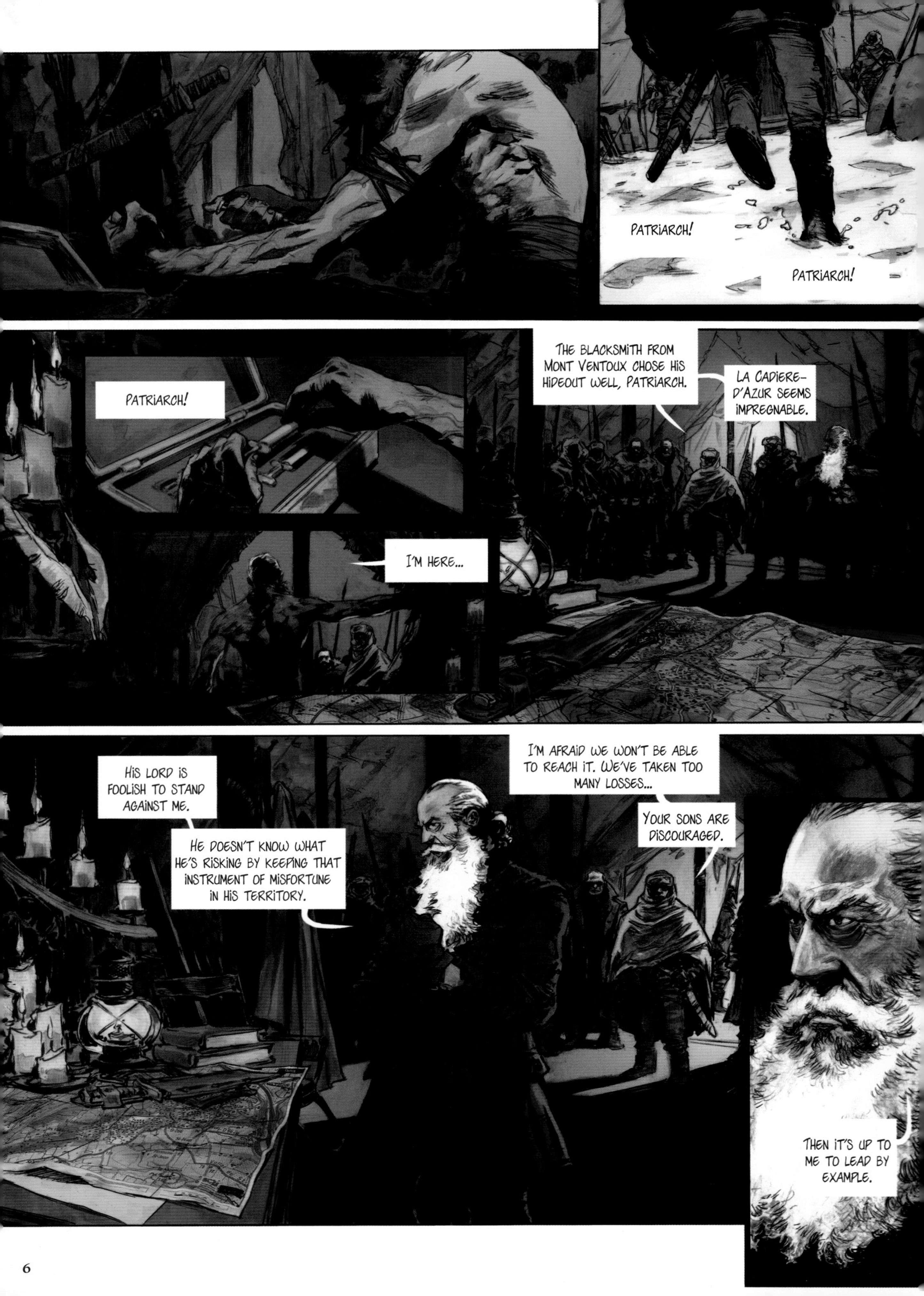
PATRIARCH!
PATRIARCH!
PATRIARCH!
THE BLACKSMITH FROM MONT VENTOUX CHOSE HIS HIDEOUT WELL, PATRIARCH.
LA CADIERE-D'AZUR SEEMS IMPREGNABLE.
I'M HERE...
HIS LORD IS FOOLISH TO STAND AGAINST ME.
HE DOESN'T KNOW WHAT HE'S RISKING BY KEEPING THAT INSTRUMENT OF MISFORTUNE IN HIS TERRITORY.
I'M AFRAID WE WON'T BE ABLE TO REACH IT. WE'VE TAKEN TOO MANY LOSSES...
YOUR SONS ARE DISCOURAGED.
THEN IT'S UP TO ME TO LEAD BY EXAMPLE.

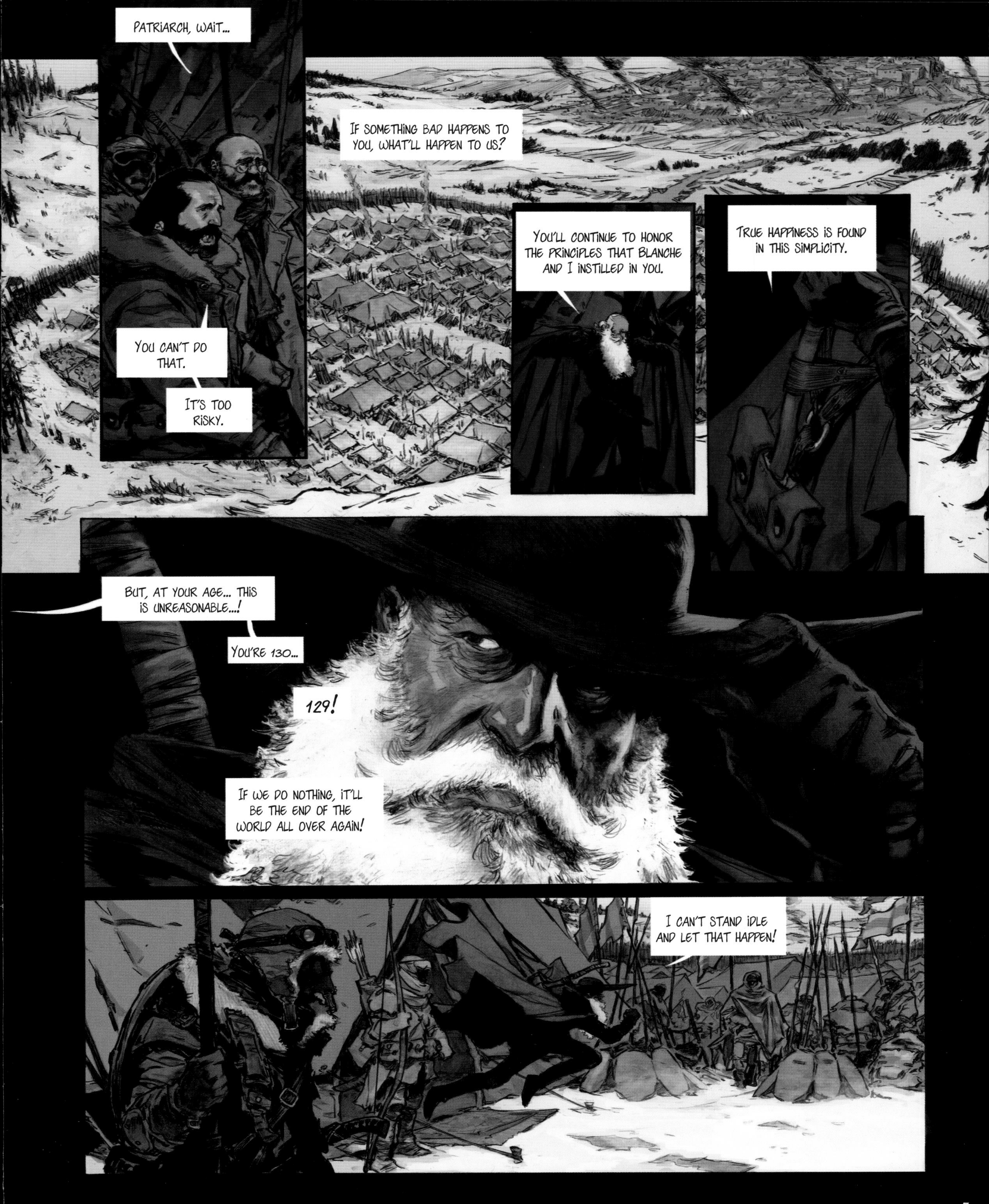
PATRIARCH, WAIT...
IF SOMETHING BAD HAPPENS TO YOU, WHAT'LL HAPPEN TO US?
YOU CAN'T DO THAT.
IT'S TOO RISKY.
YOU'LL CONTINUE TO HONOR THE PRINCIPLES THAT BLANCHE AND I INSTILLED IN YOU.
TRUE HAPPINESS IS FOUND IN THIS SIMPLICITY.
BUT, AT YOUR AGE... THIS IS UNREASONABLE...!
YOU'RE 130...
129!
IF WE DO NOTHING, IT'LL BE THE END OF THE WORLD ALL OVER AGAIN!
I CAN'T STAND IDLE AND LET THAT HAPPEN!

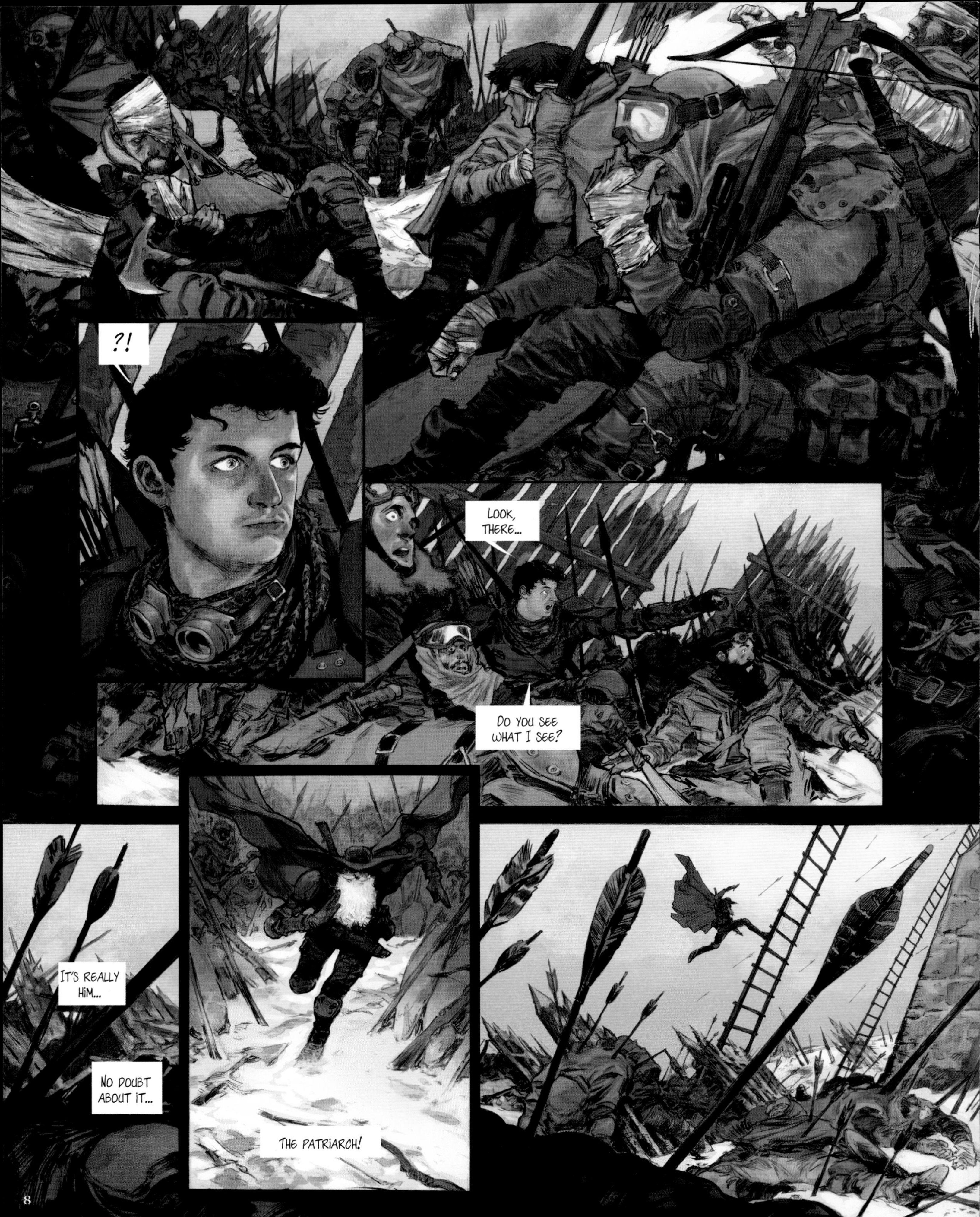
?!
LOOK, THERE...
DO YOU SEE WHAT I SEE?
IT'S REALLY HIM...
NO DOUBT ABOUT IT...
THE PATRIARCH!

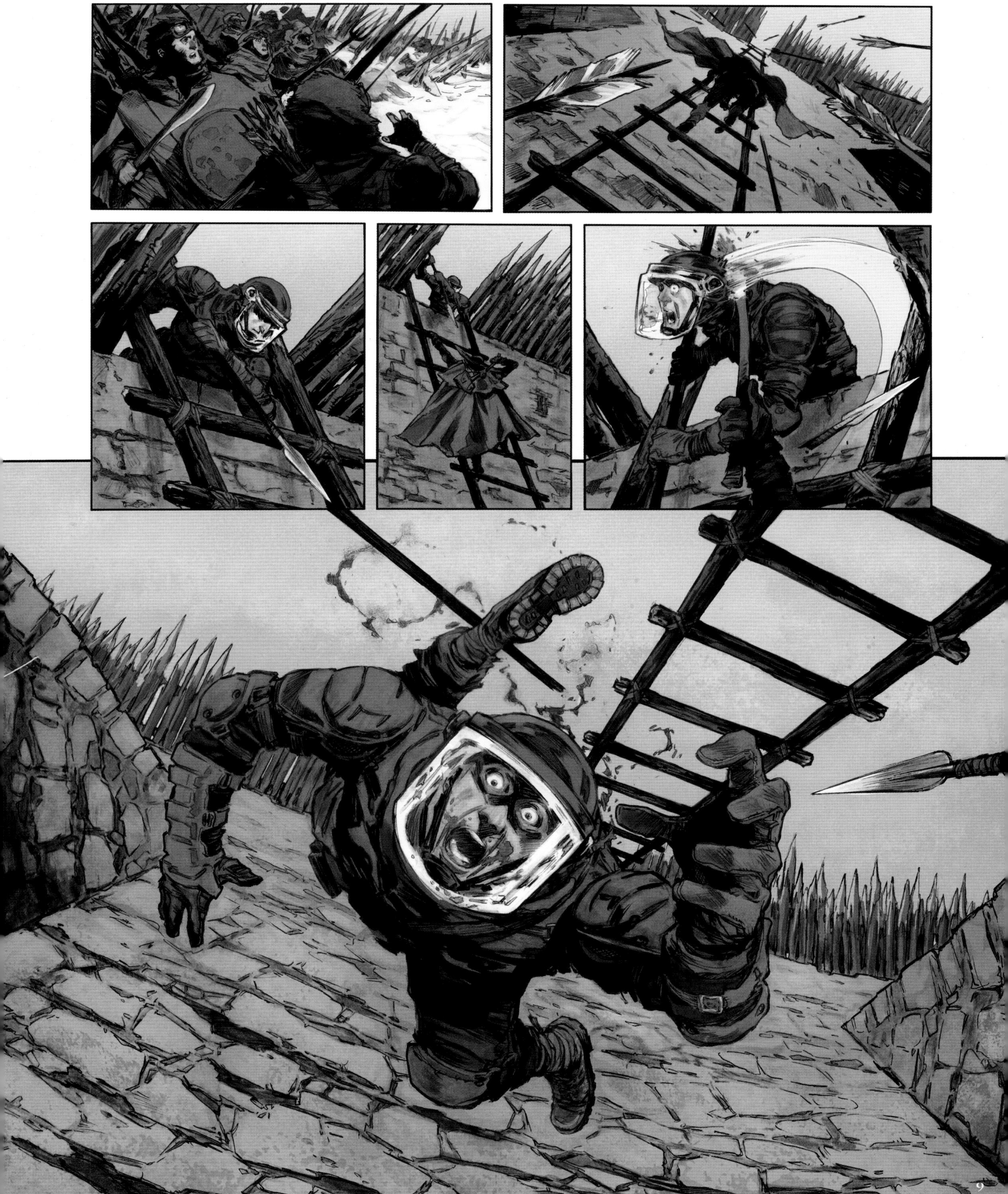

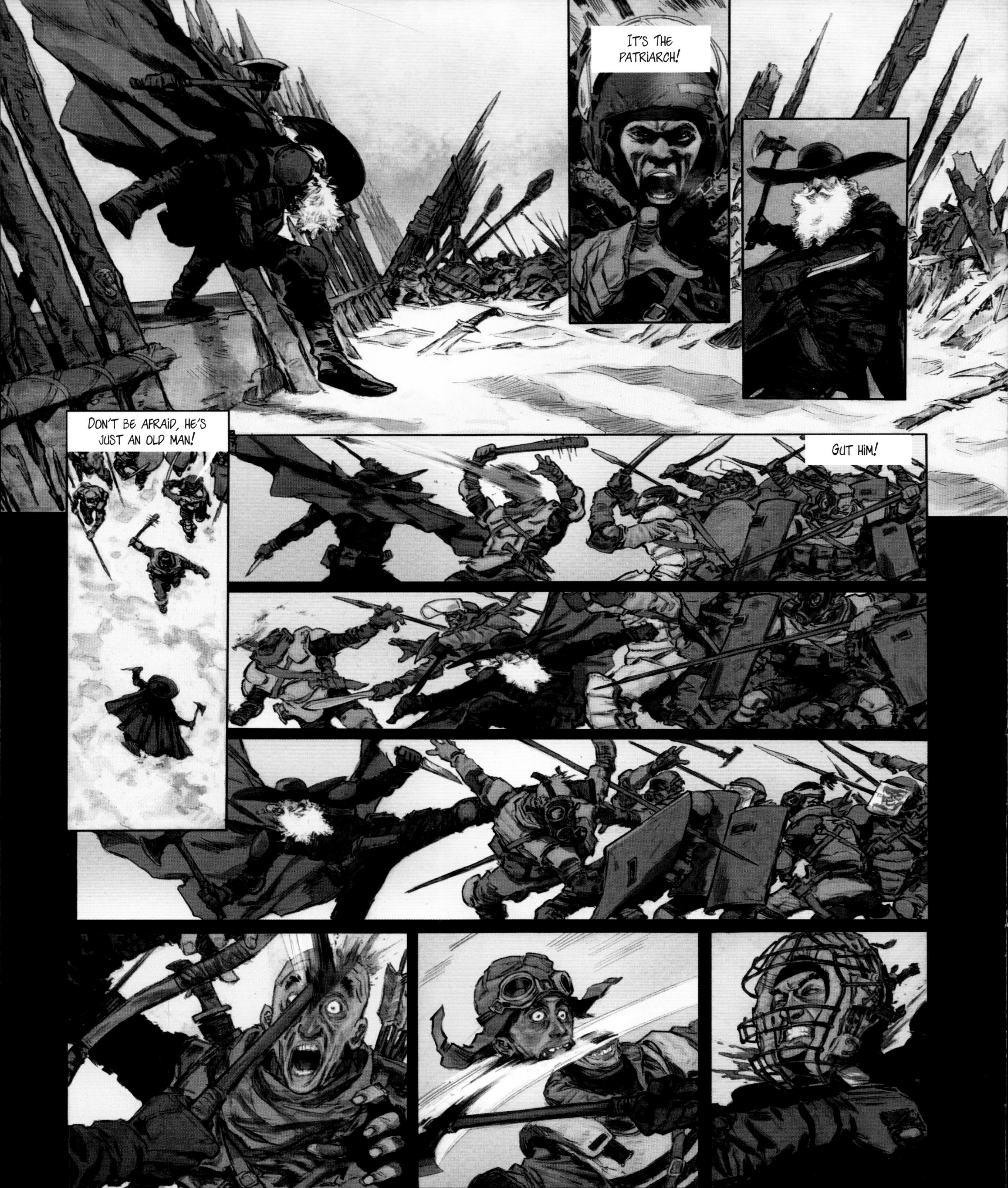

IT'S THE PATRIARCH!
DON'T BE AFRAID, HE'S JUST AN OLD MAN!
GUT HIM!

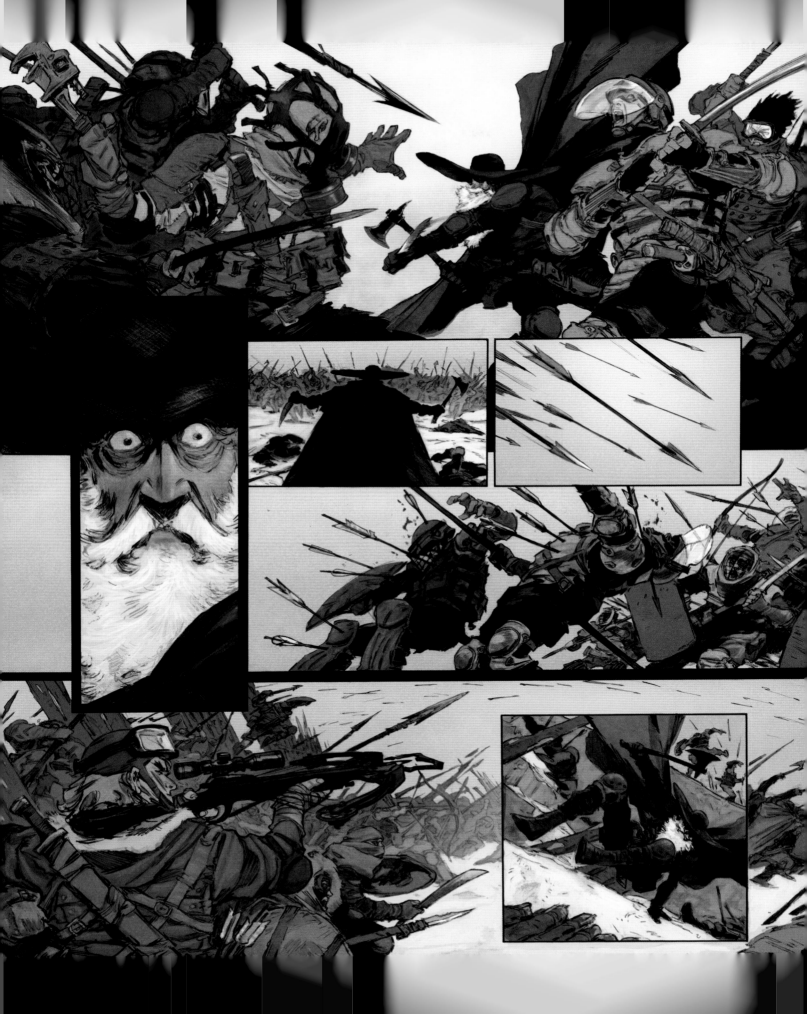

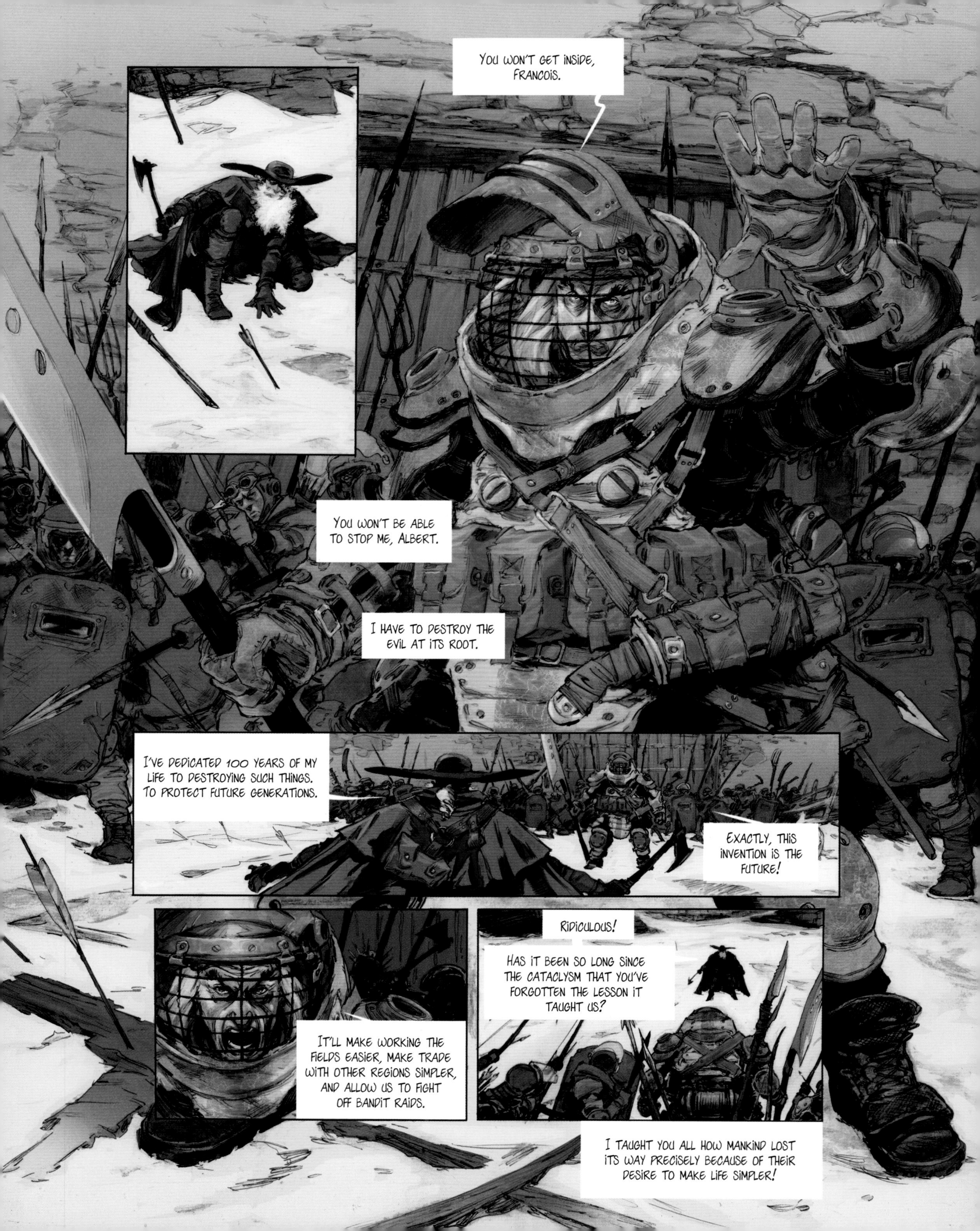
You won't get inside, Francois.
You won't be able to stop me, Albert.
I have to destroy the evil at its root.
I've dedicated 100 years of my life to destroying such things. To protect future generations.
Exactly, this invention is the future!
It'll make working the fields easier, make trade with other regions simpler, and allow us to fight off bandit raids.
Ridiculous!
Has it been so long since the cataclysm that you've forgotten the lesson it taught us?
I taught you all how mankind lost its way precisely because of their desire to make life simpler!

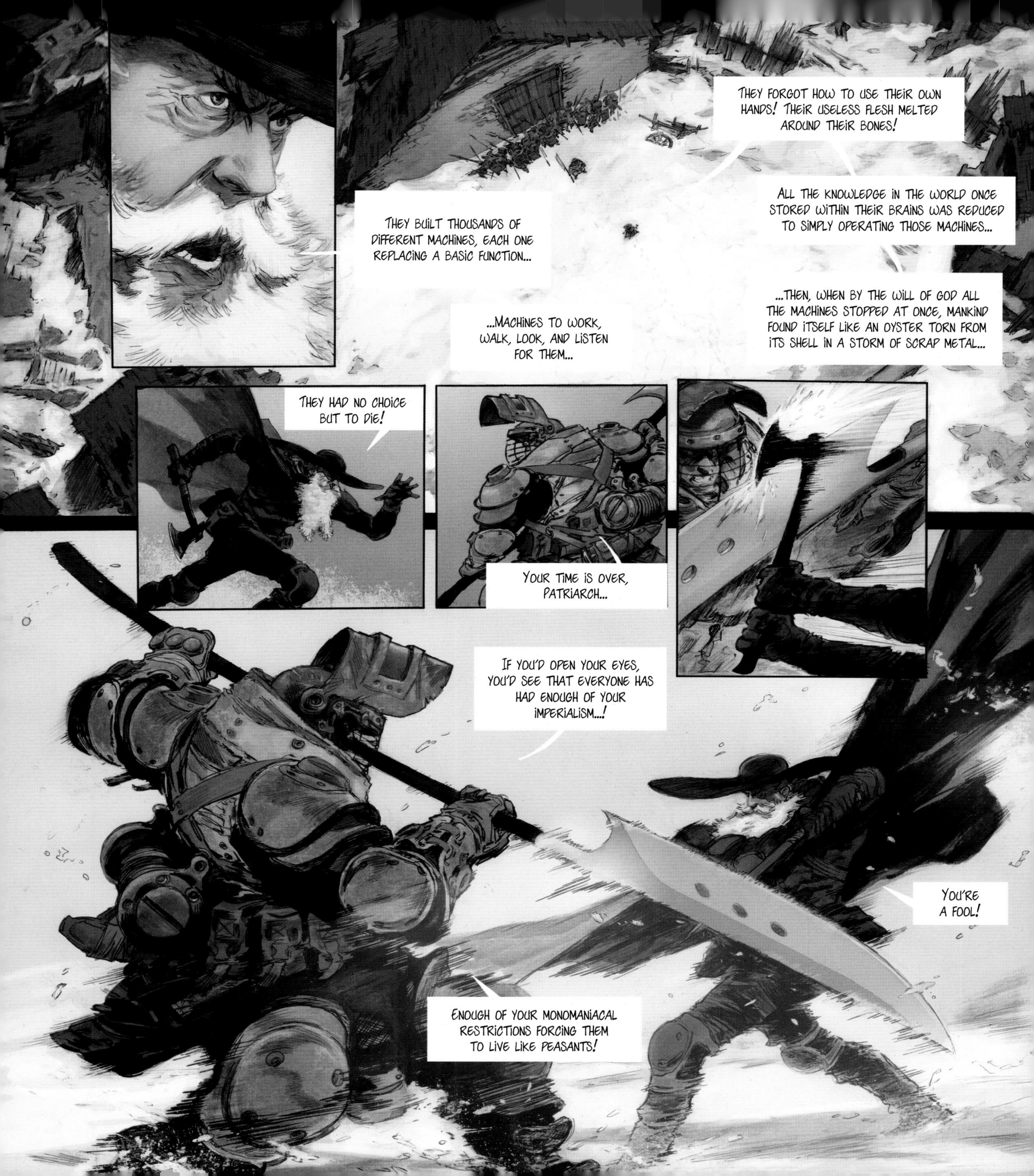

THEY BUILT THOUSANDS OF DIFFERENT MACHINES, EACH ONE REPLACING A BASIC FUNCTION...
...MACHINES TO WORK, WALK, LOOK, AND LISTEN FOR THEM...
THEY FORGOT HOW TO USE THEIR OWN HANDS! THEIR USELESS FLESH MELTED AROUND THEIR BONES!
ALL THE KNOWLEDGE IN THE WORLD ONCE STORED WITHIN THEIR BRAINS WAS REDUCED TO SIMPLY OPERATING THOSE MACHINES...
...THEN, WHEN BY THE WILL OF GOD ALL THE MACHINES STOPPED AT ONCE, MANKIND FOUND ITSELF LIKE AN OYSTER TORN FROM ITS SHELL IN A STORM OF SCRAP METAL...
THEY HAD NO CHOICE BUT TO DIE!
YOUR TIME IS OVER, PATRIARCH...
IF YOU'D OPEN YOUR EYES, YOU'D SEE THAT EVERYONE HAS HAD ENOUGH OF YOUR IMPERIALISM...!
YOU'RE A FOOL!
ENOUGH OF YOUR MONOMANIACAL RESTRICTIONS FORCING THEM TO LIVE LIKE PEASANTS!

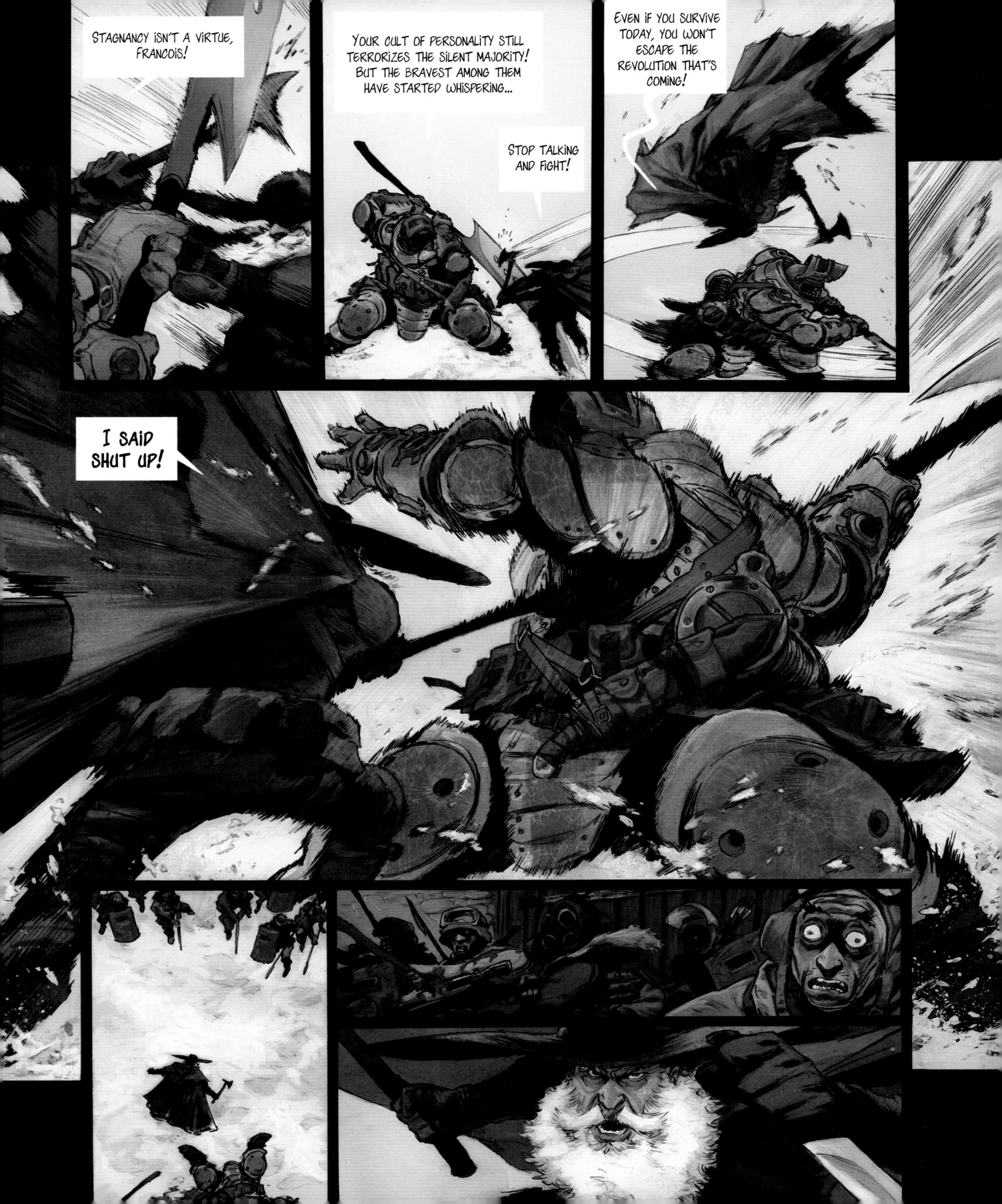
STAGNANCY ISN'T A VIRTUE, FRANCOIS!
YOUR CULT OF PERSONALITY STILL TERRORIZES THE SILENT MAJORITY! BUT THE BRAVEST AMONG THEM HAVE STARTED WHISPERING...
STOP TALKING AND FIGHT!
EVEN IF YOU SURVIVE TODAY, YOU WON'T ESCAPE THE REVOLUTION THAT'S COMING!
I SAID SHUT UP!

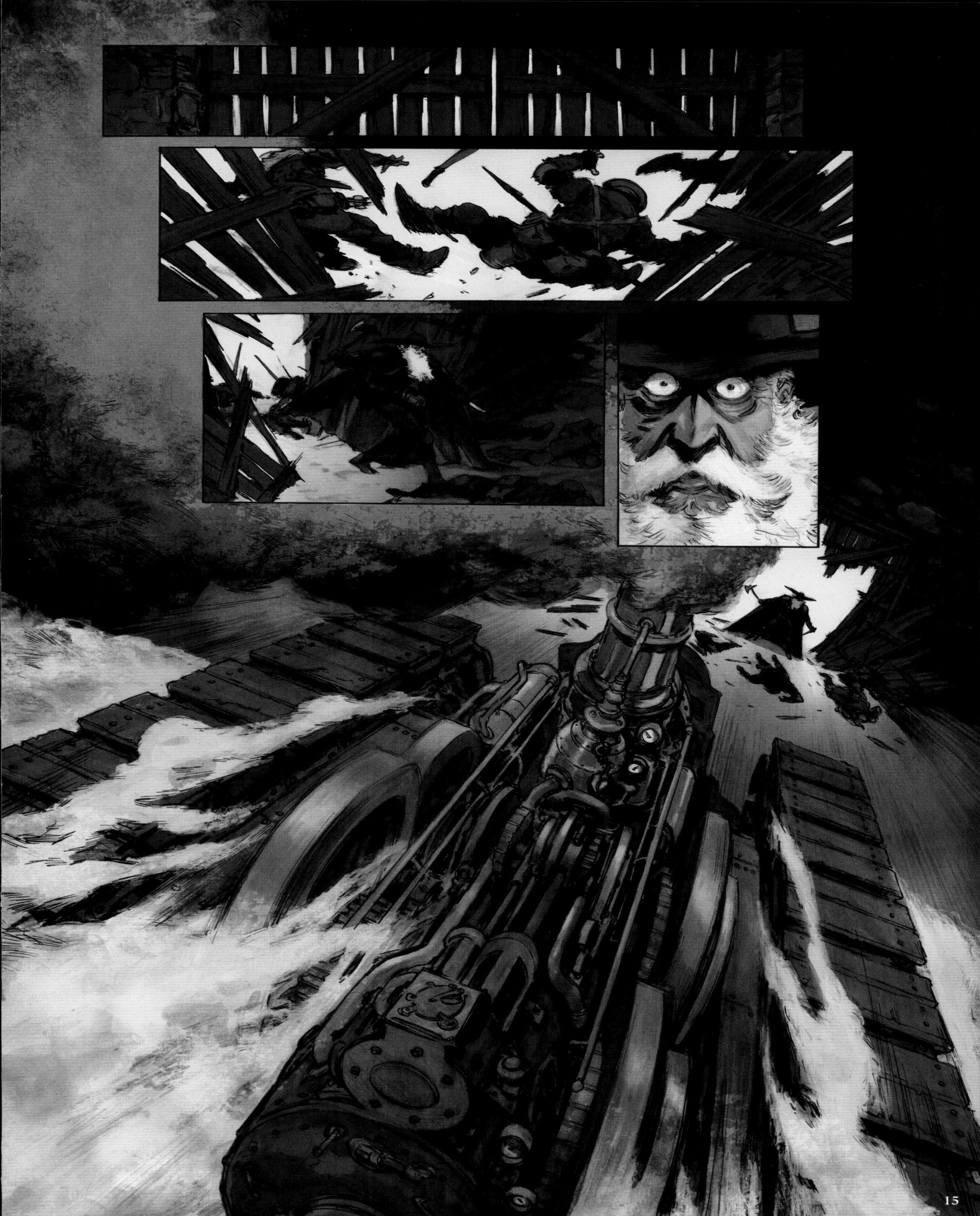

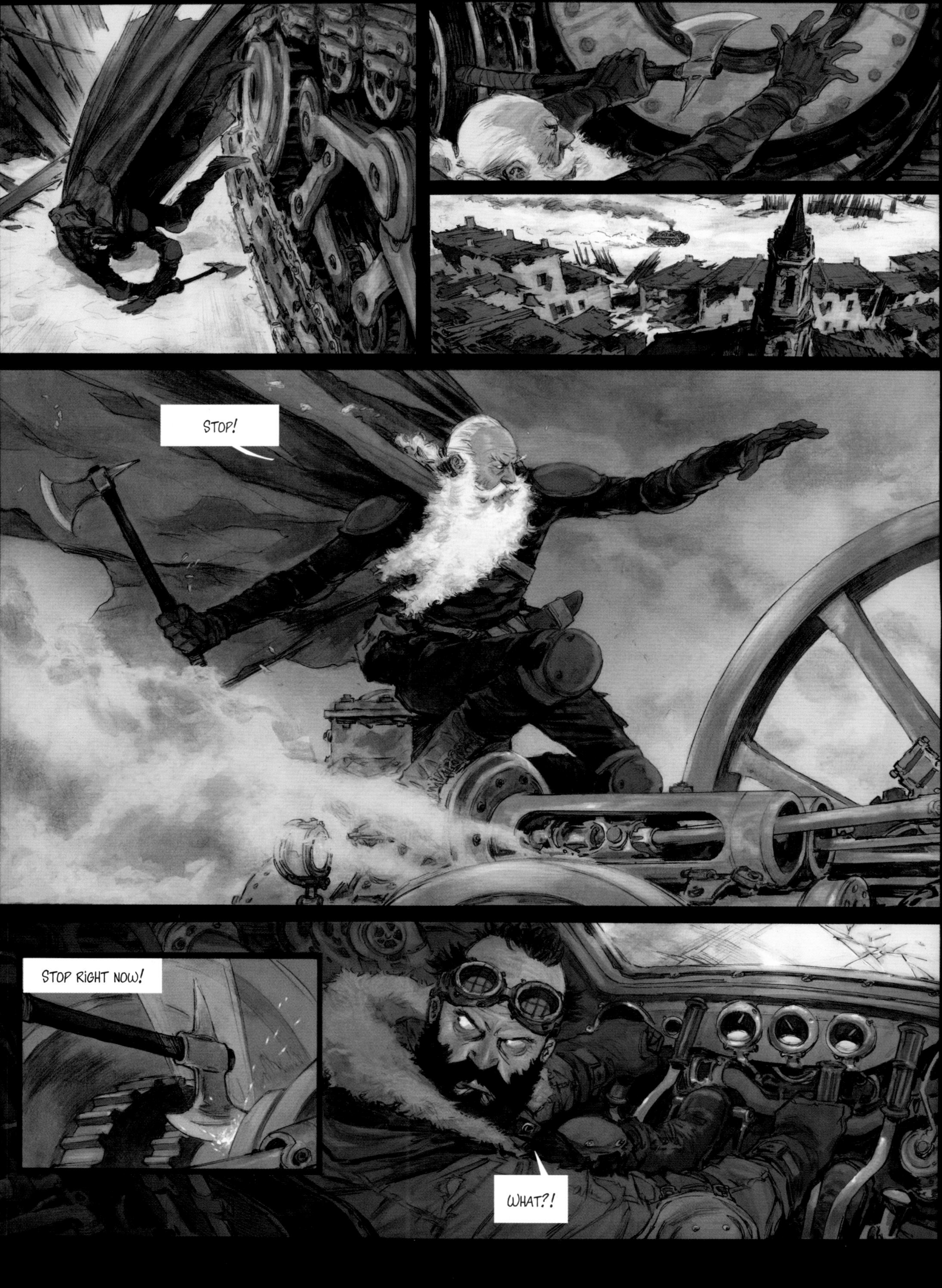
STOP!
STOP RIGHT NOW!
WHAT?!

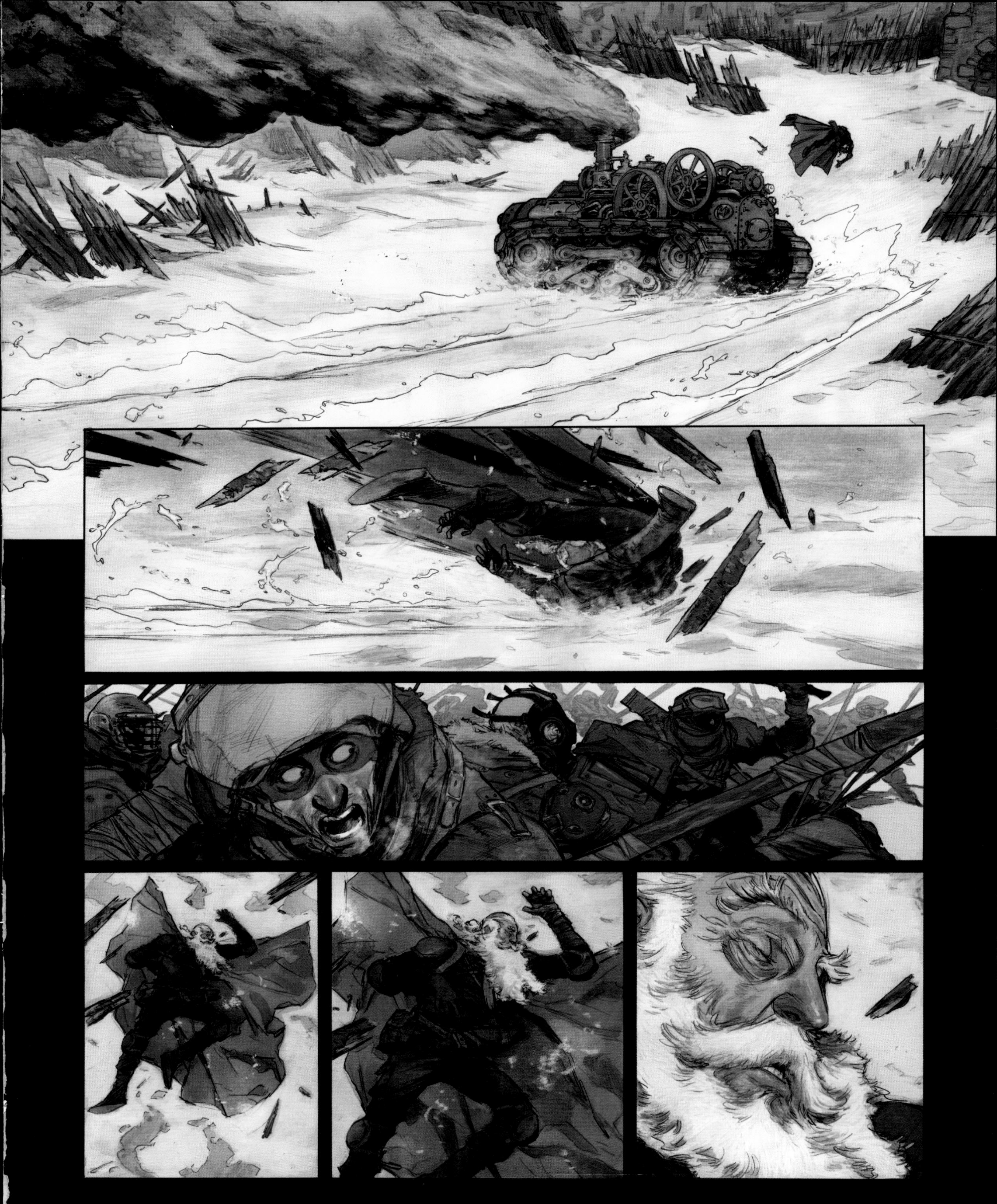

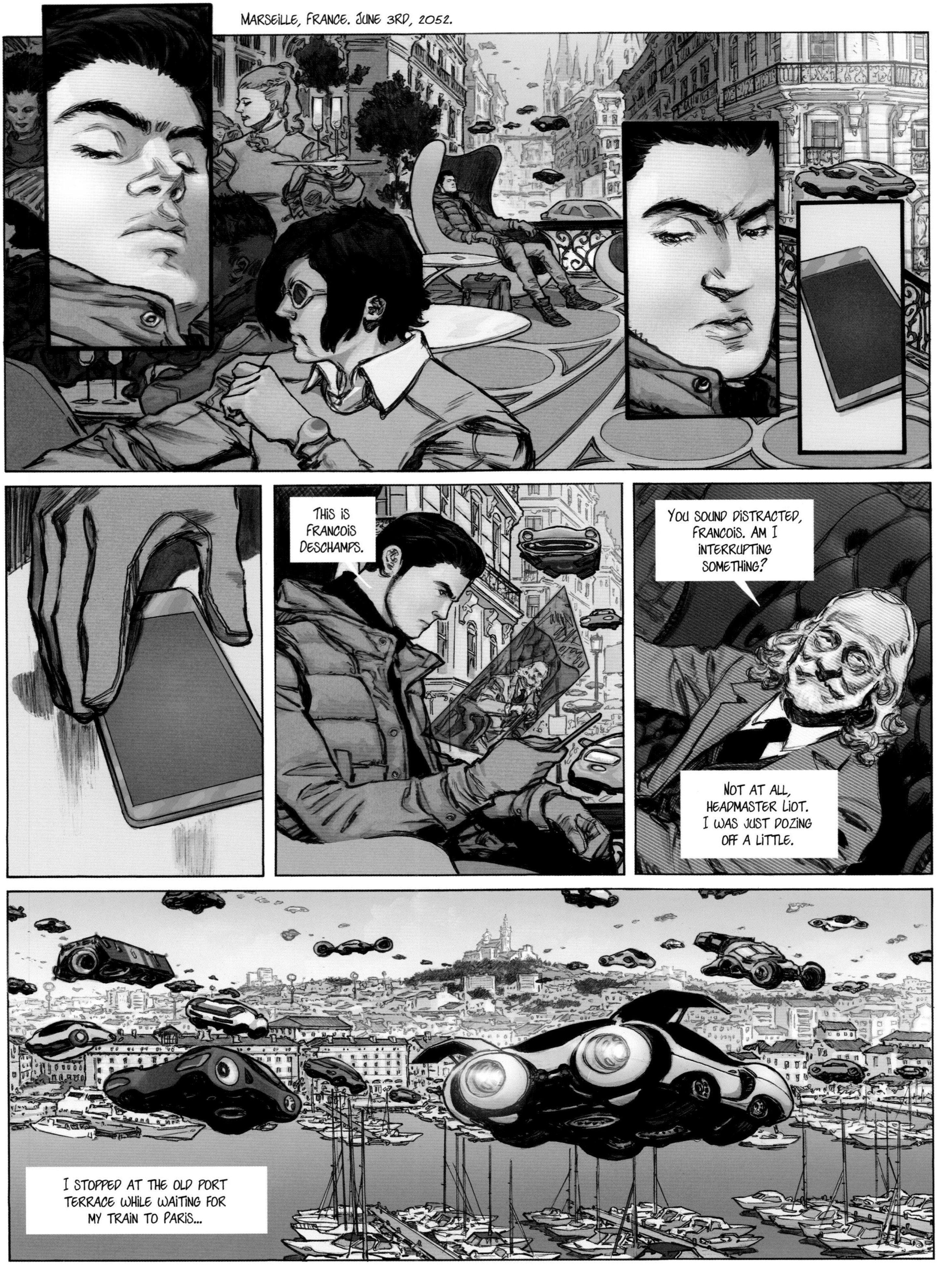
Marseille, France. June 3rd, 2052.
This is Francois Deschamps.
You sound distracted, Francois. Am I interrupting something?
Not at all, Headmaster Liot. I was just dozing off a little.
I stopped at the old port terrace while waiting for my train to Paris...

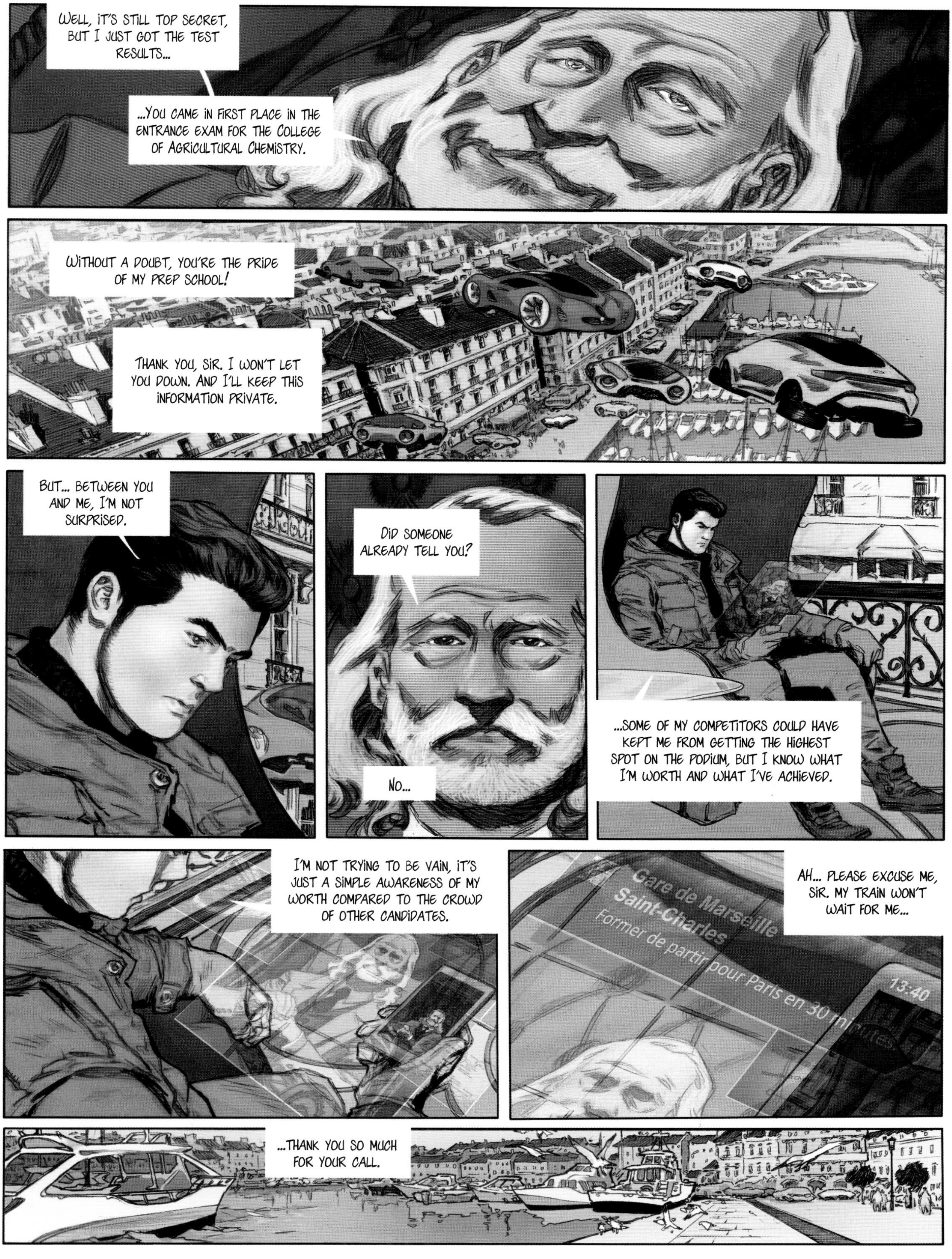

WELL, IT'S STILL TOP SECRET, BUT I JUST GOT THE TEST RESULTS...
...YOU CAME IN FIRST PLACE IN THE ENTRANCE EXAM FOR THE COLLEGE OF AGRICULTURAL CHEMISTRY.
WITHOUT A DOUBT, YOU'RE THE PRIDE OF MY PREP SCHOOL!
THANK YOU, SIR. I WON'T LET YOU DOWN. AND I'LL KEEP THIS INFORMATION PRIVATE.
BUT... BETWEEN YOU AND ME, I'M NOT SURPRISED.
DID SOMEONE ALREADY TELL YOU?
NO...
...SOME OF MY COMPETITORS COULD HAVE KEPT ME FROM GETTING THE HIGHEST SPOT ON THE PODIUM, BUT I KNOW WHAT I'M WORTH AND WHAT I'VE ACHIEVED.
I'M NOT TRYING TO BE VAIN, IT'S JUST A SIMPLE AWARENESS OF MY WORTH COMPARED TO THE CROWD OF OTHER CANDIDATES.
Gare de Marseille
Saint-Charles
Former de partir pour Paris en 30 minutes.
13:40
AH... PLEASE EXCUSE ME, SIR. MY TRAIN WON'T WAIT FOR ME...
...THANK YOU SO MUCH FOR YOUR CALL.

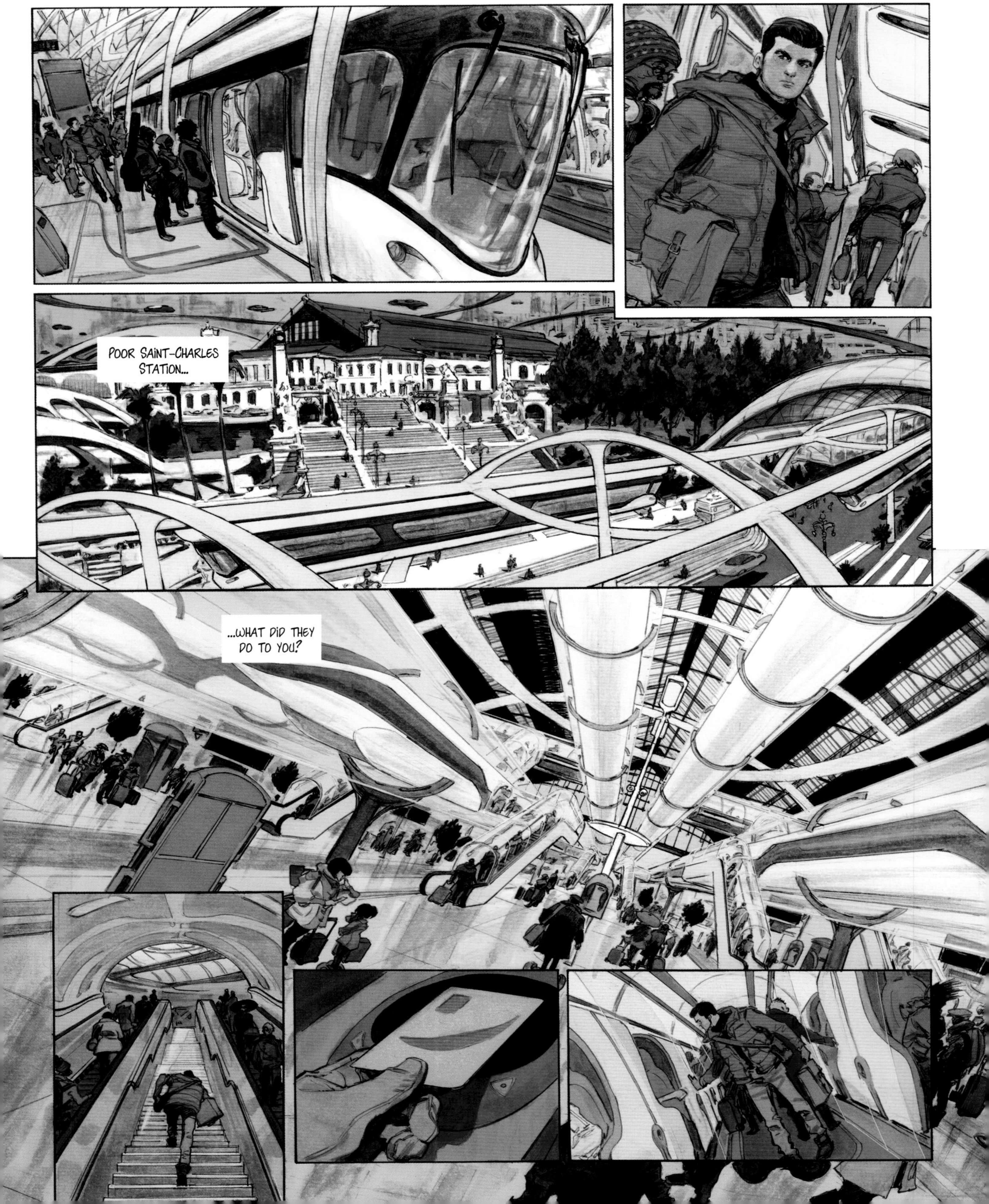
POOR SAINT-CHARLES STATION...
...WHAT DID THEY DO TO YOU?

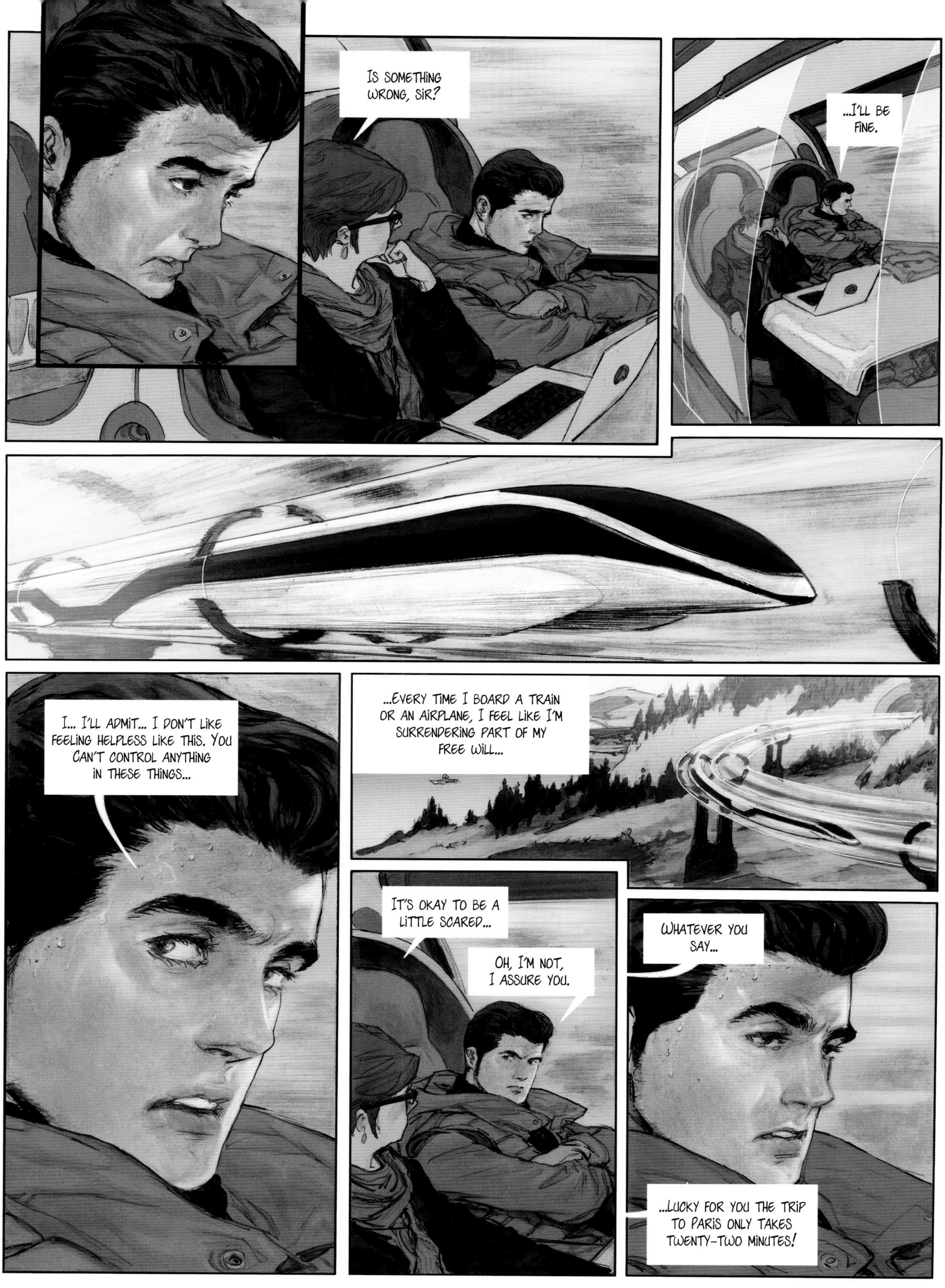
IS SOMETHING WRONG, SIR?
...I'LL BE FINE.
I... I'LL ADMIT... I DON'T LIKE FEELING HELPLESS LIKE THIS. YOU CAN'T CONTROL ANYTHING IN THESE THINGS...
...EVERY TIME I BOARD A TRAIN OR AN AIRPLANE, I FEEL LIKE I'M SURRENDERING PART OF MY FREE WILL...
IT'S OKAY TO BE A LITTLE SCARED...
OH, I'M NOT, I ASSURE YOU.
WHATEVER YOU SAY...
...LUCKY FOR YOU THE TRIP TO PARIS ONLY TAKES TWENTY-TWO MINUTES!

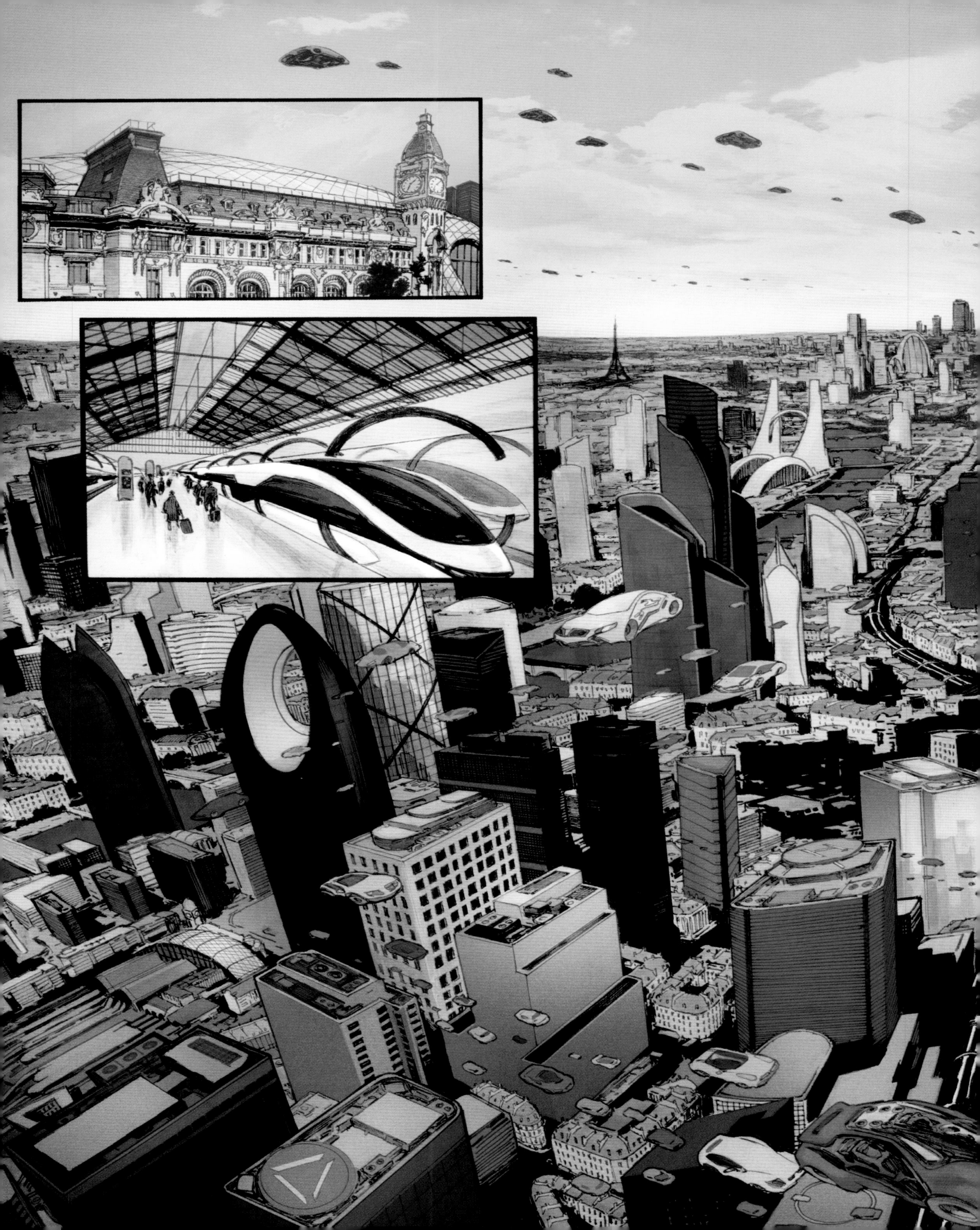

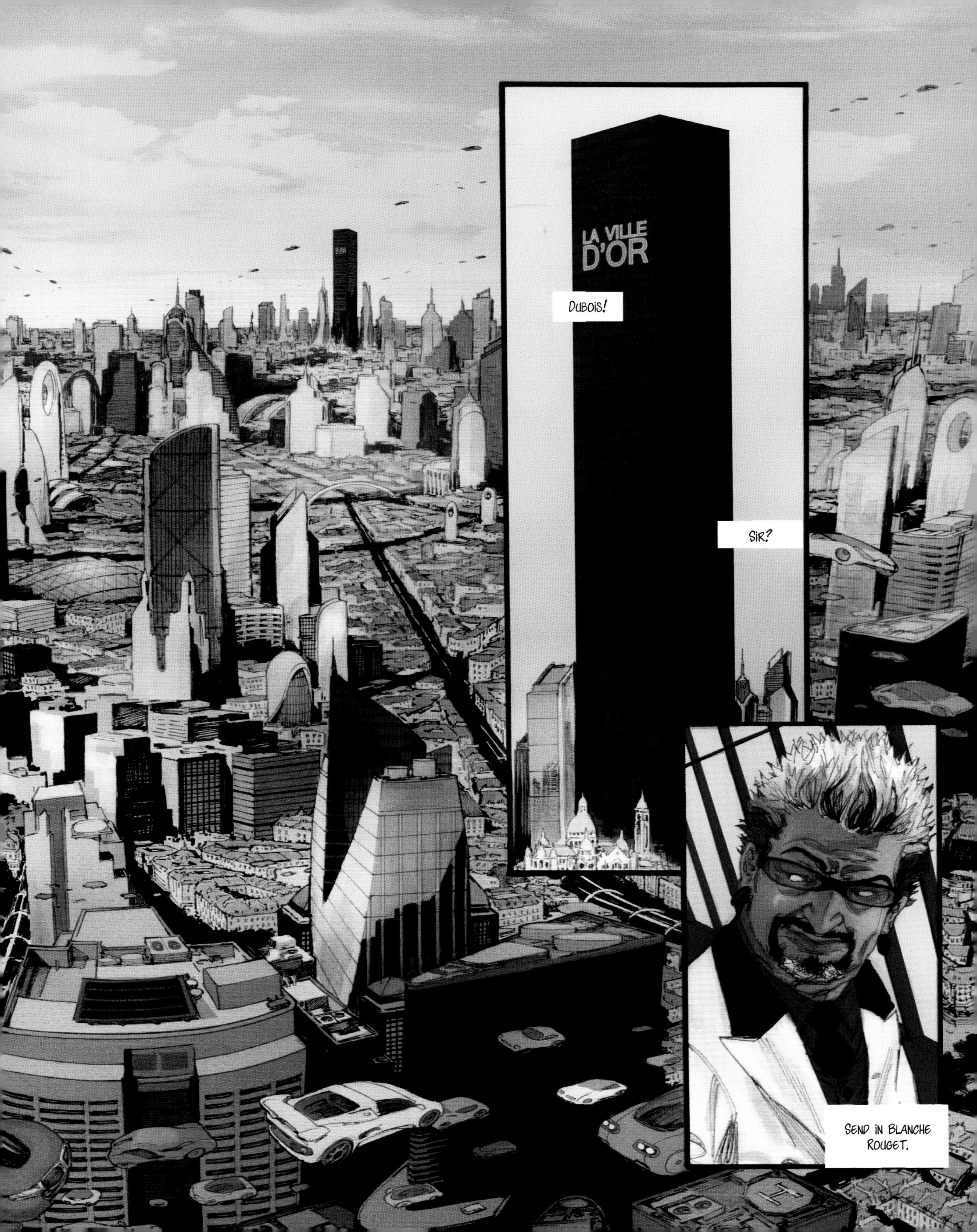
LA VILLE D'OR
DUBOIS!
SIR?
SEND IN BLANCHE ROUGET.

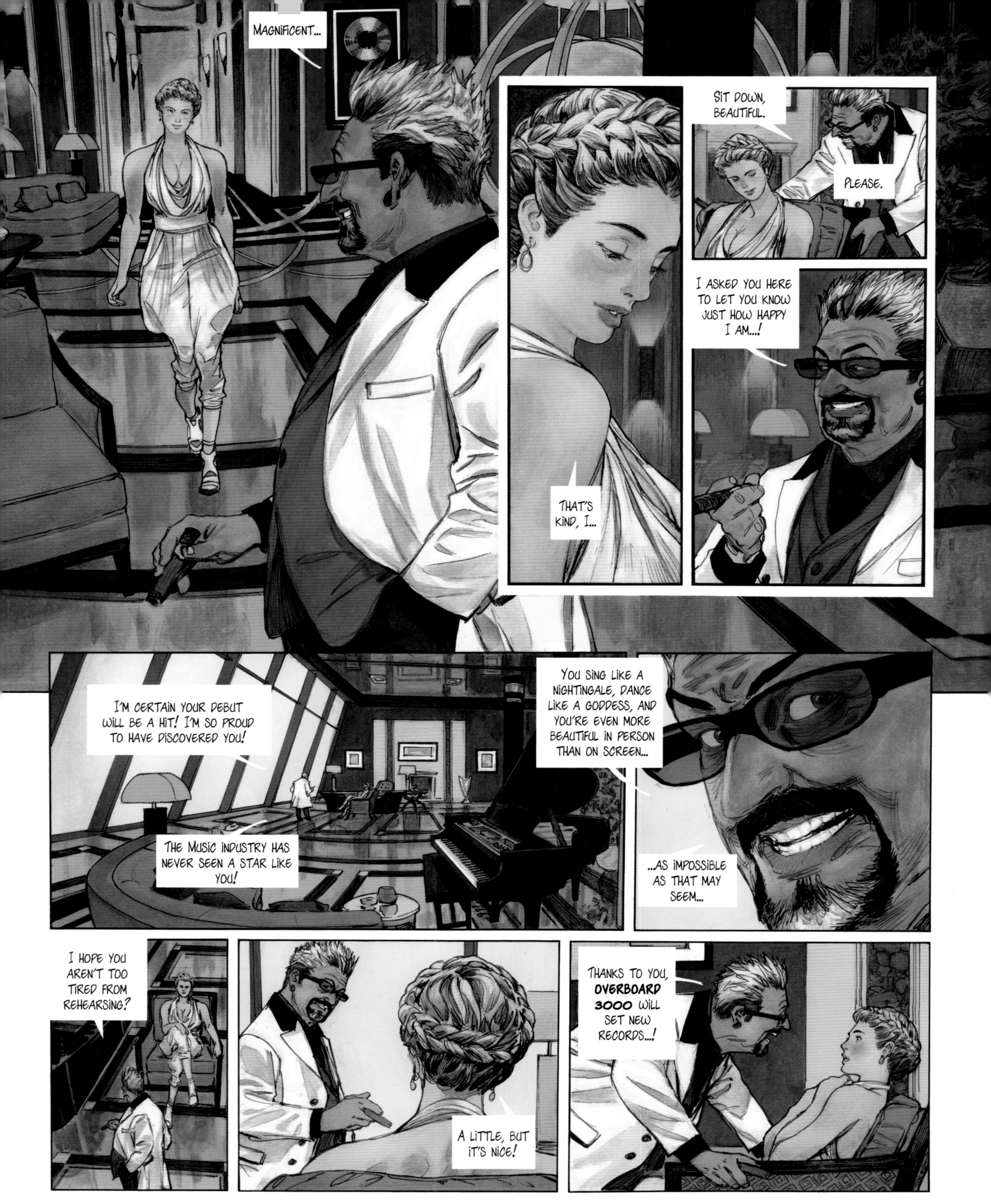
MAGNIFICENT...
SIT DOWN, BEAUTIFUL.
PLEASE.
THAT'S KIND, I...
I ASKED YOU HERE TO LET YOU KNOW JUST HOW HAPPY I AM...!
I'M CERTAIN YOUR DEBUT WILL BE A HIT! I'M SO PROUD TO HAVE DISCOVERED YOU!
THE MUSIC INDUSTRY HAS NEVER SEEN A STAR LIKE YOU!
YOU SING LIKE A NIGHTINGALE, DANCE LIKE A GODDESS, AND YOU'RE EVEN MORE BEAUTIFUL IN PERSON THAN ON SCREEN...
...AS IMPOSSIBLE AS THAT MAY SEEM...
I HOPE YOU AREN'T TOO TIRED FROM REHEARSING?
A LITTLE, BUT IT'S NICE!
THANKS TO YOU, **OVERBOARD 3000** WILL SET NEW RECORDS...!

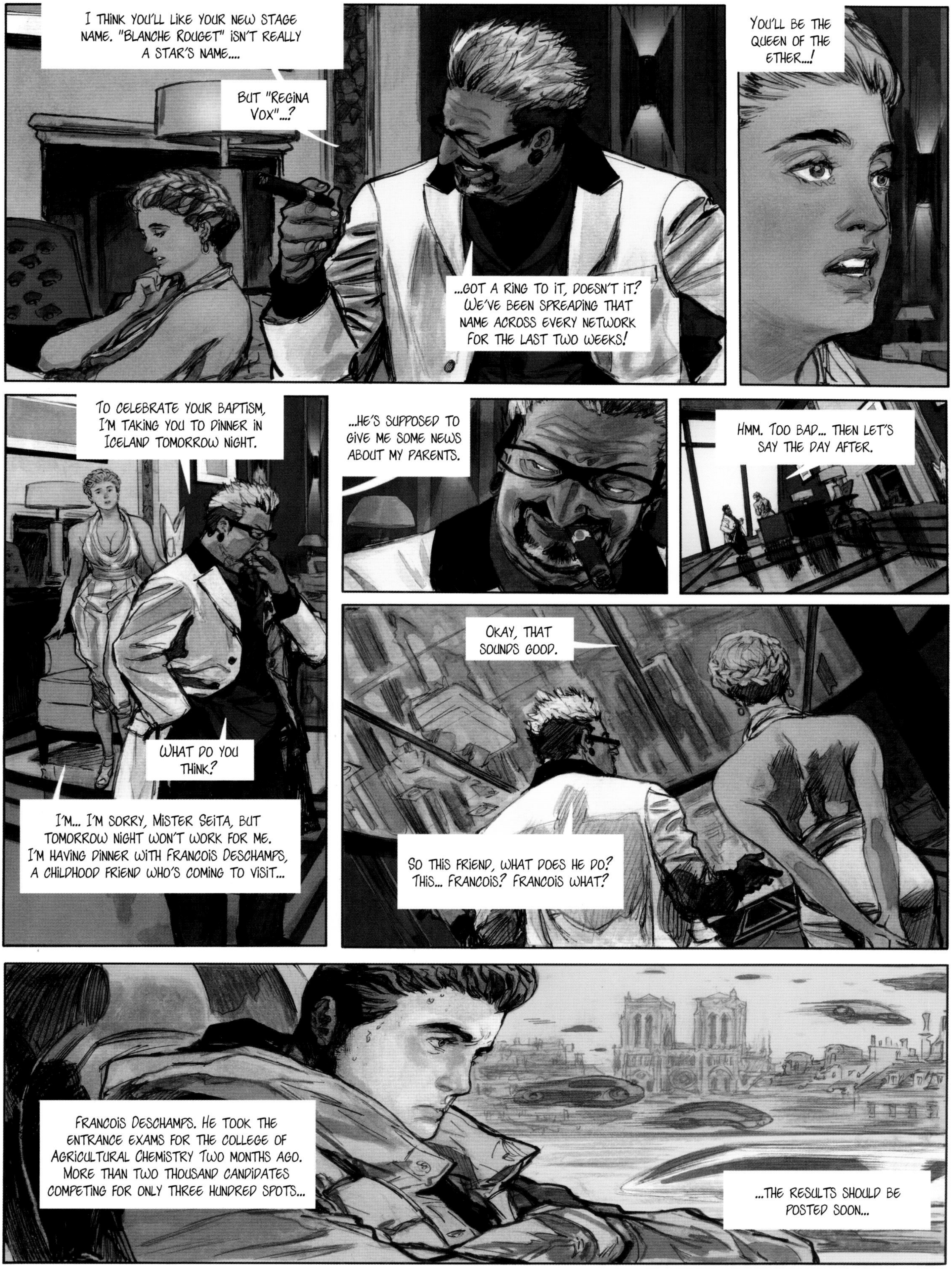
I THINK YOU'LL LIKE YOUR NEW STAGE NAME. "BLANCHE ROUGET" ISN'T REALLY A STAR'S NAME....
BUT "REGINA VOX"...?
...GOT A RING TO IT, DOESN'T IT? WE'VE BEEN SPREADING THAT NAME ACROSS EVERY NETWORK FOR THE LAST TWO WEEKS!
YOU'LL BE THE QUEEN OF THE ETHER...!
TO CELEBRATE YOUR BAPTISM, I'M TAKING YOU TO DINNER IN ICELAND TOMORROW NIGHT.
WHAT DO YOU THINK?
I'M... I'M SORRY, MISTER SEITA, BUT TOMORROW NIGHT WON'T WORK FOR ME. I'M HAVING DINNER WITH FRANCOIS DESCHAMPS, A CHILDHOOD FRIEND WHO'S COMING TO VISIT...
...HE'S SUPPOSED TO GIVE ME SOME NEWS ABOUT MY PARENTS.
HMM. TOO BAD... THEN LET'S SAY THE DAY AFTER.
OKAY, THAT SOUNDS GOOD.
SO THIS FRIEND, WHAT DOES HE DO? THIS... FRANCOIS? FRANCOIS WHAT?
FRANCOIS DESCHAMPS. HE TOOK THE ENTRANCE EXAMS FOR THE COLLEGE OF AGRICULTURAL CHEMISTRY TWO MONTHS AGO. MORE THAN TWO THOUSAND CANDIDATES COMPETING FOR ONLY THREE HUNDRED SPOTS...
...THE RESULTS SHOULD BE POSTED SOON...

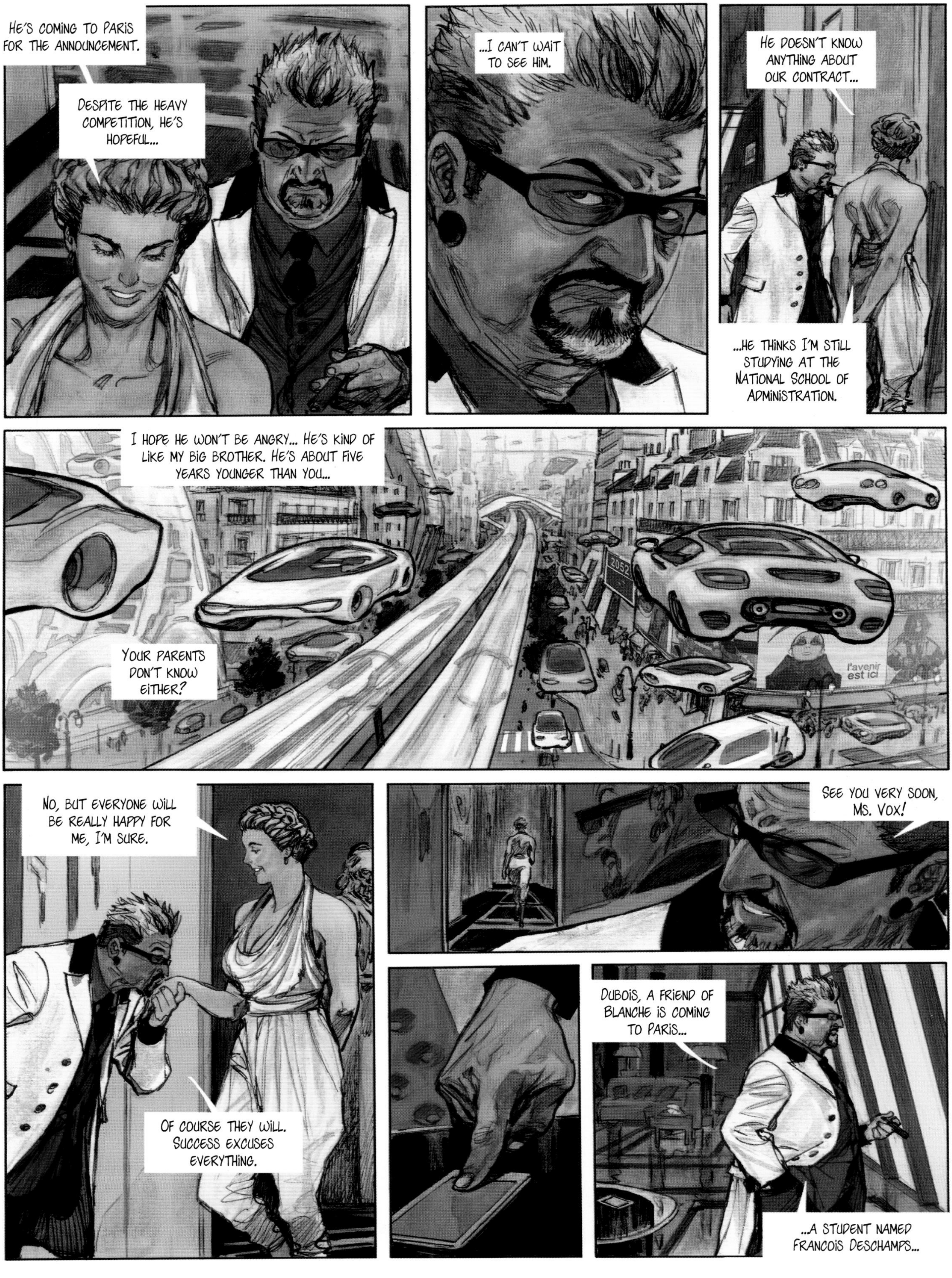
He's coming to Paris for the announcement.
Despite the heavy competition, he's hopeful...
...I can't wait to see him.
He doesn't know anything about our contract...
...he thinks I'm still studying at the National School of Administration.
I hope he won't be angry... He's kind of like my big brother. He's about five years younger than you...
Your parents don't know either?
2052
l'avenir est ici
No, but everyone will be really happy for me, I'm sure.
Of course they will. Success excuses everything.
See you very soon, Ms. Vox!
Dubois, a friend of Blanche is coming to Paris...
...a student named Francois Deschamps...

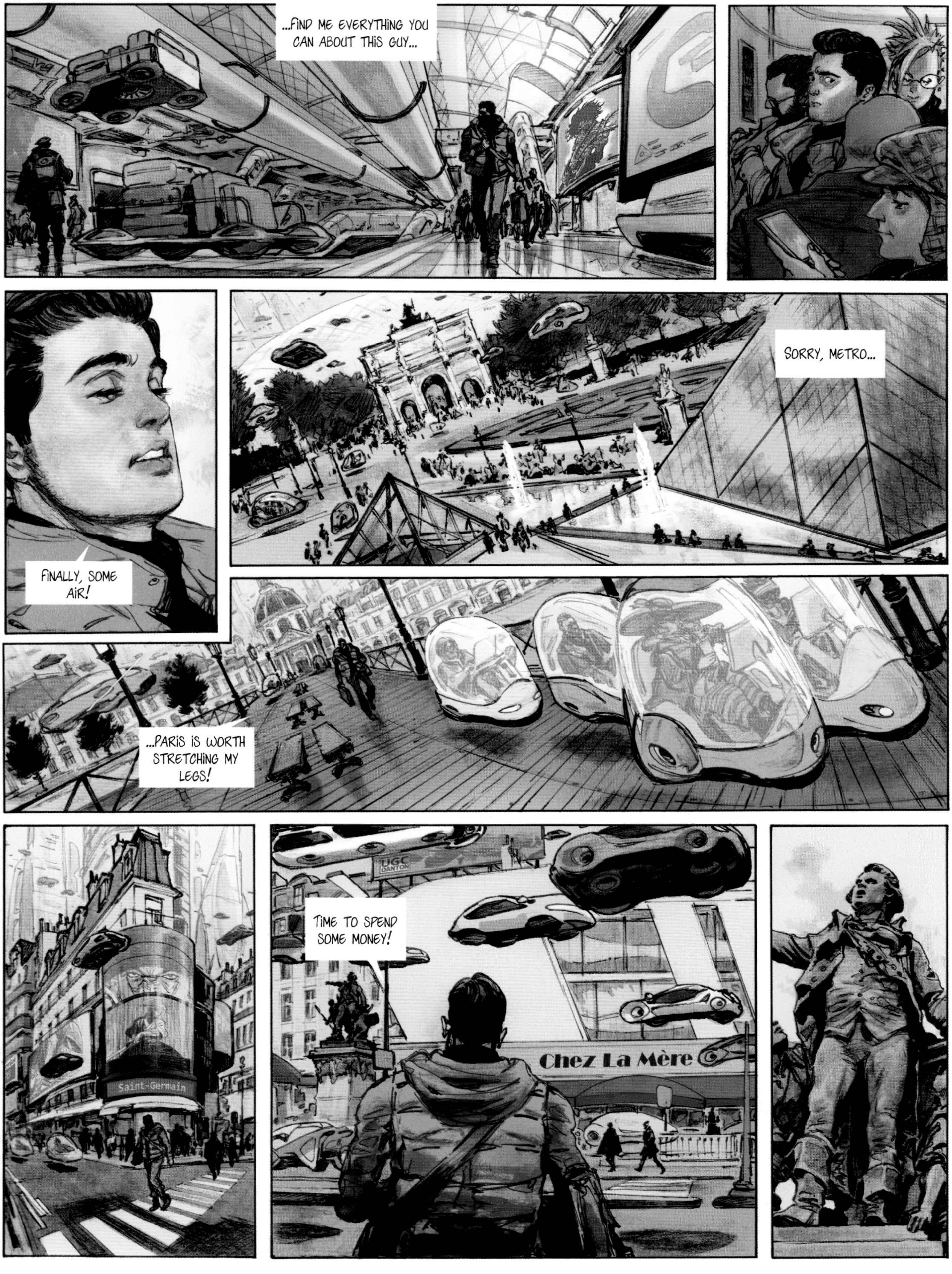
...FIND ME EVERYTHING YOU CAN ABOUT THIS GUY...
FINALLY, SOME AIR!
SORRY, METRO...
...PARIS IS WORTH STRETCHING MY LEGS!
UGC DANTON
Saint-Germain
TIME TO SPEND SOME MONEY!
Chez La Mère

Bienvenue Chez La Mère

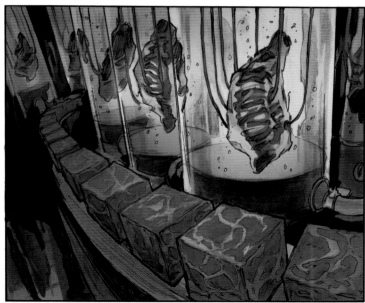

Filet de bœuf saignant

Filet de bœuf saignant

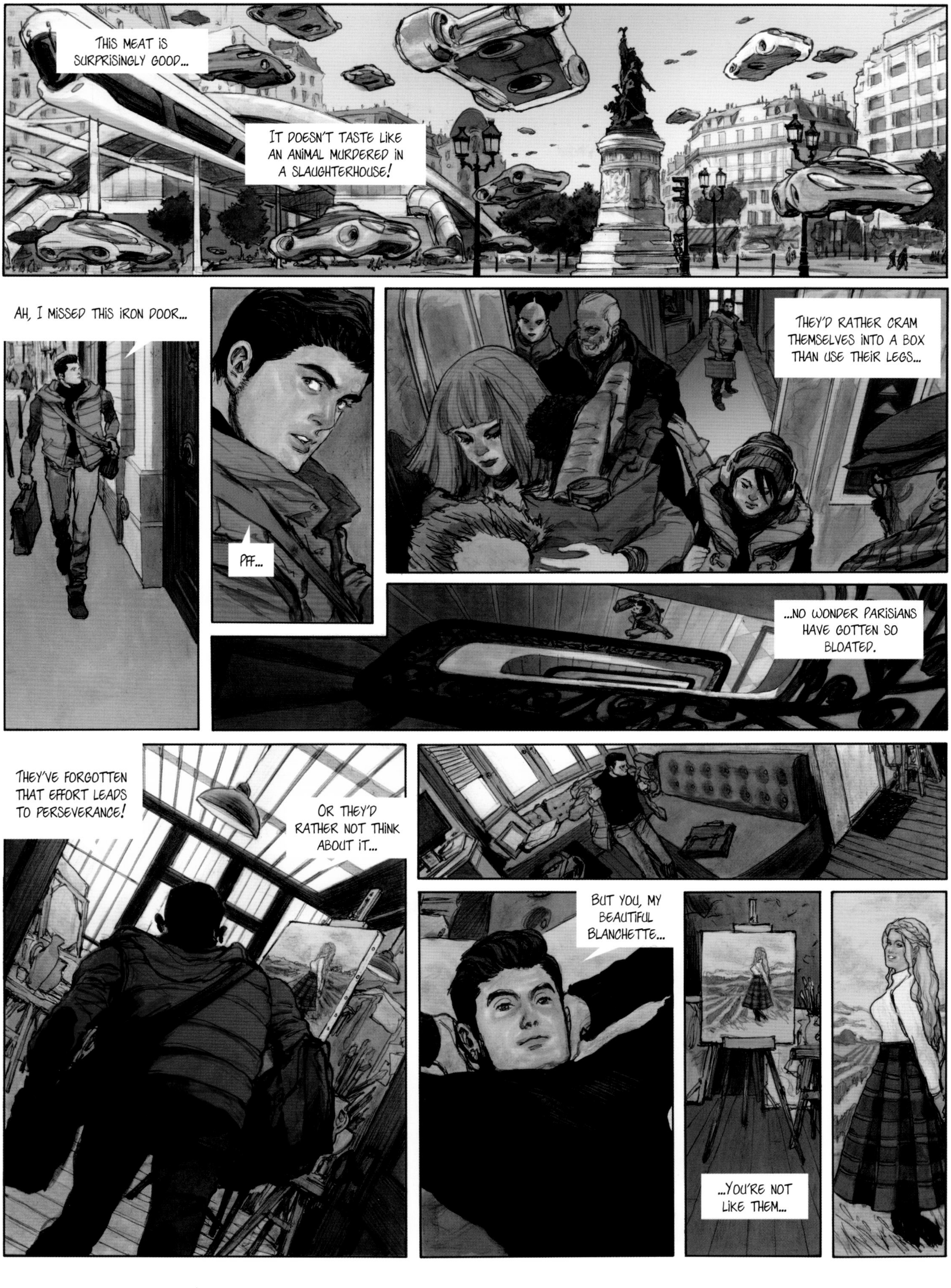

THIS MEAT IS SURPRISINGLY GOOD...
IT DOESN'T TASTE LIKE AN ANIMAL MURDERED IN A SLAUGHTERHOUSE!
AH, I MISSED THIS IRON DOOR...
PFF...
THEY'D RATHER CRAM THEMSELVES INTO A BOX THAN USE THEIR LEGS...
...NO WONDER PARISIANS HAVE GOTTEN SO BLOATED.
THEY'VE FORGOTTEN THAT EFFORT LEADS TO PERSEVERANCE!
OR THEY'D RATHER NOT THINK ABOUT IT...
BUT YOU, MY BEAUTIFUL BLANCHETTE...
...YOU'RE NOT LIKE THEM...

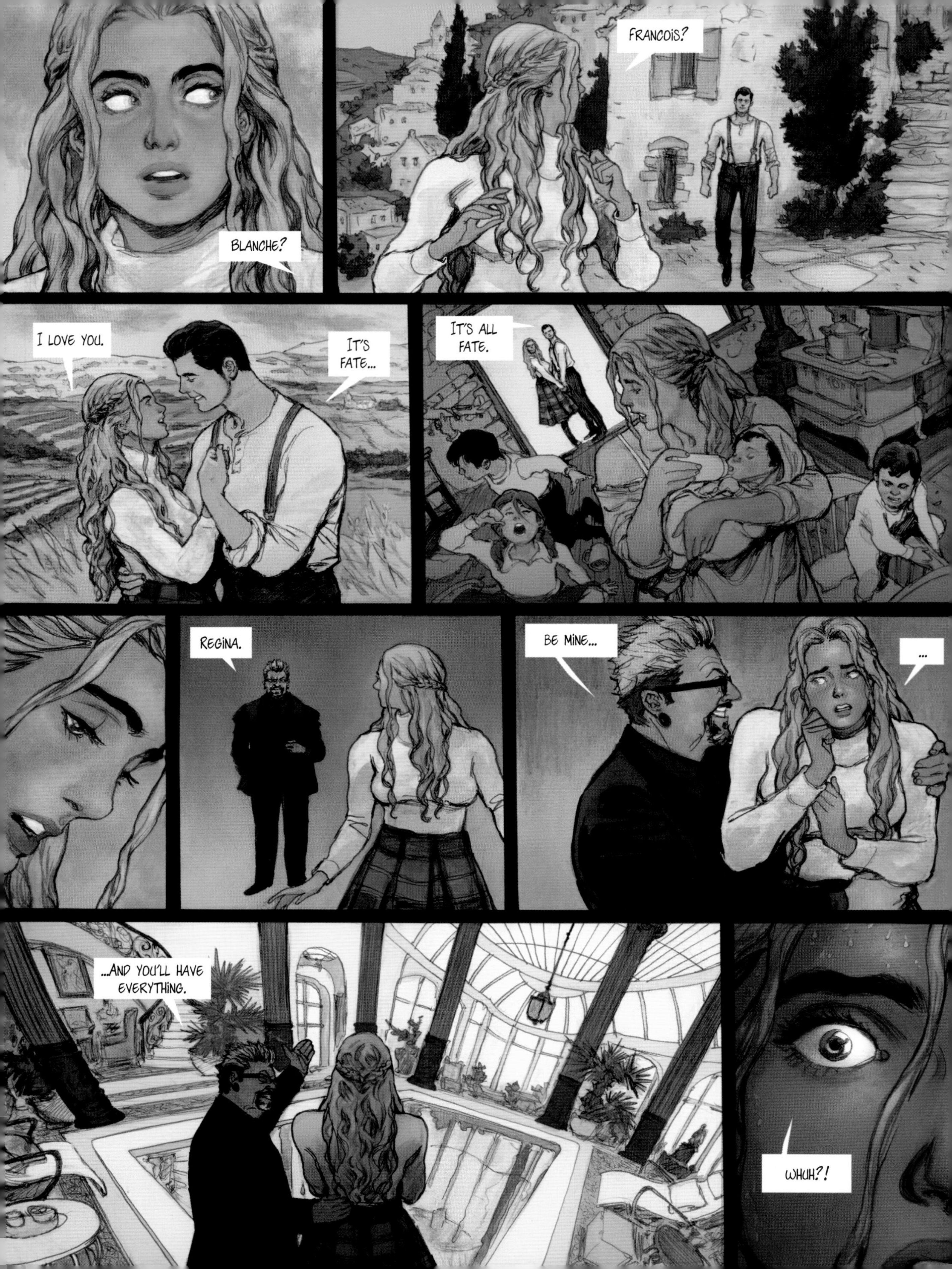
BLANCHE?
FRANCOIS?
I LOVE YOU.
IT'S FATE...
IT'S ALL FATE.
REGINA.
BE MINE...
...
...AND YOU'LL HAVE EVERYTHING.
WHUH?!

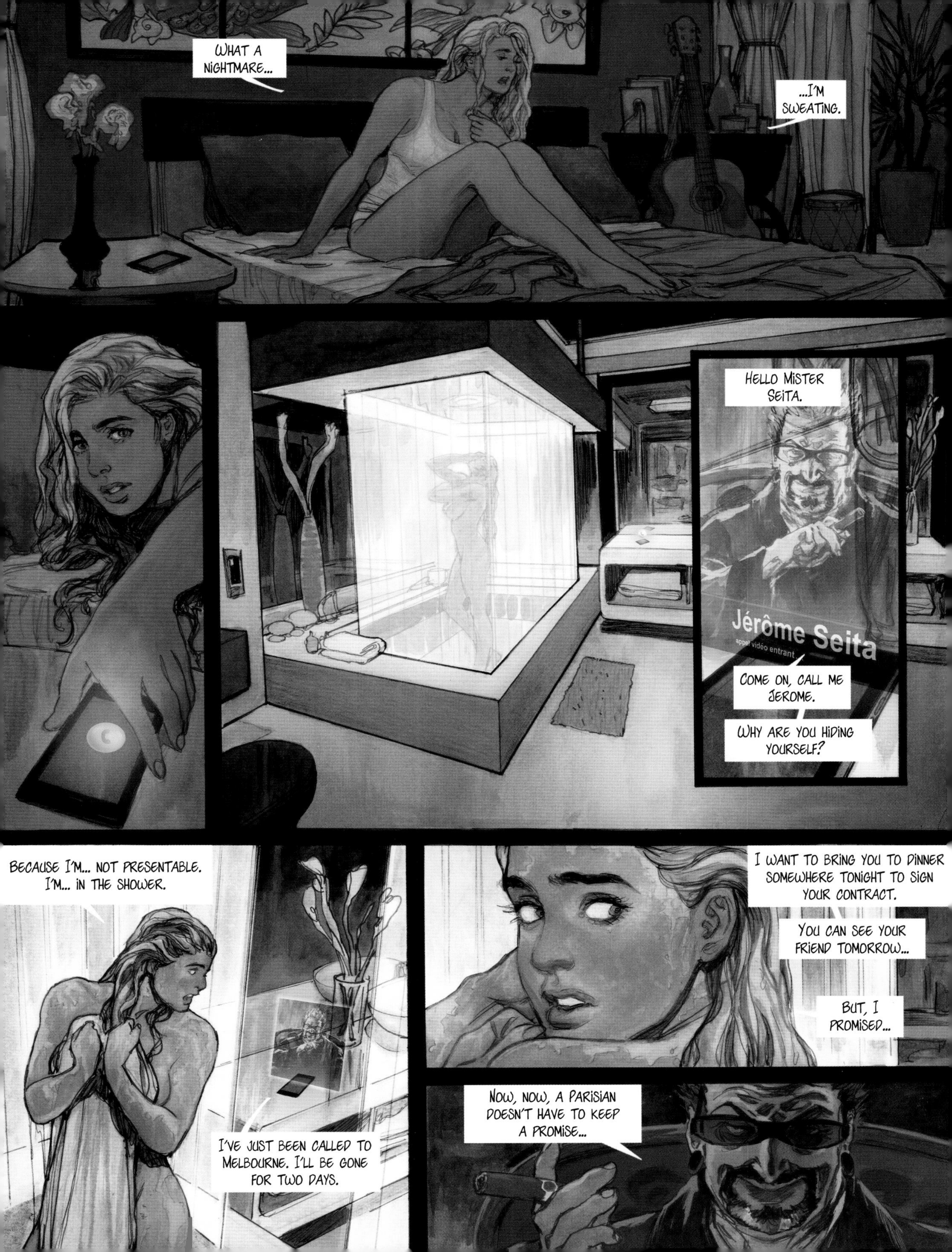

WHAT A NIGHTMARE...
...I'M SWEATING.
HELLO MISTER SEITA.
Jérôme Seita
appel vidéo entrant
COME ON, CALL ME JEROME.
WHY ARE YOU HIDING YOURSELF?
BECAUSE I'M... NOT PRESENTABLE. I'M... IN THE SHOWER.
I'VE JUST BEEN CALLED TO MELBOURNE. I'LL BE GONE FOR TWO DAYS.
I WANT TO BRING YOU TO DINNER SOMEWHERE TONIGHT TO SIGN YOUR CONTRACT.
YOU CAN SEE YOUR FRIEND TOMORROW...
BUT, I PROMISED...
NOW, NOW, A PARISIAN DOESN'T HAVE TO KEEP A PROMISE...

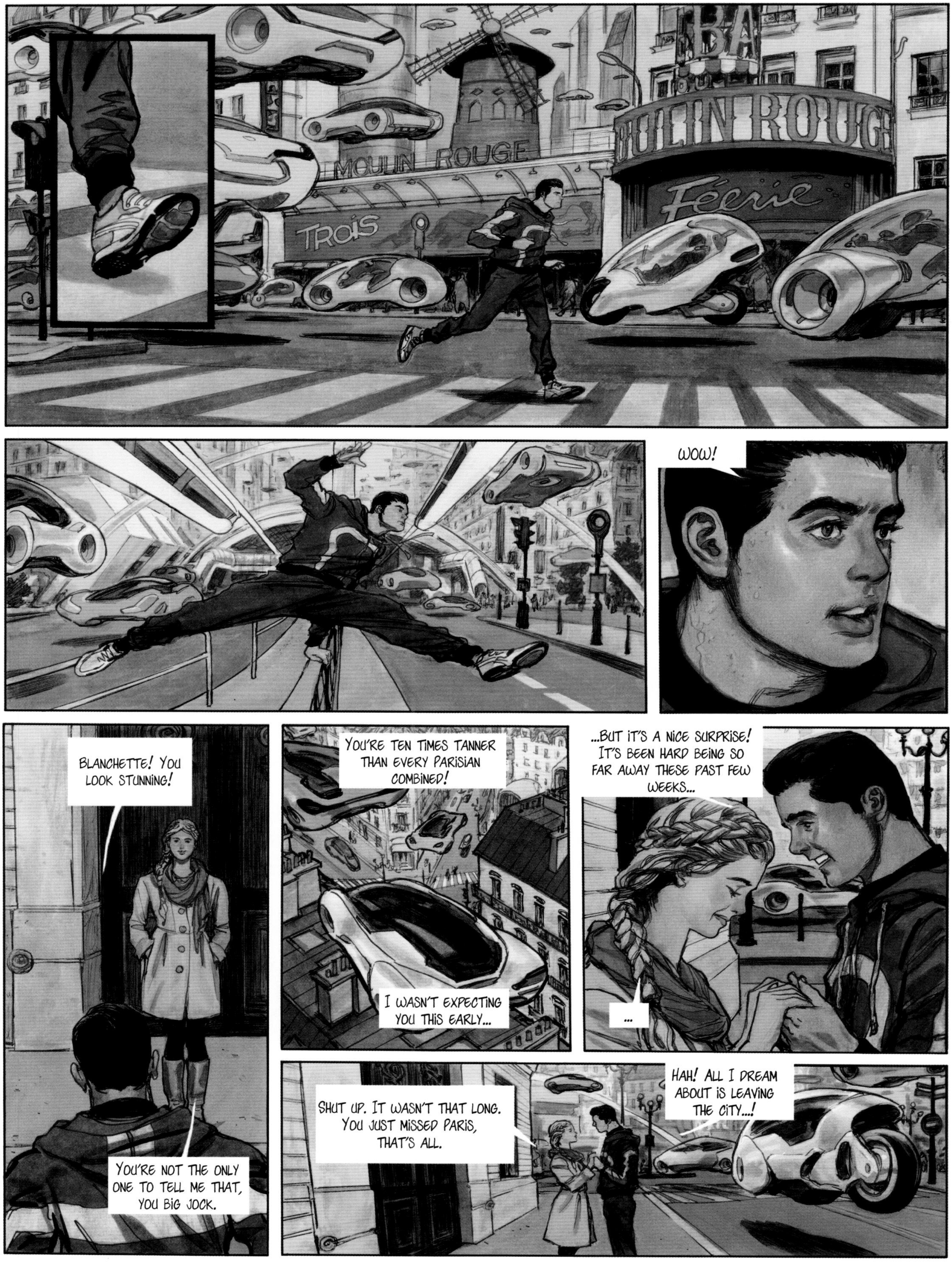
MOULIN ROUGE
TROIS
MOULIN ROUGE
Féerie
WOW!
BLANCHETTE! YOU LOOK STUNNING!
YOU'RE NOT THE ONLY ONE TO TELL ME THAT, YOU BIG JOCK.
YOU'RE TEN TIMES TANNER THAN EVERY PARISIAN COMBINED!
I WASN'T EXPECTING YOU THIS EARLY...
...BUT IT'S A NICE SURPRISE! IT'S BEEN HARD BEING SO FAR AWAY THESE PAST FEW WEEKS...
...
SHUT UP. IT WASN'T THAT LONG. YOU JUST MISSED PARIS, THAT'S ALL.
HAH! ALL I DREAM ABOUT IS LEAVING THE CITY...!

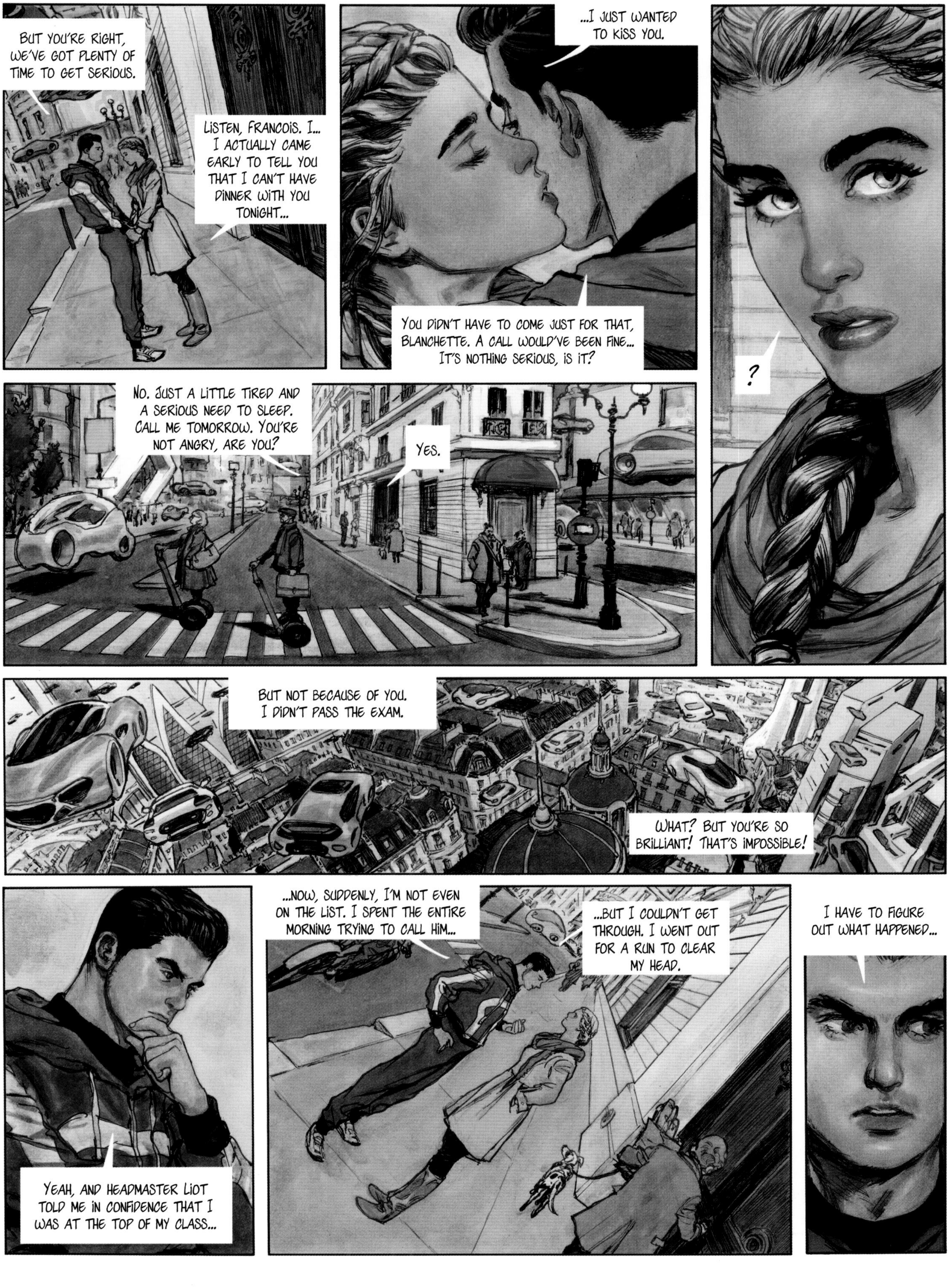
BUT YOU'RE RIGHT, WE'VE GOT PLENTY OF TIME TO GET SERIOUS.
LISTEN, FRANCOIS. I... I ACTUALLY CAME EARLY TO TELL YOU THAT I CAN'T HAVE DINNER WITH YOU TONIGHT...
...I JUST WANTED TO KISS YOU.
YOU DIDN'T HAVE TO COME JUST FOR THAT, BLANCHETTE. A CALL WOULD'VE BEEN FINE... IT'S NOTHING SERIOUS, IS IT?
?
NO. JUST A LITTLE TIRED AND A SERIOUS NEED TO SLEEP. CALL ME TOMORROW. YOU'RE NOT ANGRY, ARE YOU?
YES.
BUT NOT BECAUSE OF YOU. I DIDN'T PASS THE EXAM.
WHAT? BUT YOU'RE SO BRILLIANT! THAT'S IMPOSSIBLE!
YEAH, AND HEADMASTER LIOT TOLD ME IN CONFIDENCE THAT I WAS AT THE TOP OF MY CLASS...
...NOW, SUDDENLY, I'M NOT EVEN ON THE LIST. I SPENT THE ENTIRE MORNING TRYING TO CALL HIM...
...BUT I COULDN'T GET THROUGH. I WENT OUT FOR A RUN TO CLEAR MY HEAD.
I HAVE TO FIGURE OUT WHAT HAPPENED...

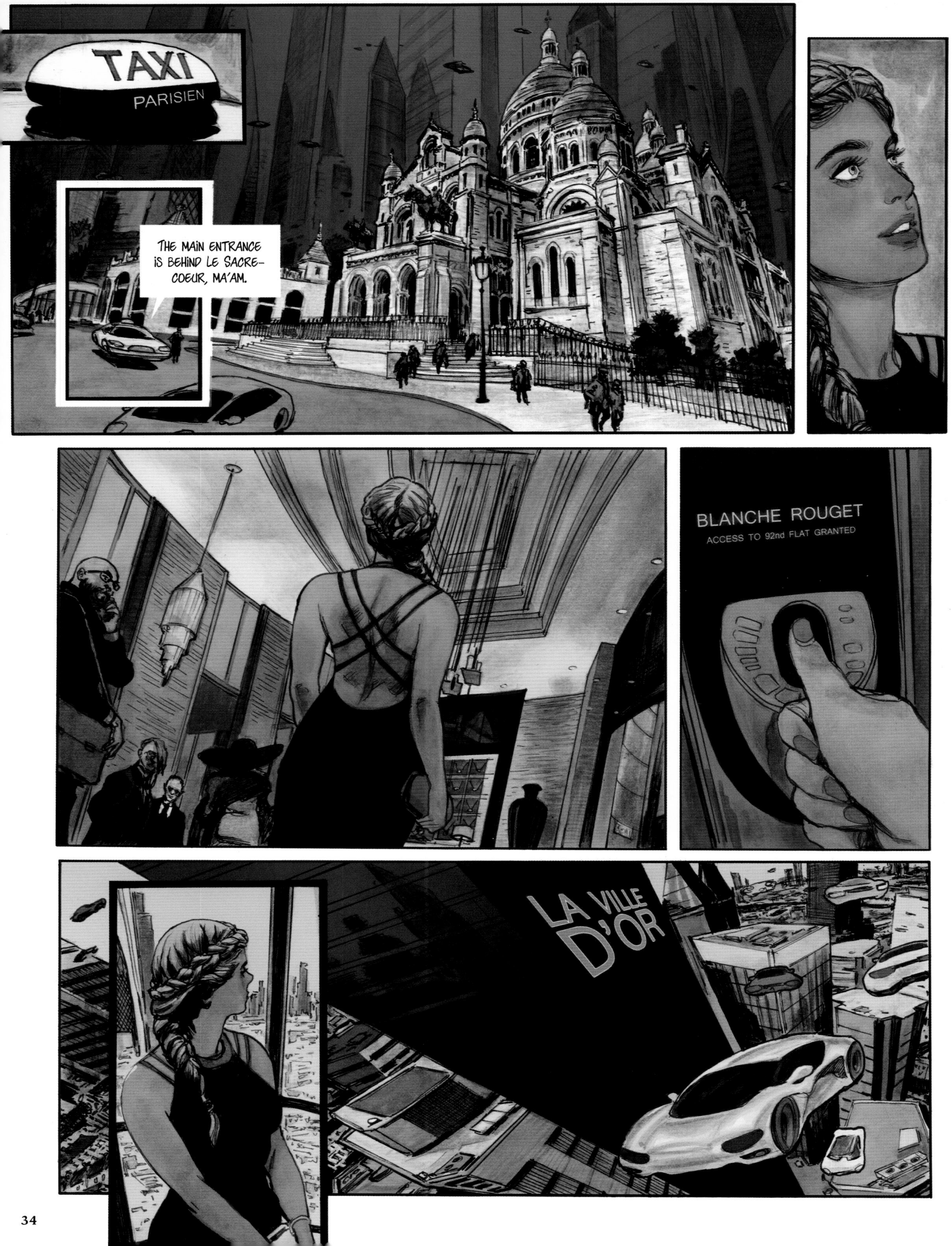
TAXI
PARISIEN
THE MAIN ENTRANCE IS BEHIND LE SACRE-COEUR, MA'AM.
BLANCHE ROUGET
ACCESS TO 92nd FLAT GRANTED
LA VILLE D'OR

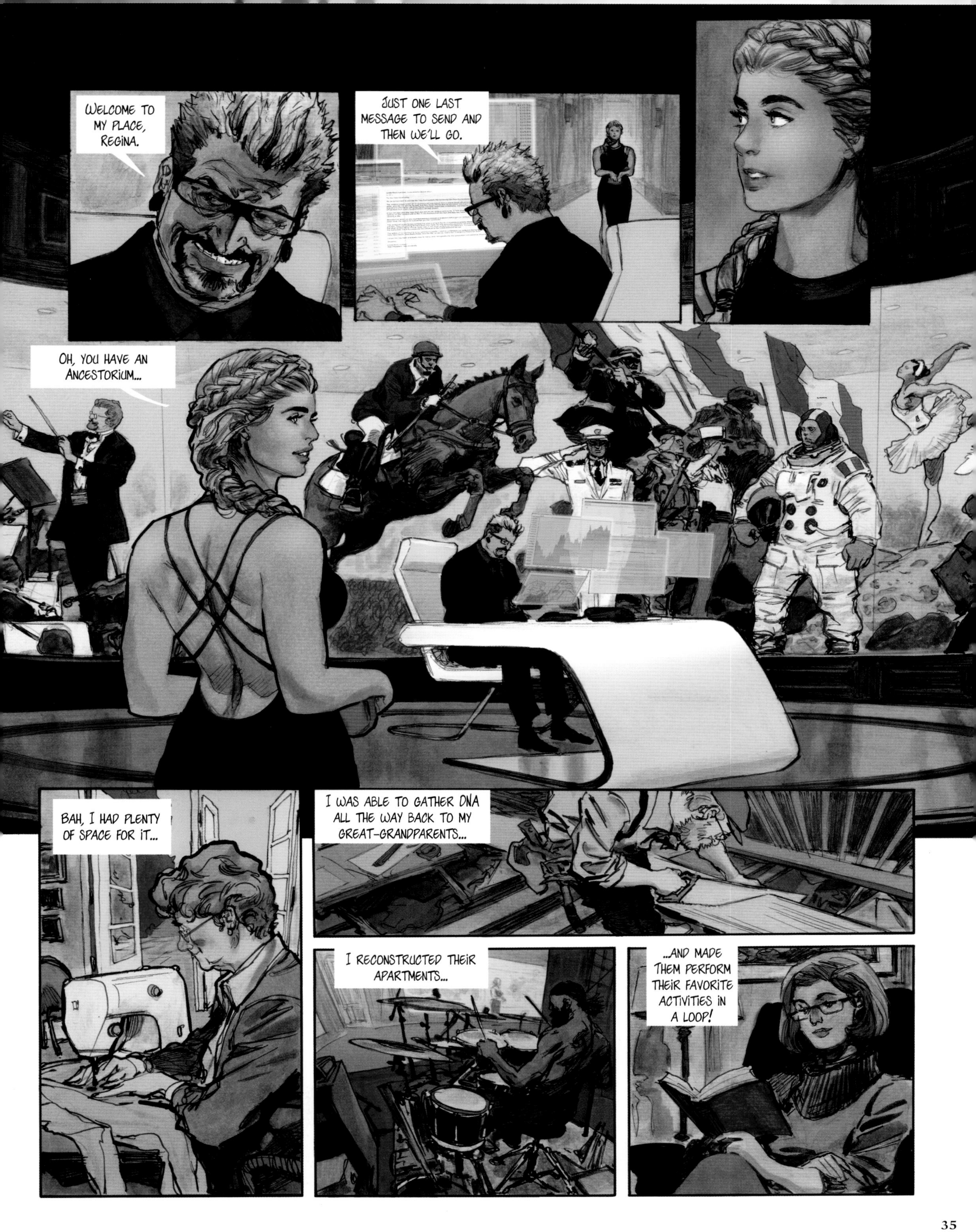
WELCOME TO MY PLACE, REGINA.
JUST ONE LAST MESSAGE TO SEND AND THEN WE'LL GO.
OH, YOU HAVE AN ANCESTORIUM...
BAH, I HAD PLENTY OF SPACE FOR IT...
I WAS ABLE TO GATHER DNA ALL THE WAY BACK TO MY GREAT-GRANDPARENTS...
I RECONSTRUCTED THEIR APARTMENTS...
...AND MADE THEM PERFORM THEIR FAVORITE ACTIVITIES IN A LOOP!

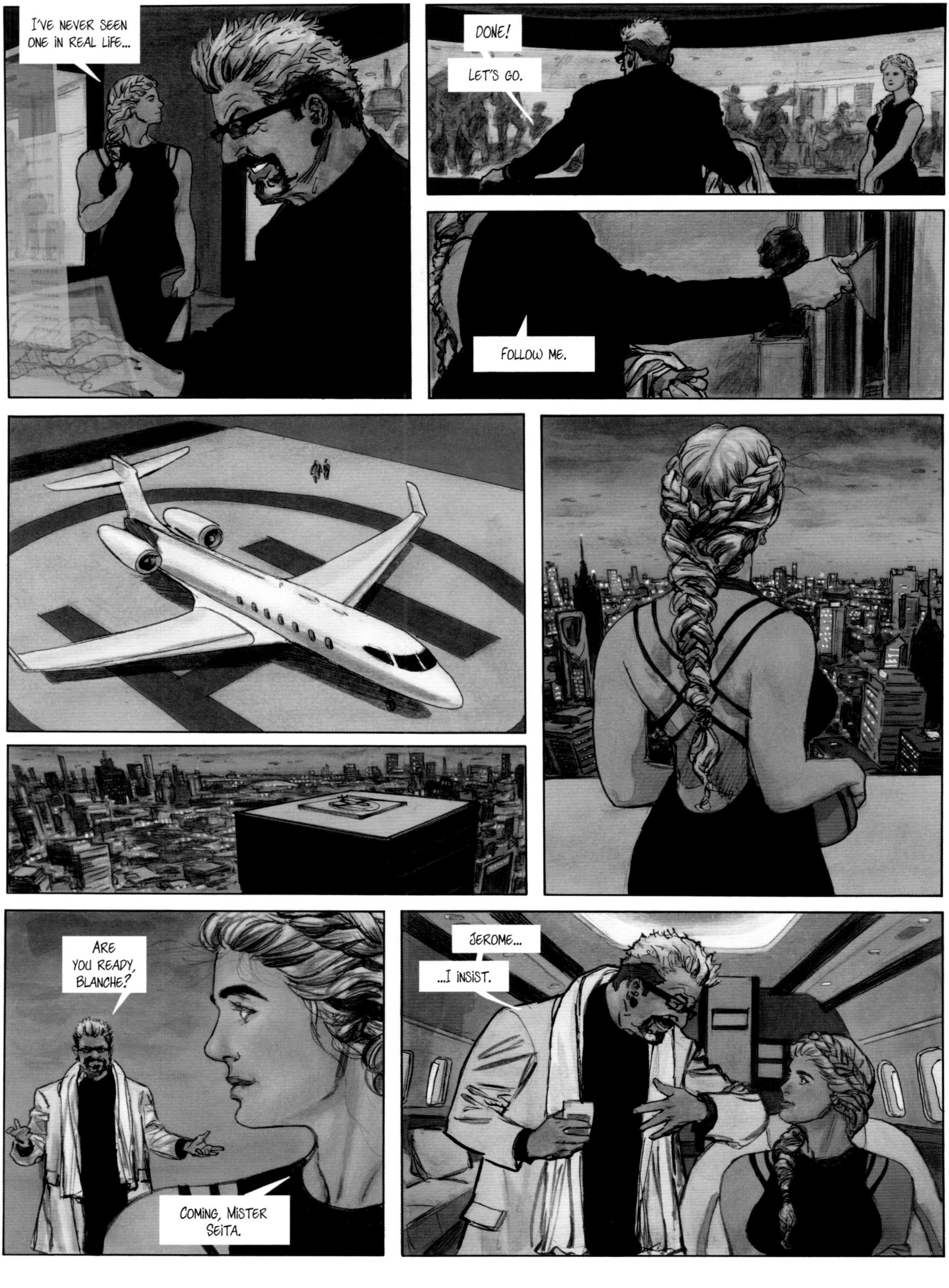
I'VE NEVER SEEN ONE IN REAL LIFE...
DONE!
LET'S GO.
FOLLOW ME.
ARE YOU READY, BLANCHE?
COMING, MISTER SEITA.
JEROME...
...I INSIST.

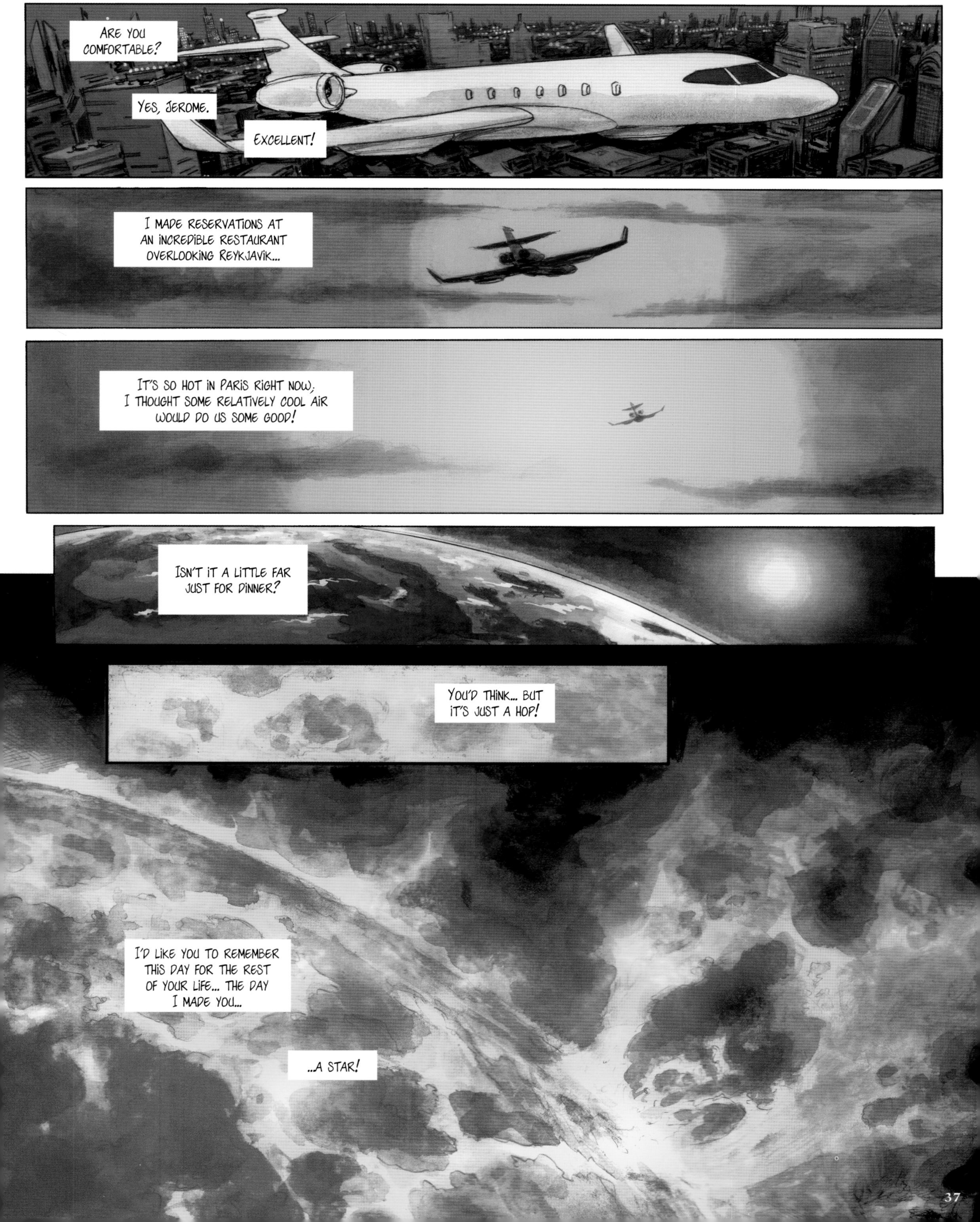
Are you comfortable?
Yes, Jerome.
Excellent!
I made reservations at an incredible restaurant overlooking Reykjavik...
It's so hot in Paris right now; I thought some relatively cool air would do us some good!
Isn't it a little far just for dinner?
You'd think... but it's just a hop!
I'd like you to remember this day for the rest of your life... the day I made you...
...a star!

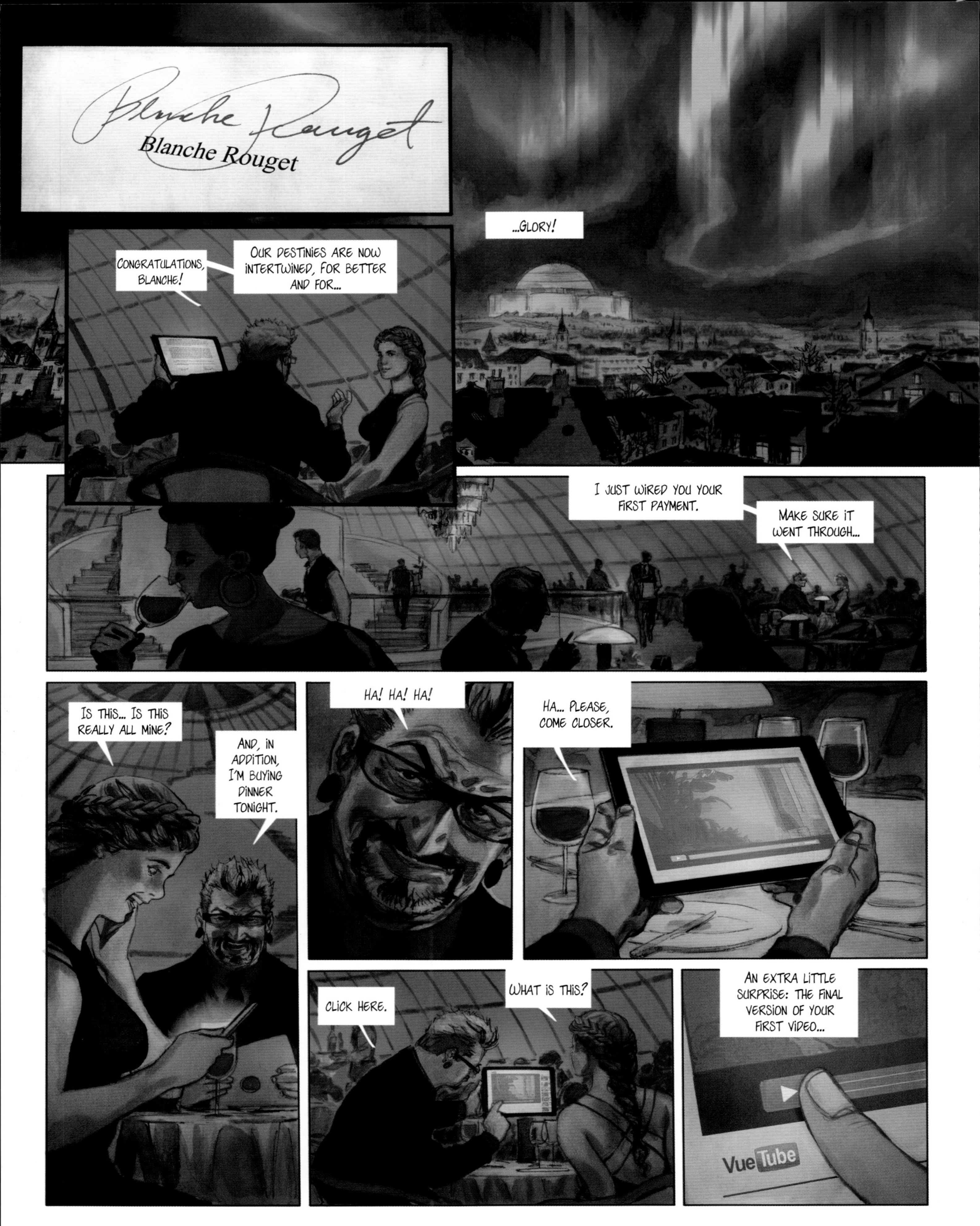
Blanche Rouget
...GLORY!
CONGRATULATIONS, BLANCHE!
OUR DESTINIES ARE NOW INTERTWINED, FOR BETTER AND FOR...
I JUST WIRED YOU YOUR FIRST PAYMENT.
MAKE SURE IT WENT THROUGH...
IS THIS... IS THIS REALLY ALL MINE?
AND, IN ADDITION, I'M BUYING DINNER TONIGHT.
HA! HA! HA!
HA... PLEASE, COME CLOSER.
CLICK HERE.
WHAT IS THIS?
AN EXTRA LITTLE SURPRISE: THE FINAL VERSION OF YOUR FIRST VIDEO...
VueTube

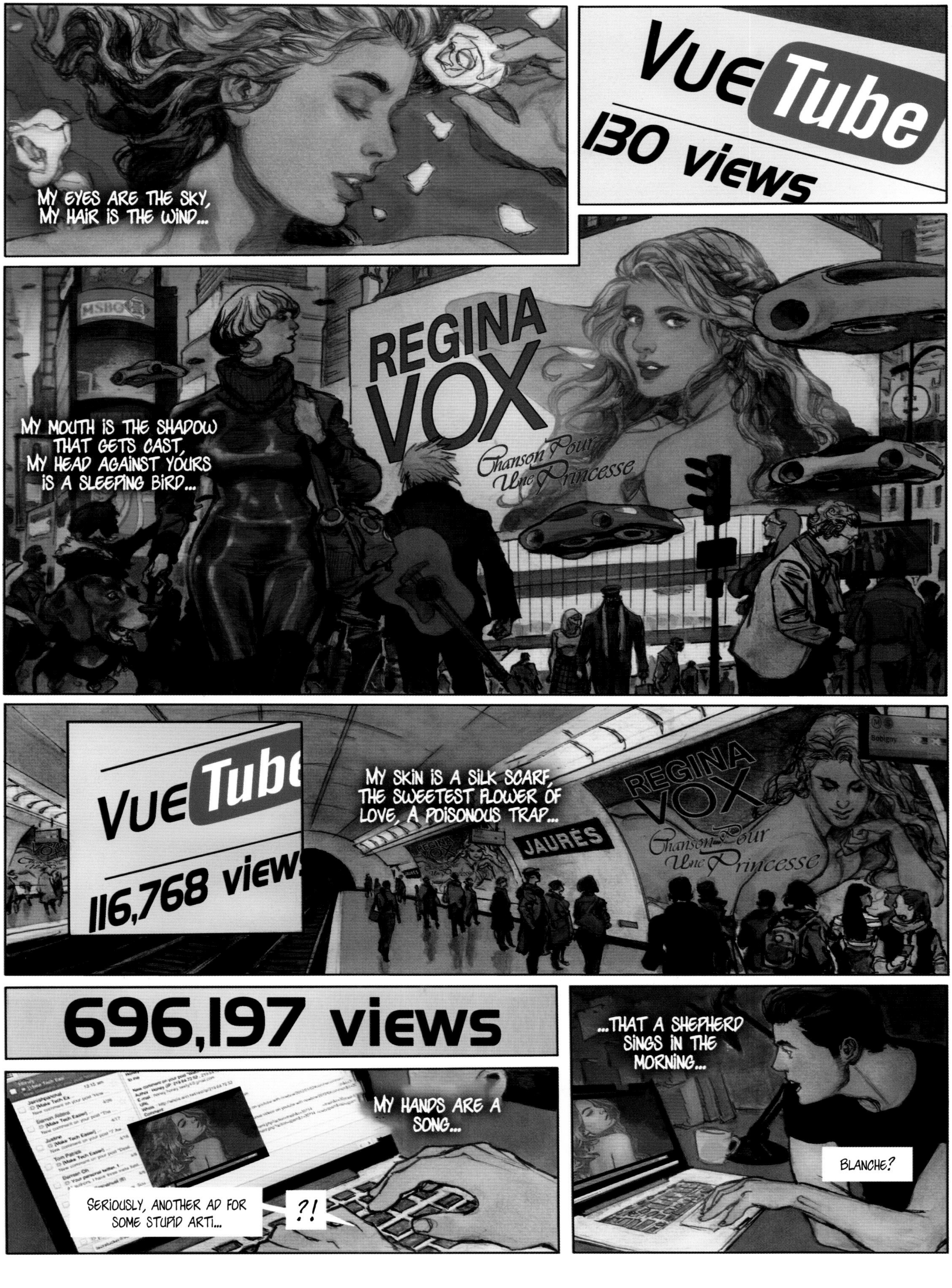

VueTube
130 views
My eyes are the sky, my hair is the wind...
REGINA VOX
Chanson Pour Une Princesse
My mouth is the shadow that gets cast, my head against yours is a sleeping bird...
VueTube
116,768 views
My skin is a silk scarf, the sweetest flower of love, a poisonous trap...
JAURÈS
REGINA VOX
Chanson Pour Une Princesse
696,197 views
My hands are a song...
Seriously, another ad for some stupid arti...
?!
...that a shepherd sings in the morning...
Blanche?

ARE YOU SEEING THESE NUMBERS, BLANCHE?
WE'RE A HIT!
THIS IS INCREDI...
IS SOMETHING WRONG?
NO... I'M JUST TIRED ALL OF A SUDDEN...
YOU MUST BE OVERWHELMED.
Appel entrant...
François Deschamps
Refuser
Répondre
MUST BE.
WE'RE BLOWING PAST TWO MILLION ALREADY!
I DIDN'T LIE TO YOU, MY LITTLE BLANCHE!
François Deschamps
Nouveau message texte
I've been trying to call you, but that hasn't worked, so I'm writing instead. I just saw your video on my computer. Now I understand why you couldn't meet tonight. I can't believe it. You... Regina Vox.
I'd be lying if I said that I'm happy for your change in circumstances. There's no doubt you'll make more money than a minister, but I hope you won't let yourself be misled by all of the compliments and praise you'll no doubt accumulate. Stay nice, Blanchette. Try to avoid becoming one of those stars who are nothing more than puppets with silly smiles. Don't forget that your new life is fake.
Just because you can now get whatever you want with the press of a button, it doesn't mean that you're a goddess. Your legs are no more beautiful dancing on all the screens of the world than when they were mine alone to love. Stay yourself. Love your work. But don't be vain. Remember: only one thing matters: effort.

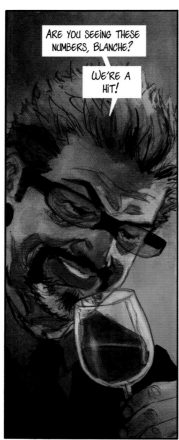

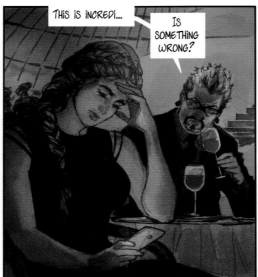

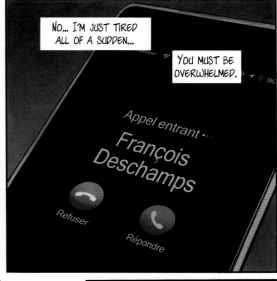

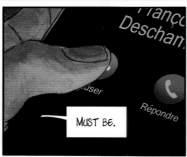

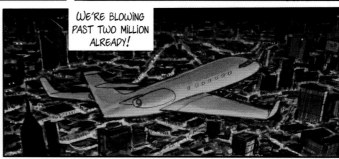

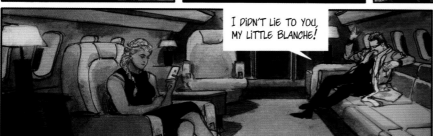

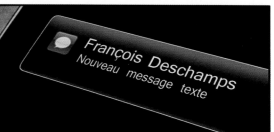

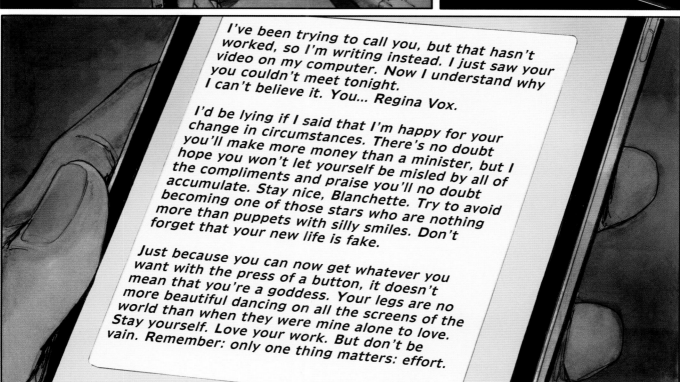

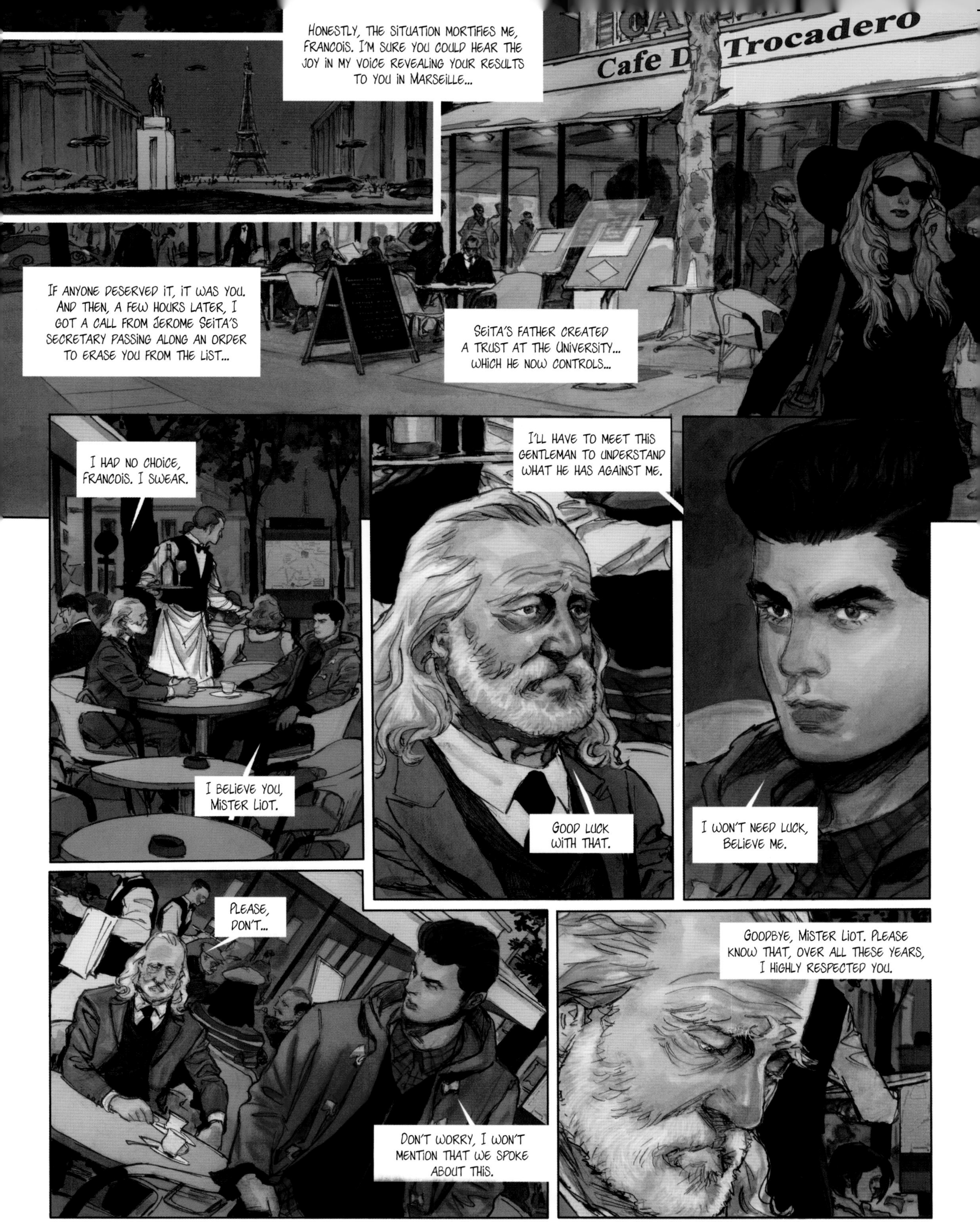

Honestly, the situation mortifies me, Francois. I'm sure you could hear the joy in my voice revealing your results to you in Marseille...
Cafe D Trocadero
If anyone deserved it, it was you. And then, a few hours later, I got a call from Jerome Seita's secretary passing along an order to erase you from the list...
Seita's father created a trust at the University... which he now controls...
I had no choice, Francois. I swear.
I believe you, Mister Liot.
I'll have to meet this gentleman to understand what he has against me.
Good luck with that.
I won't need luck, believe me.
Please, don't...
Don't worry, I won't mention that we spoke about this.
Goodbye, Mister Liot. Please know that, over all these years, I highly respected you.

YOU DON'T HAVE TO GO RIGHT NOW...

I REALLY DON'T FEEL WELL.

ALL THE MORE REASON TO STAY. REST HERE A WHILE.

I PROMISE, I'LL CALL A TAXI FOR YOU AS SOON AS WE CROSS THE 3 MILLION MARK!

HERE, TAKE THIS.

BLANCHE. MY NAME IS BLANCHE.

YOU'RE SO PRETTY, REGINA.

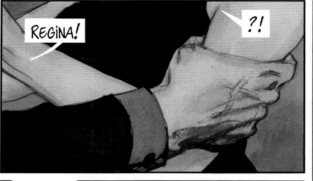

REGINA!

?!

YOU OWE ME EVERYTHING! BE NICE TO ME!

WHAT'S WRONG WITH YOU?

LET GO OF ME!

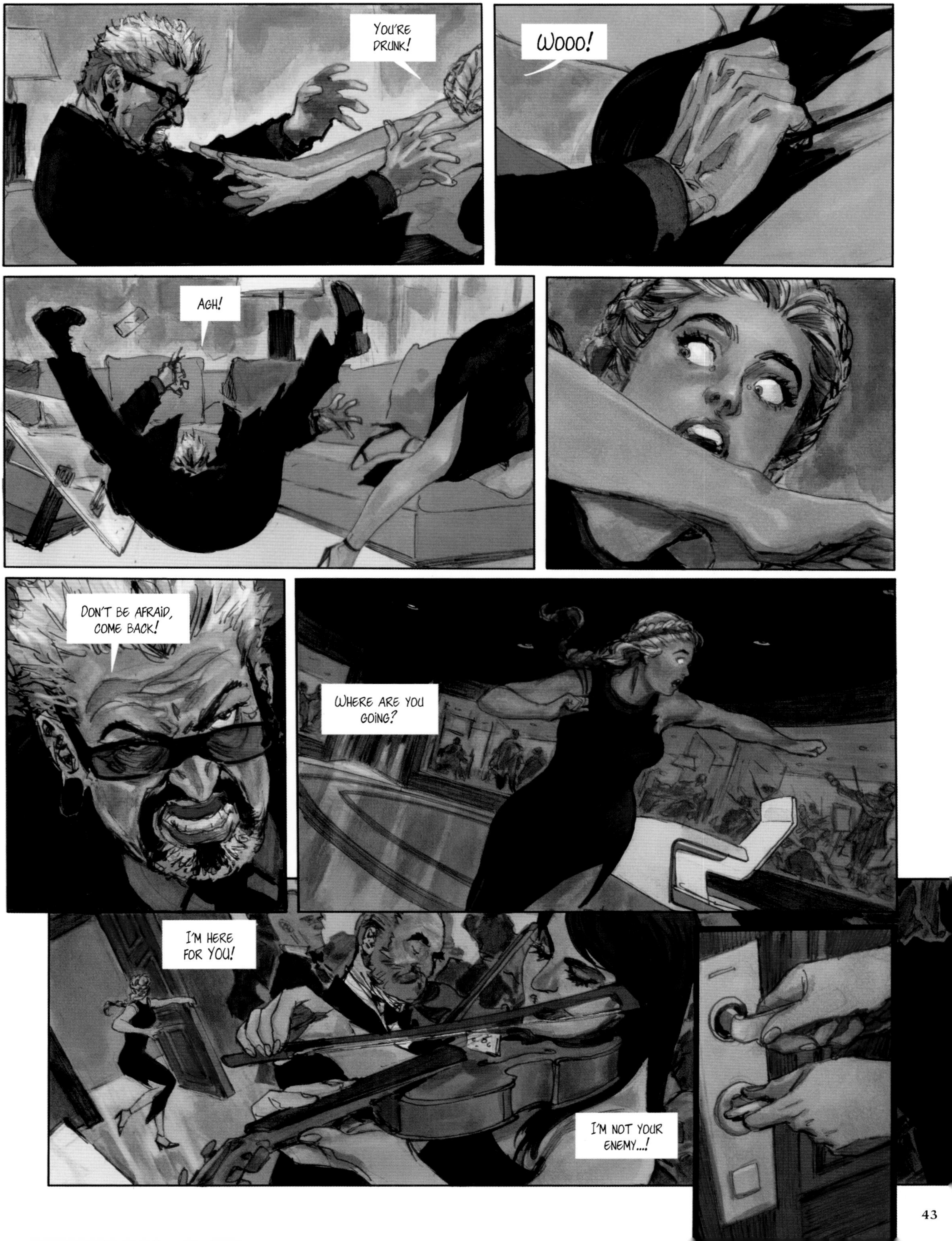
YOU'RE DRUNK!
WOOO!
AGH!
DON'T BE AFRAID, COME BACK!
WHERE ARE YOU GOING?
I'M HERE FOR YOU!
I'M NOT YOUR ENEMY...!

YOU'RE ACTING CRAZY!

OPEN UP!

THIS IS INSANE...

HOW AM I GOING TO GET OUT OF HERE?

FRANÇOIS...

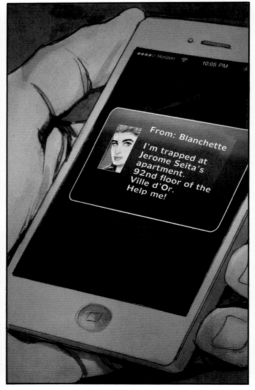

From: Blanchette

I'm trapped at Jerome Seita's apartment. 92nd floor of the Ville d'Or. Help me!

44

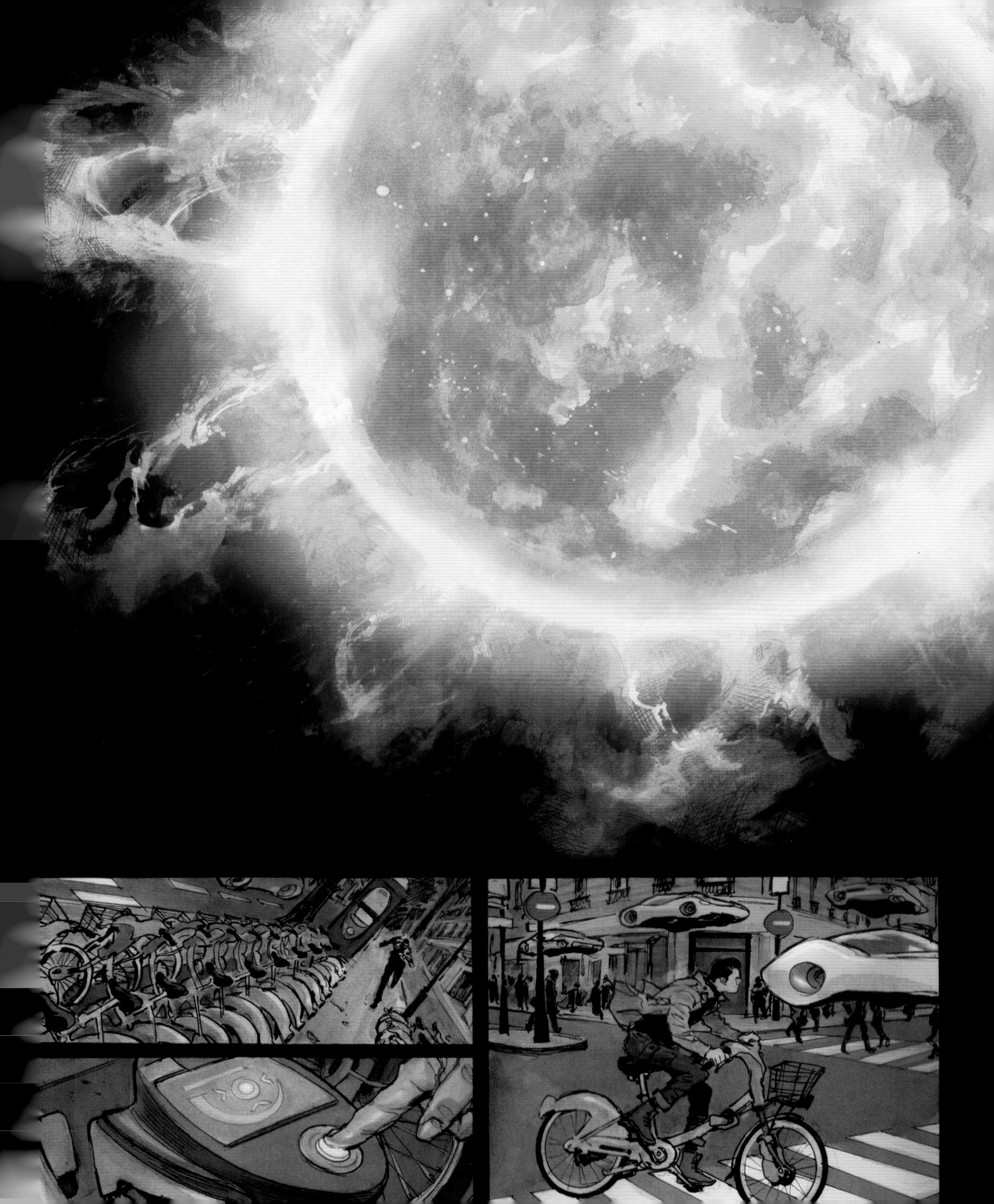

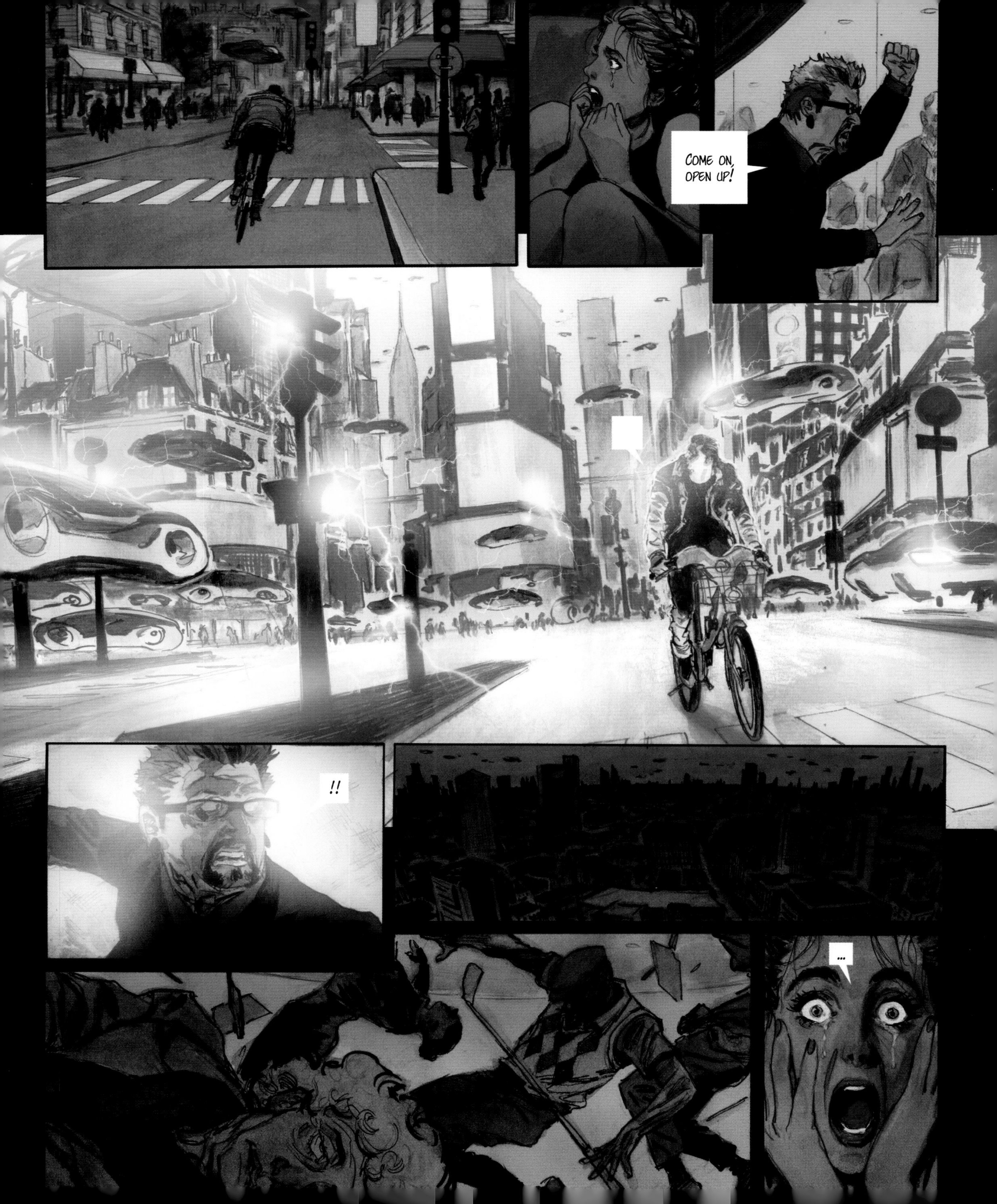
COME ON,
OPEN UP!
!!
...

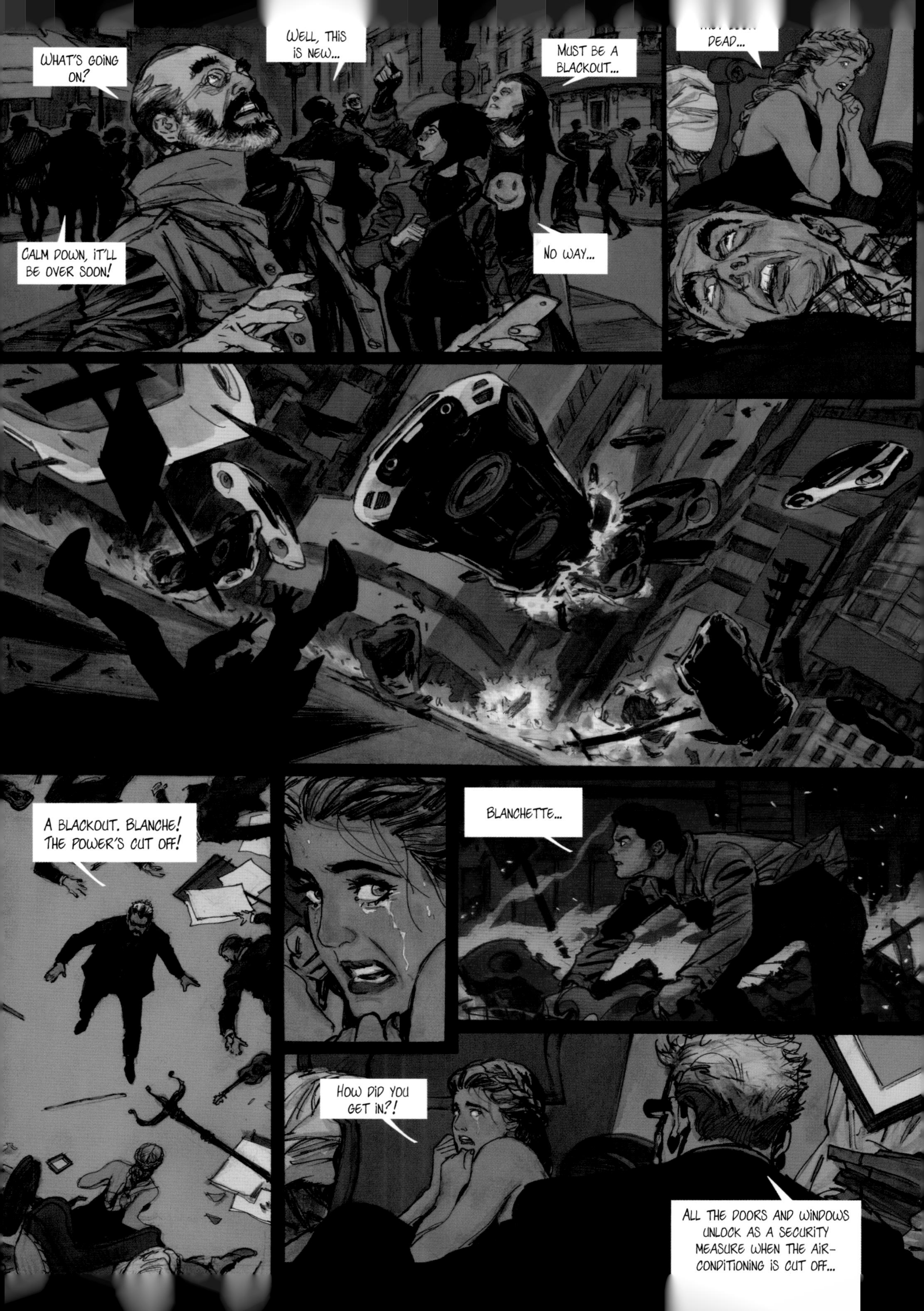
WHAT'S GOING ON?
WELL, THIS IS NEW...
MUST BE A BLACKOUT...
CALM DOWN, IT'LL BE OVER SOON!
NO WAY...
DEAD...
A BLACKOUT. BLANCHE! THE POWER'S CUT OFF!
BLANCHETTE...
HOW DID YOU GET IN?!
ALL THE DOORS AND WINDOWS UNLOCK AS A SECURITY MEASURE WHEN THE AIR-CONDITIONING IS CUT OFF...

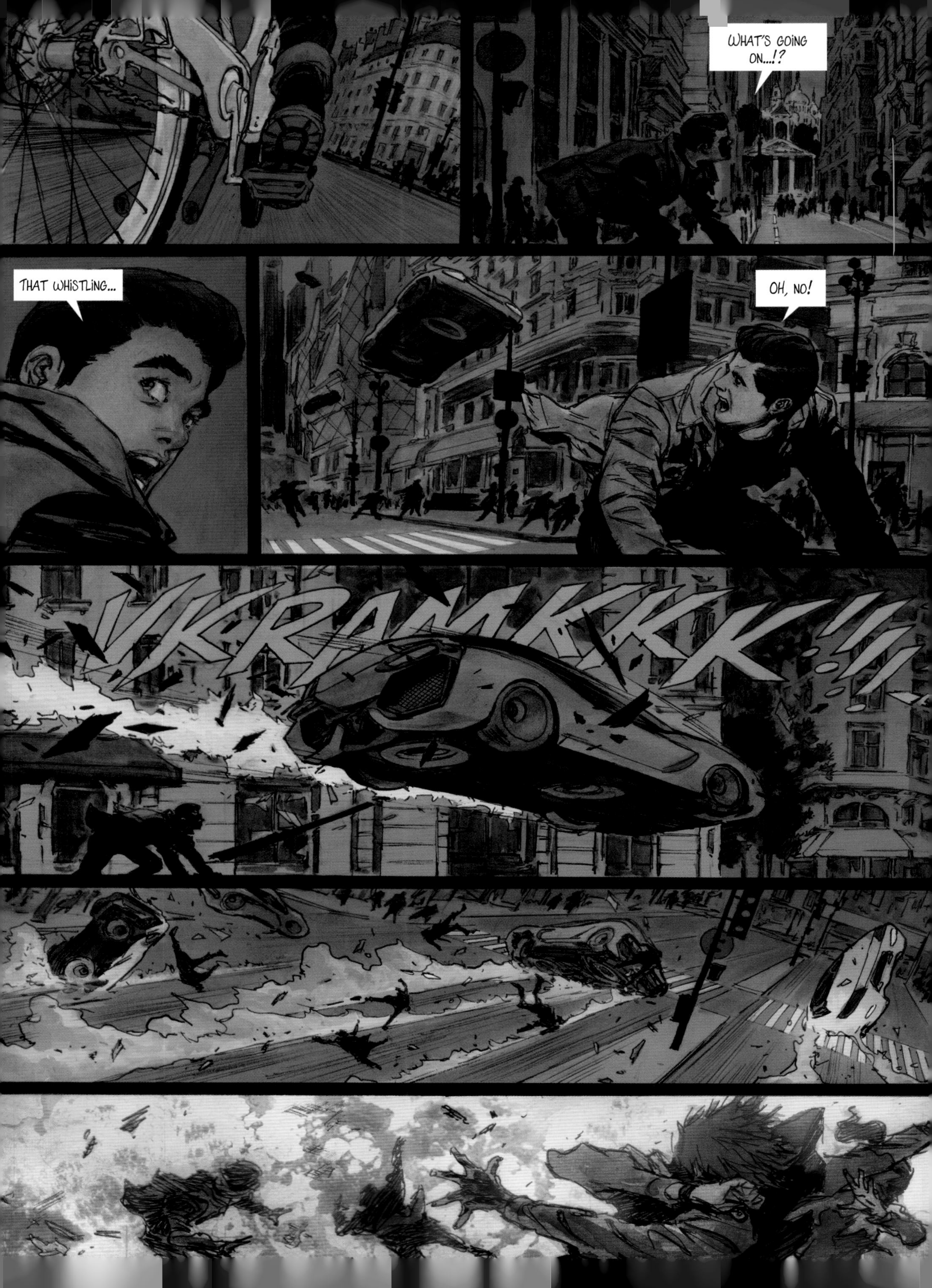
WHAT'S GOING ON...!?
THAT WHISTLING...
OH, NO!
VKRAMKKK!!!

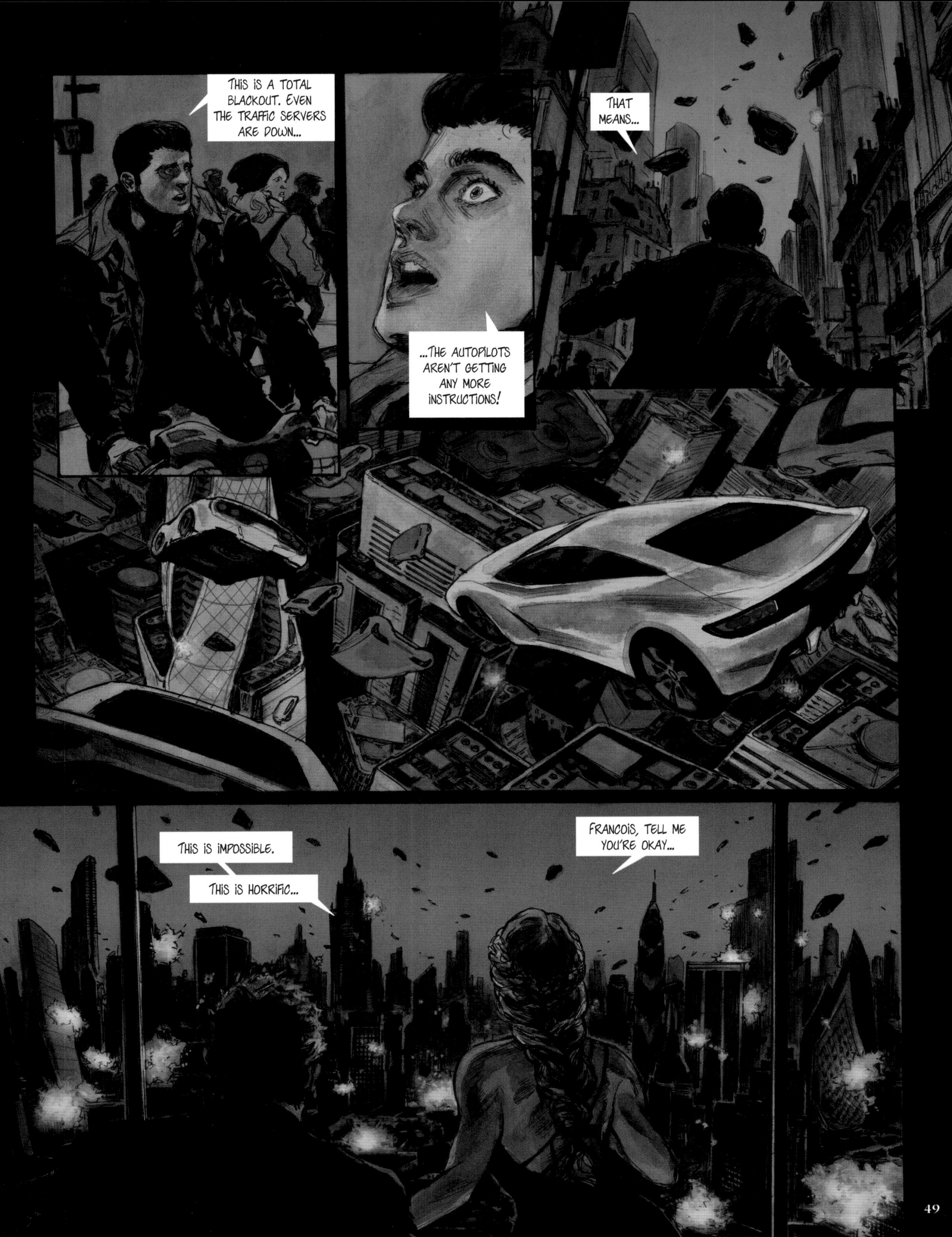
THIS IS A TOTAL BLACKOUT. EVEN THE TRAFFIC SERVERS ARE DOWN...
THAT MEANS...
...THE AUTOPILOTS AREN'T GETTING ANY MORE INSTRUCTIONS!
THIS IS IMPOSSIBLE.
THIS IS HORRIFIC...
FRANCOIS, TELL ME YOU'RE OKAY...

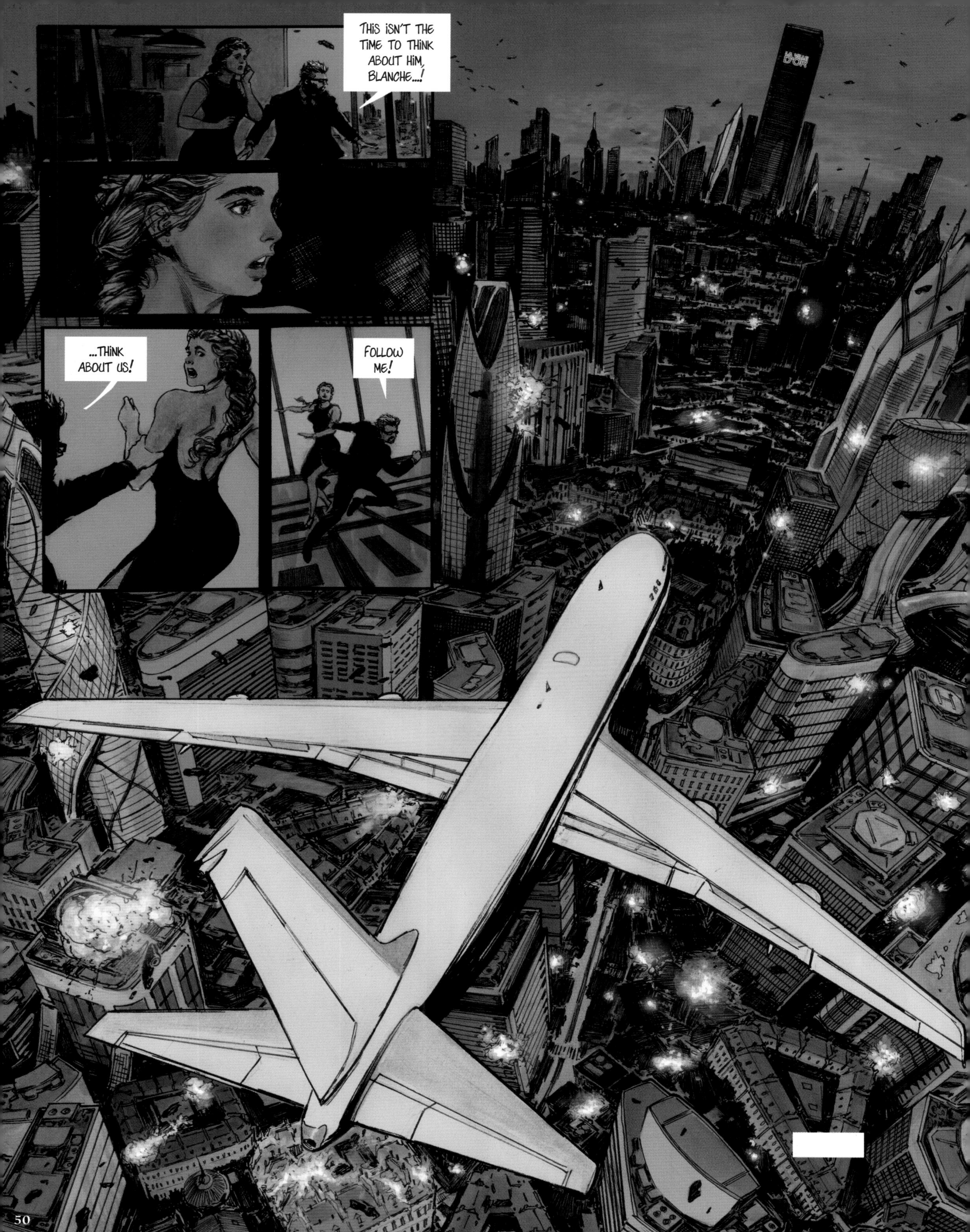
THIS ISN'T THE TIME TO THINK ABOUT HIM, BLANCHE...!
...THINK ABOUT US!
FOLLOW ME!

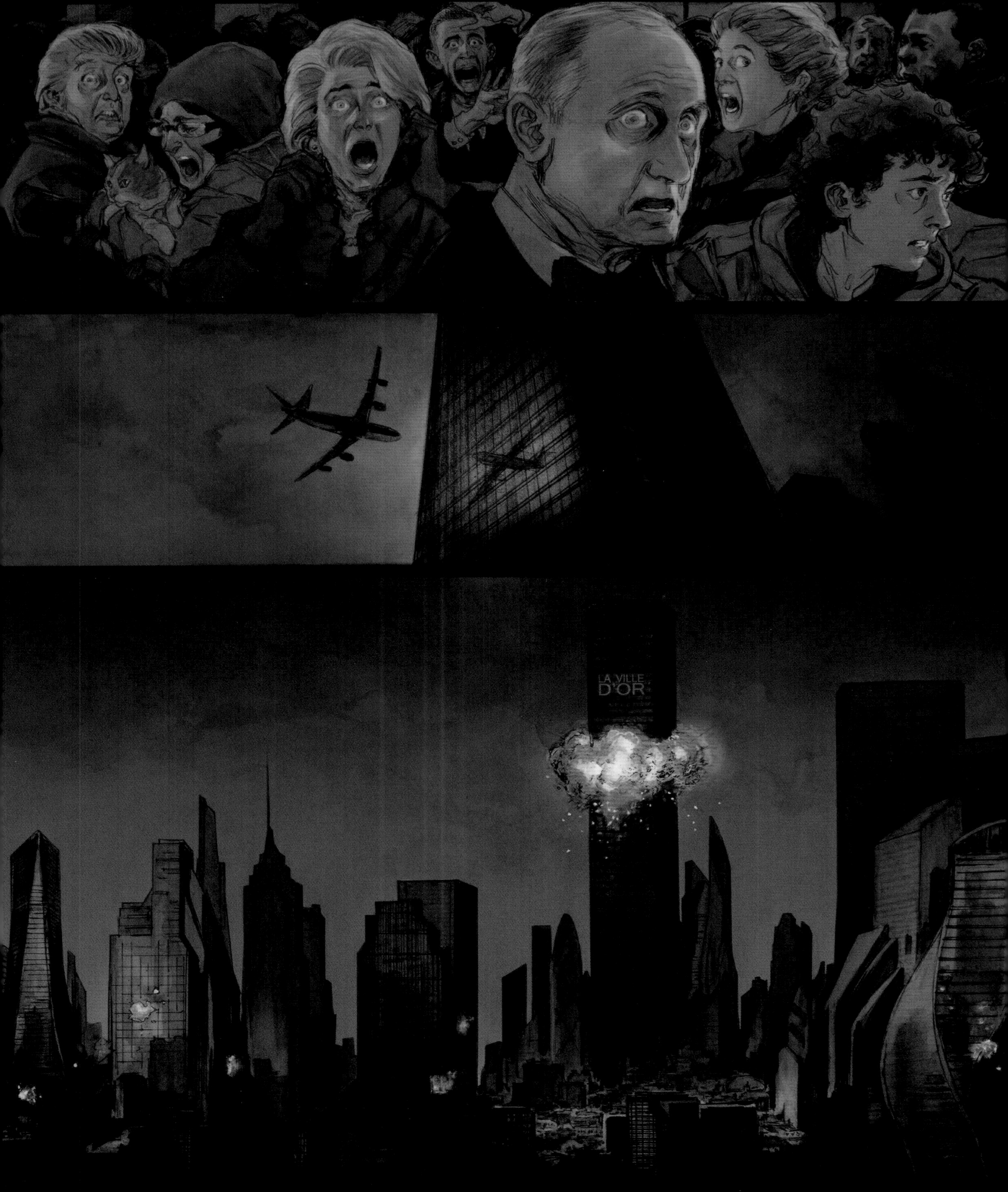
LA VILLE
D'OR

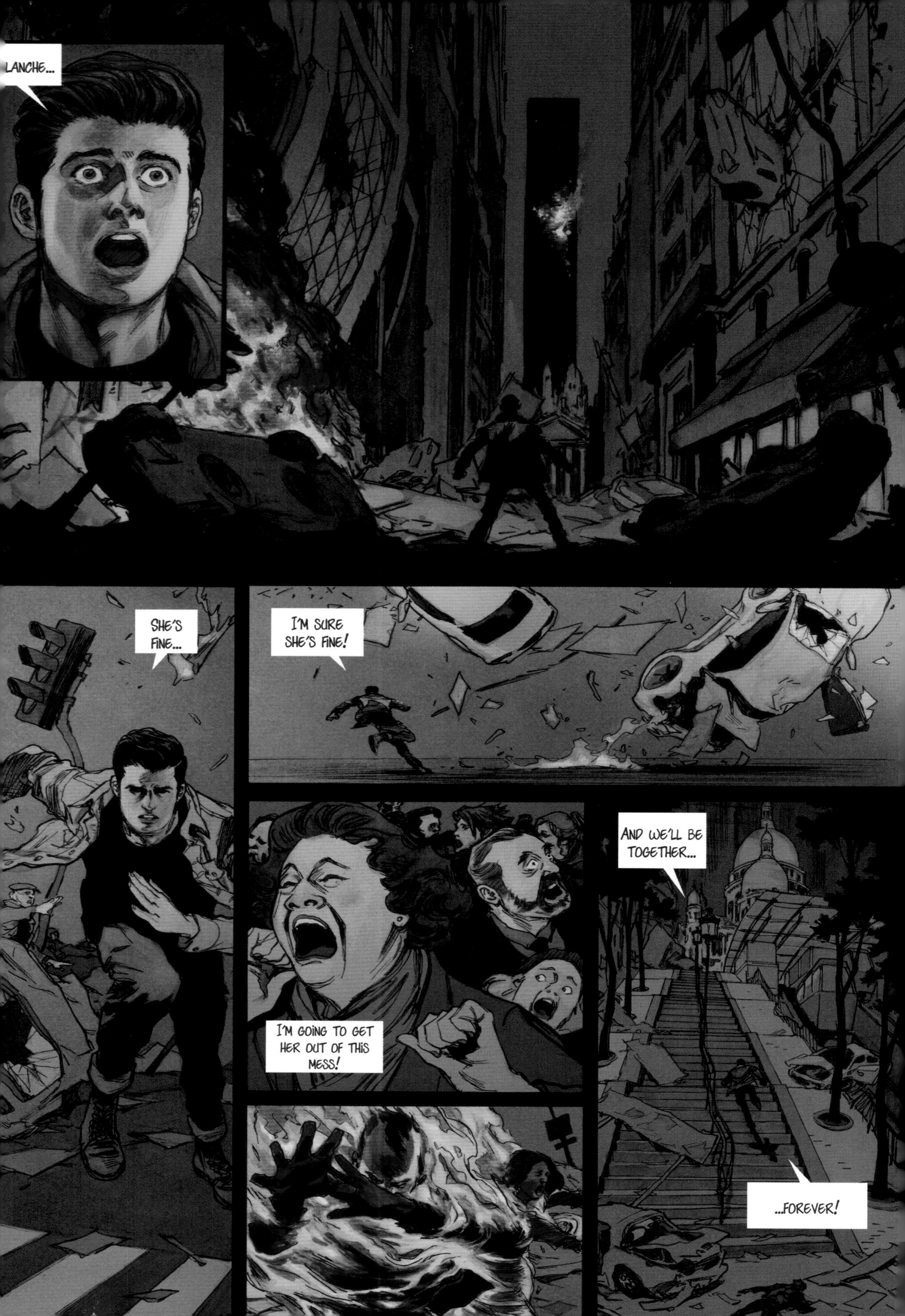
LANCHE...
SHE'S FINE...
I'M SURE SHE'S FINE!
I'M GOING TO GET HER OUT OF THIS MESS!
AND WE'LL BE TOGETHER...
...FOREVER!

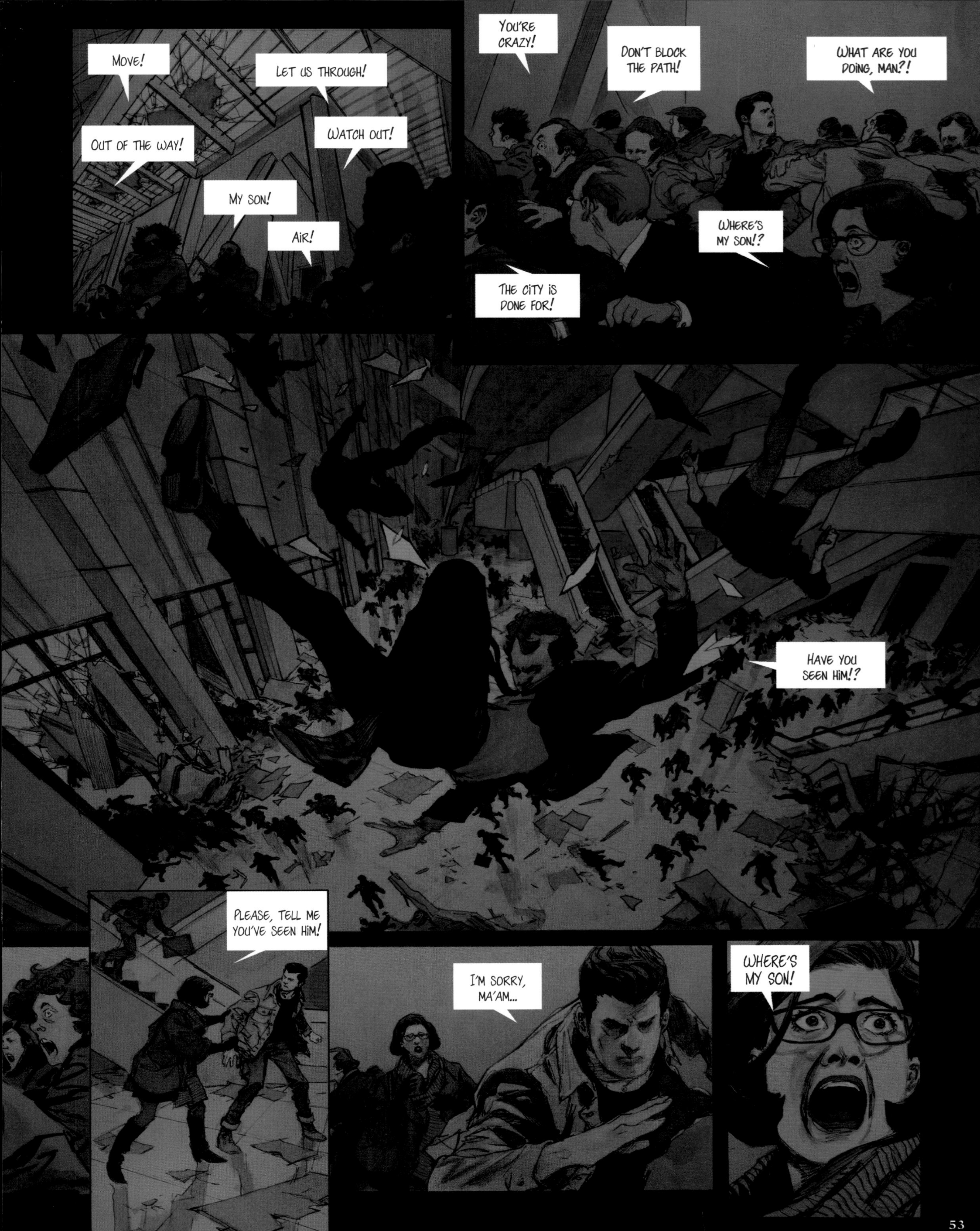
Move!
Let us through!
Out of the way!
Watch out!
My son!
Air!
You're crazy!
Don't block the path!
What are you doing, man?!
Where's my son!?
The city is done for!
Have you seen him!?
Please, tell me you've seen him!
I'm sorry, ma'am...
Where's my son!

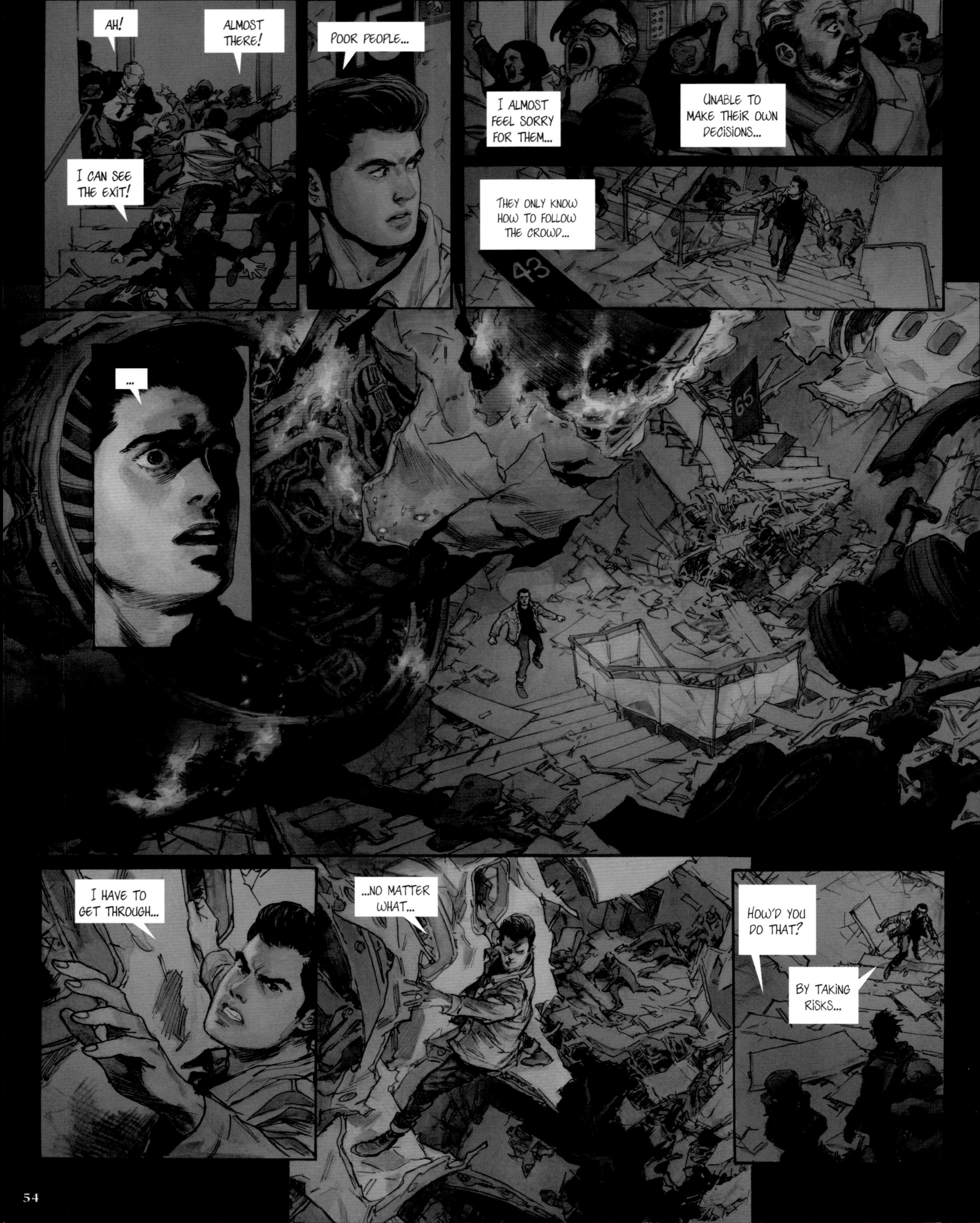
AH!
ALMOST THERE!
I CAN SEE THE EXIT!
POOR PEOPLE...
I ALMOST FEEL SORRY FOR THEM...
UNABLE TO MAKE THEIR OWN DECISIONS...
THEY ONLY KNOW HOW TO FOLLOW THE CROWD...
...
I HAVE TO GET THROUGH...
...NO MATTER WHAT...
HOW'D YOU DO THAT?
BY TAKING RISKS...

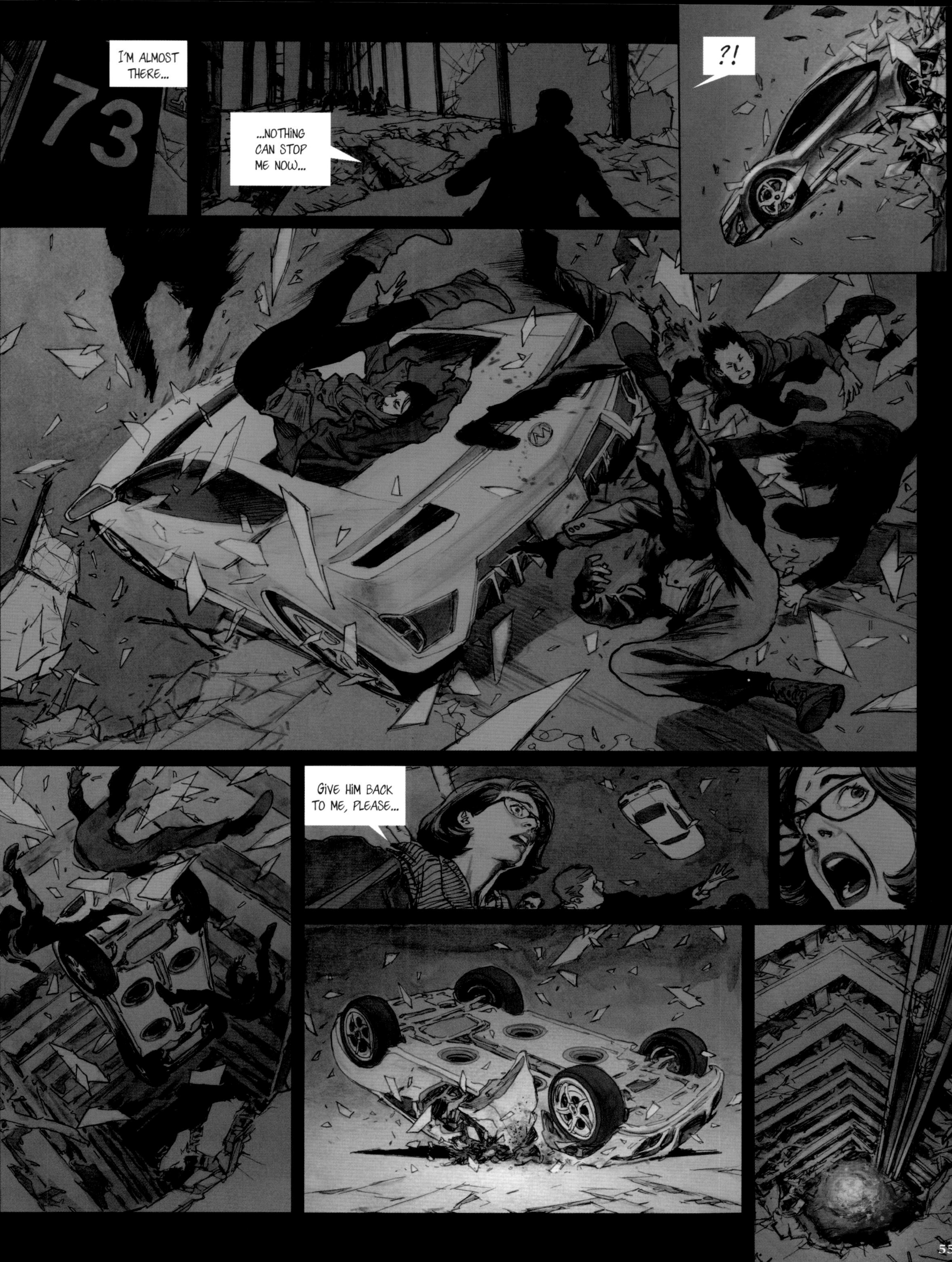
73
I'M ALMOST THERE...
...NOTHING CAN STOP ME NOW...
?!
GIVE HIM BACK TO ME, PLEASE...

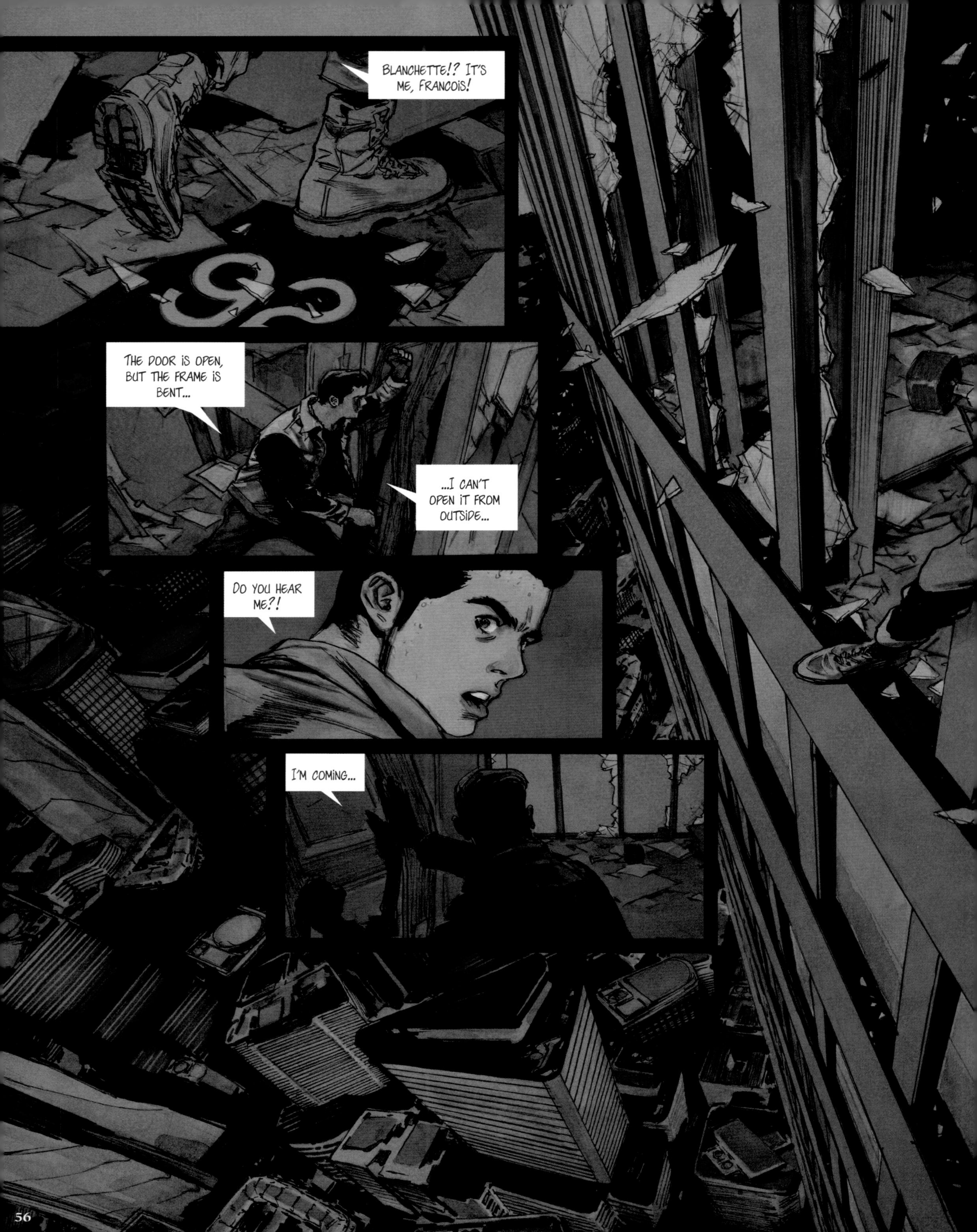
BLANCHETTE!? IT'S ME, FRANCOIS!
THE DOOR IS OPEN, BUT THE FRAME IS BENT...
...I CAN'T OPEN IT FROM OUTSIDE...
DO YOU HEAR ME?!
I'M COMING...

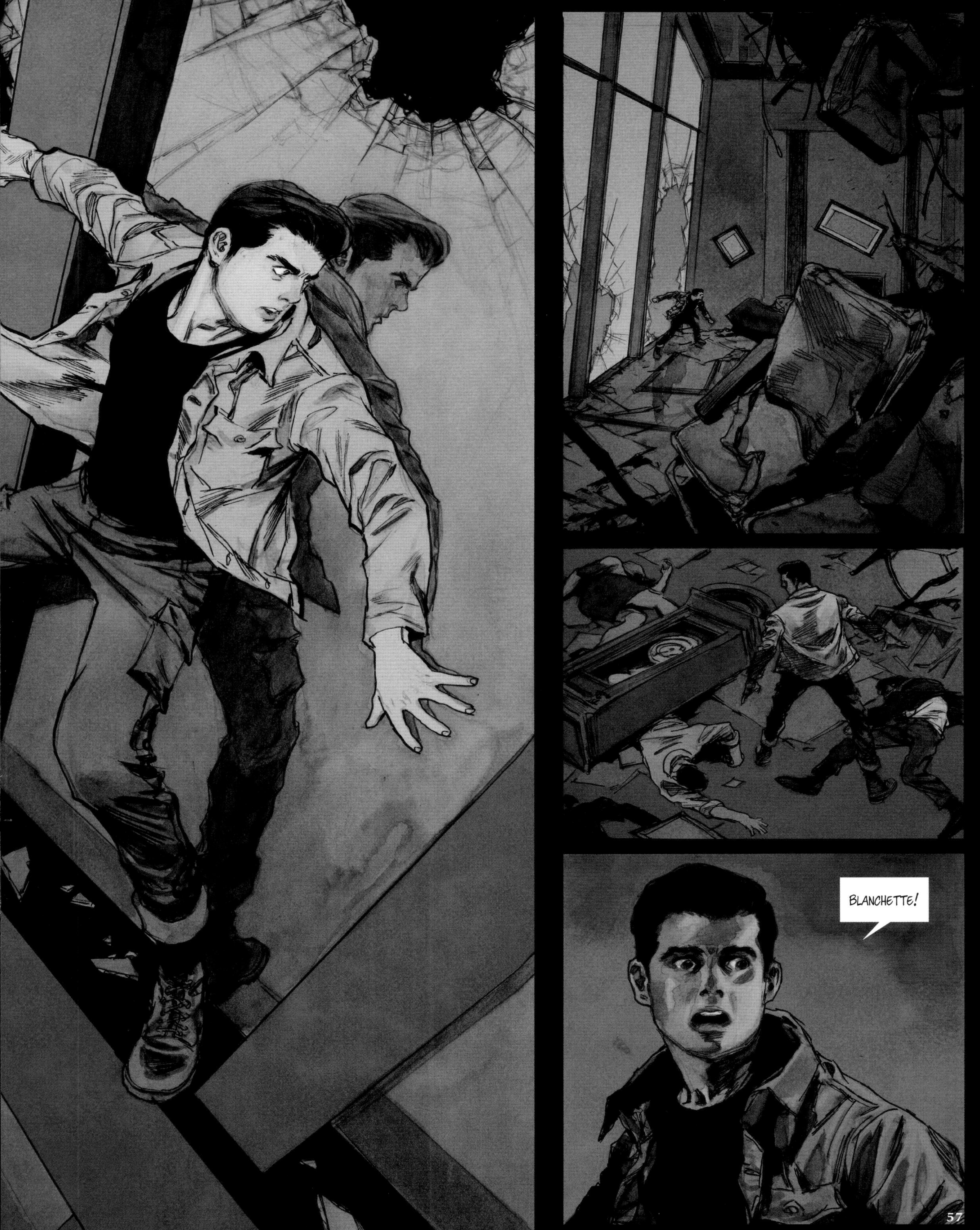
BLANCHETTE!

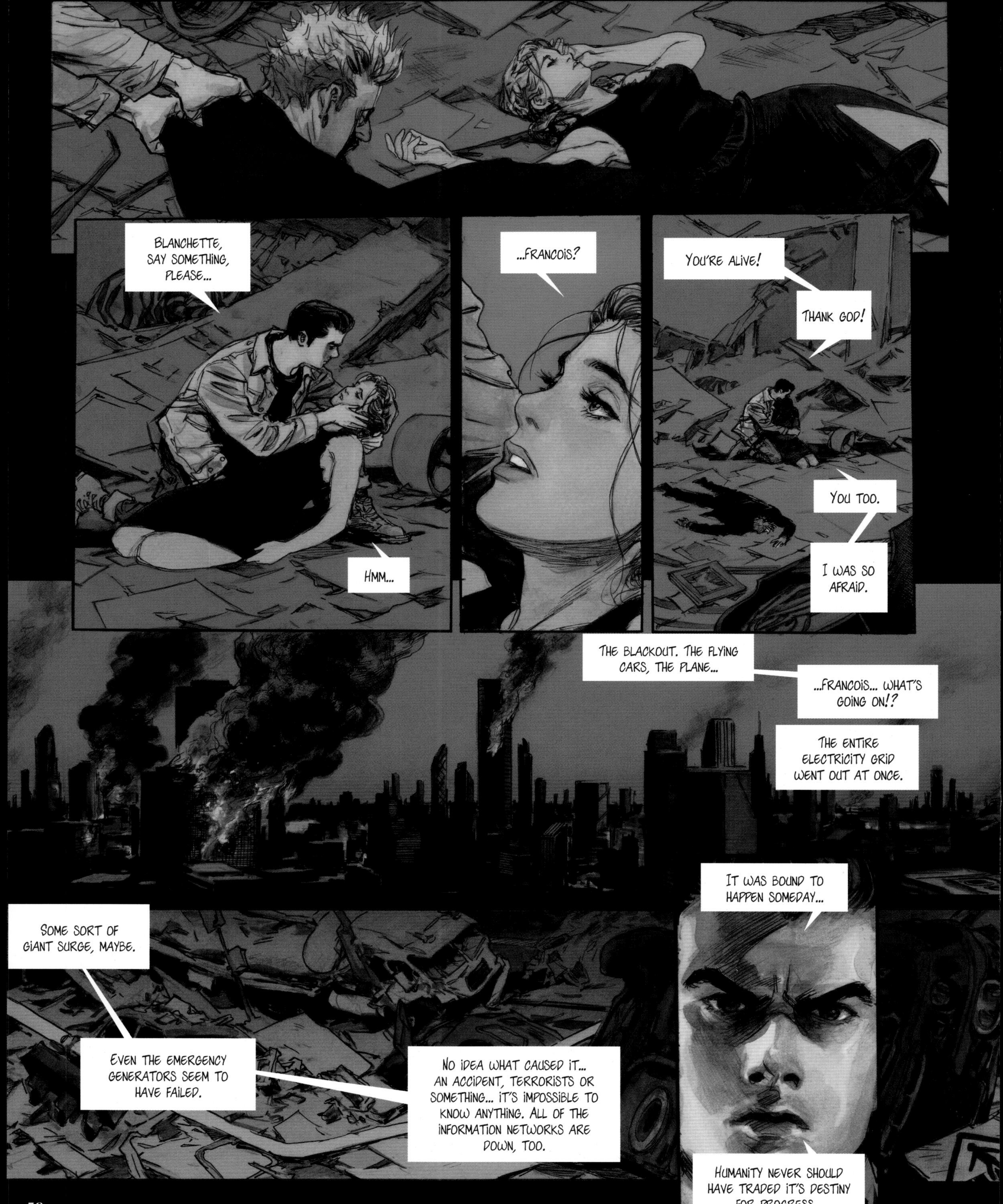
BLANCHETTE, SAY SOMETHING, PLEASE...
HMM...
...FRANCOIS?
YOU'RE ALIVE!
THANK GOD!
YOU TOO.
I WAS SO AFRAID.
THE BLACKOUT. THE FLYING CARS, THE PLANE...
...FRANCOIS... WHAT'S GOING ON!?
THE ENTIRE ELECTRICITY GRID WENT OUT AT ONCE.
SOME SORT OF GIANT SURGE, MAYBE.
EVEN THE EMERGENCY GENERATORS SEEM TO HAVE FAILED.
NO IDEA WHAT CAUSED IT... AN ACCIDENT, TERRORISTS OR SOMETHING... IT'S IMPOSSIBLE TO KNOW ANYTHING. ALL OF THE INFORMATION NETWORKS ARE DOWN, TOO.
IT WAS BOUND TO HAPPEN SOMEDAY...
HUMANITY NEVER SHOULD HAVE TRADED IT'S DESTINY FOR PROGRESS...

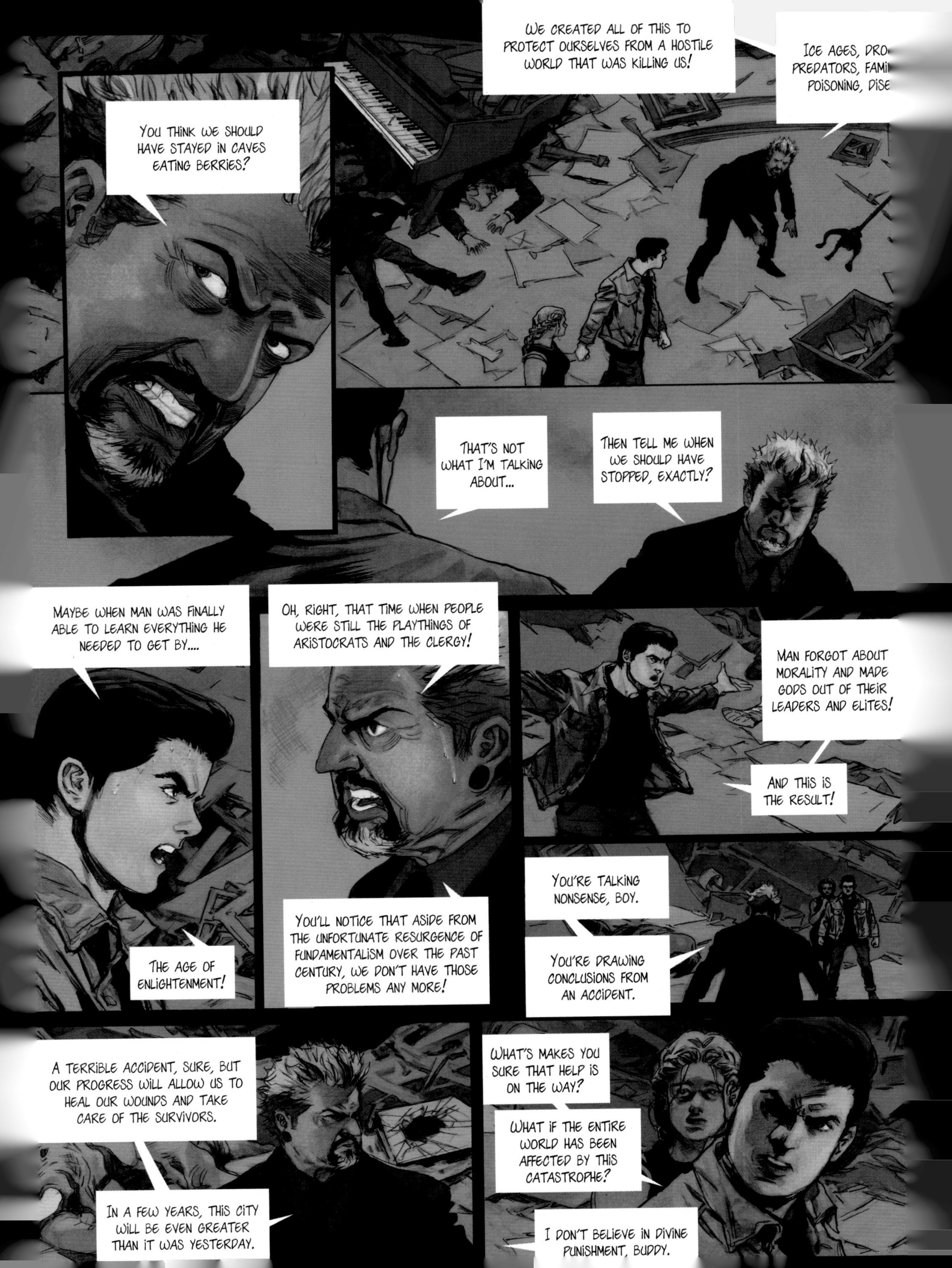

You think we should have stayed in caves eating berries?
We created all of this to protect ourselves from a hostile world that was killing us!
Ice ages, dro predators, fami poisoning, dise
That's not what I'm talking about...
Then tell me when we should have stopped, exactly?
Maybe when man was finally able to learn everything he needed to get by....
The age of enlightenment!
Oh, right, that time when people were still the playthings of aristocrats and the clergy!
You'll notice that aside from the unfortunate resurgence of fundamentalism over the past century, we don't have those problems any more!
Man forgot about morality and made gods out of their leaders and elites!
And this is the result!
You're talking nonsense, boy.
You're drawing conclusions from an accident.
A terrible accident, sure, but our progress will allow us to heal our wounds and take care of the survivors.
In a few years, this city will be even greater than it was yesterday.
What's makes you sure that help is on the way?
What if the entire world has been affected by this catastrophe?
I don't believe in divine punishment, buddy.

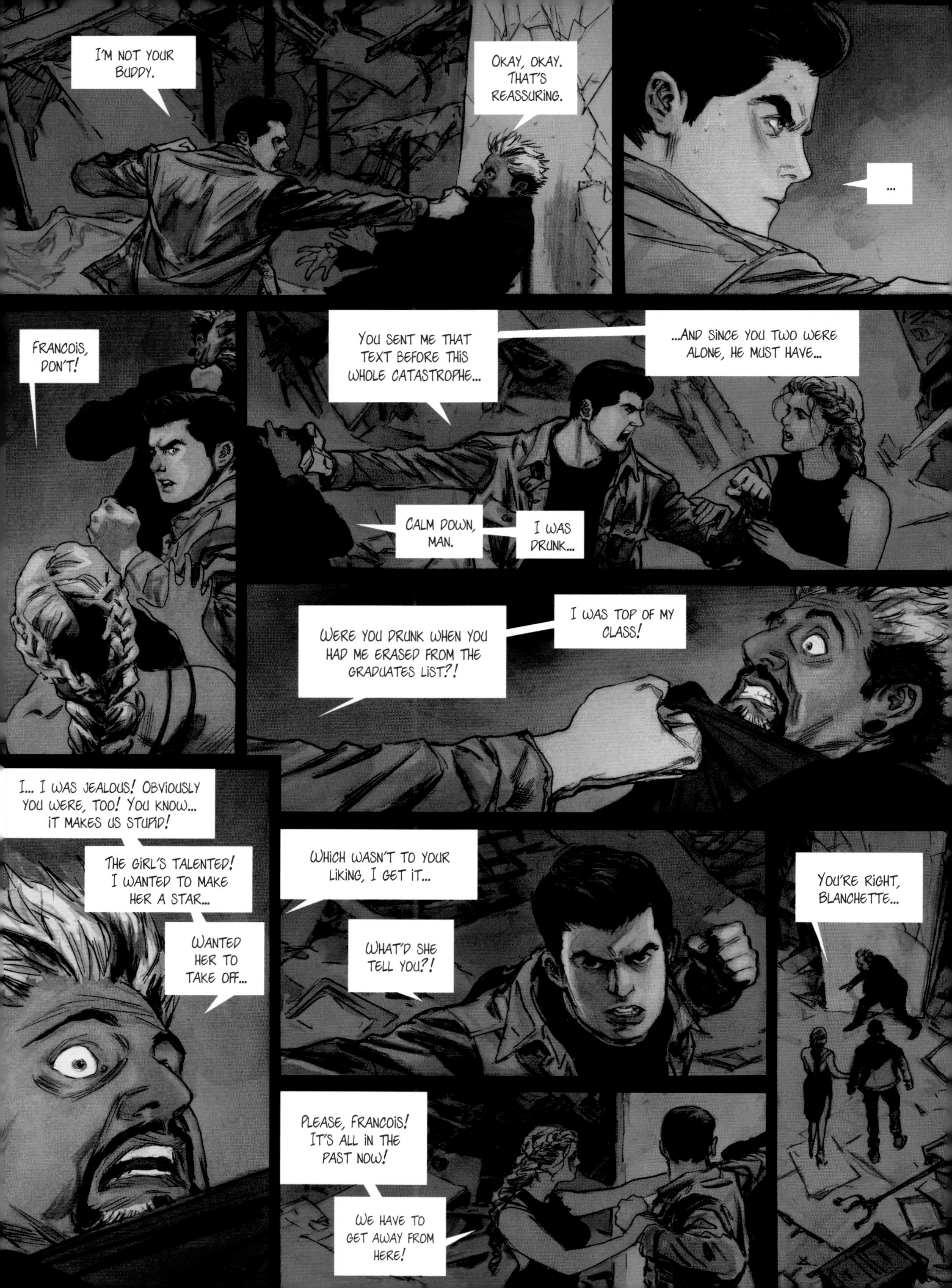
I'M NOT YOUR BUDDY.
OKAY, OKAY. THAT'S REASSURING.
...
FRANCOIS, DON'T!
YOU SENT ME THAT TEXT BEFORE THIS WHOLE CATASTROPHE...
...AND SINCE YOU TWO WERE ALONE, HE MUST HAVE...
CALM DOWN, MAN.
I WAS DRUNK...
WERE YOU DRUNK WHEN YOU HAD ME ERASED FROM THE GRADUATES LIST?!
I WAS TOP OF MY CLASS!
I... I WAS JEALOUS! OBVIOUSLY YOU WERE, TOO! YOU KNOW... IT MAKES US STUPID!
THE GIRL'S TALENTED! I WANTED TO MAKE HER A STAR...
WANTED HER TO TAKE OFF...
WHICH WASN'T TO YOUR LIKING, I GET IT...
WHAT'D SHE TELL YOU?!
PLEASE, FRANCOIS! IT'S ALL IN THE PAST NOW!
WE HAVE TO GET AWAY FROM HERE!
YOU'RE RIGHT, BLANCHETTE...

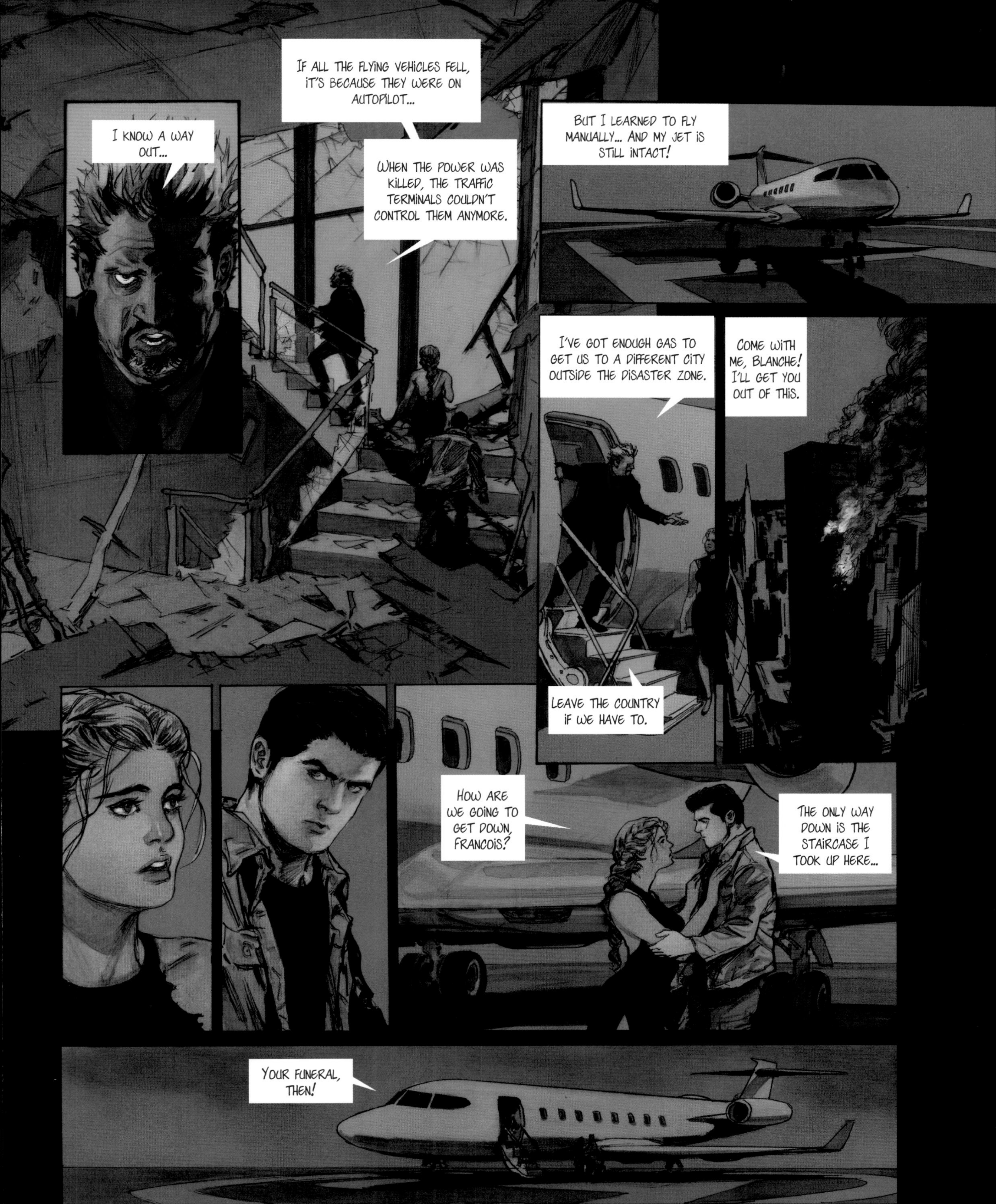
I KNOW A WAY OUT...
IF ALL THE FLYING VEHICLES FELL, IT'S BECAUSE THEY WERE ON AUTOPILOT...
WHEN THE POWER WAS KILLED, THE TRAFFIC TERMINALS COULDN'T CONTROL THEM ANYMORE.
BUT I LEARNED TO FLY MANUALLY... AND MY JET IS STILL INTACT!
I'VE GOT ENOUGH GAS TO GET US TO A DIFFERENT CITY OUTSIDE THE DISASTER ZONE.
LEAVE THE COUNTRY IF WE HAVE TO.
COME WITH ME, BLANCHE! I'LL GET YOU OUT OF THIS.
HOW ARE WE GOING TO GET DOWN, FRANCOIS?
THE ONLY WAY DOWN IS THE STAIRCASE I TOOK UP HERE...
YOUR FUNERAL, THEN!

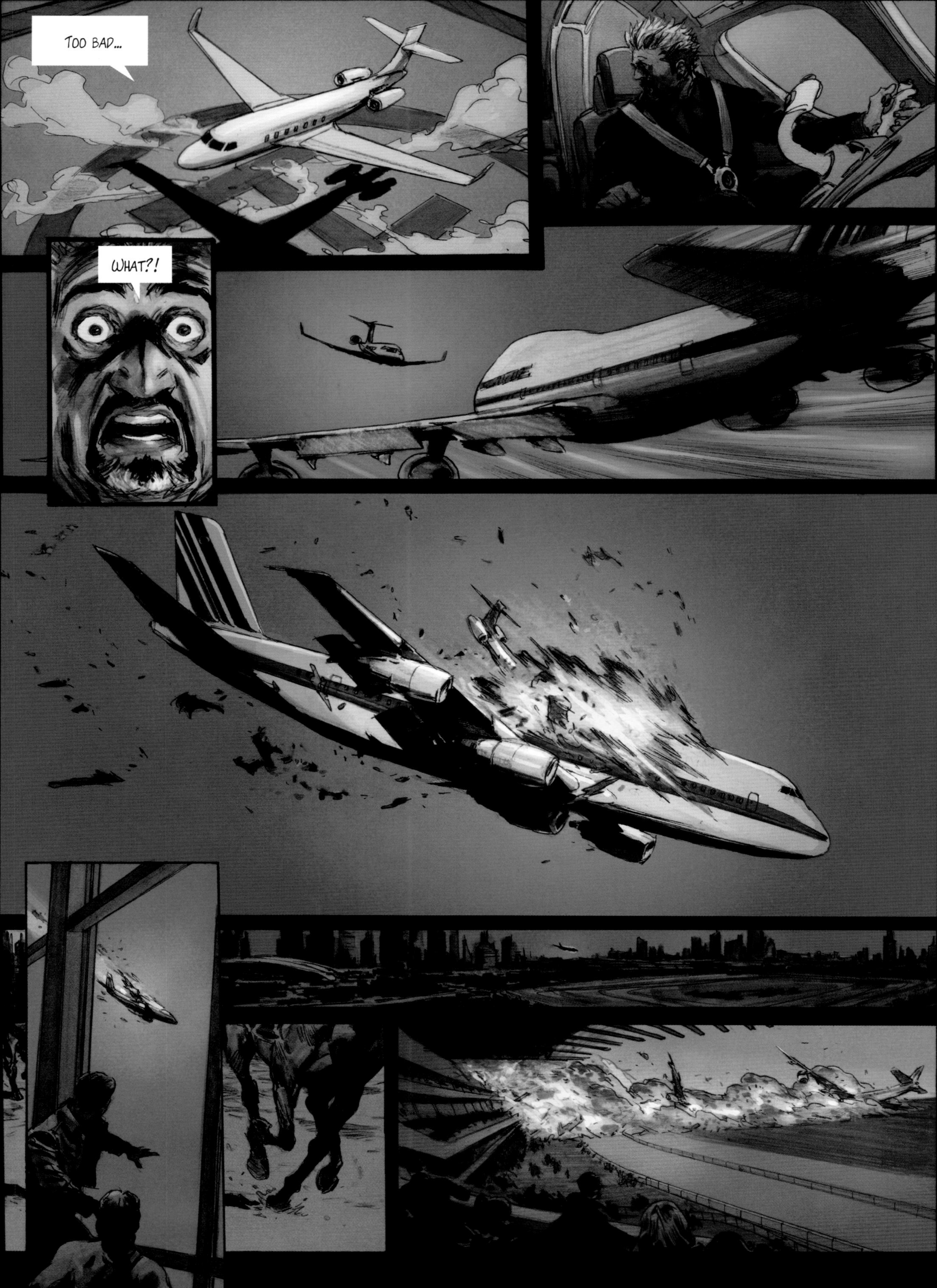
TOO BAD...
WHAT?!

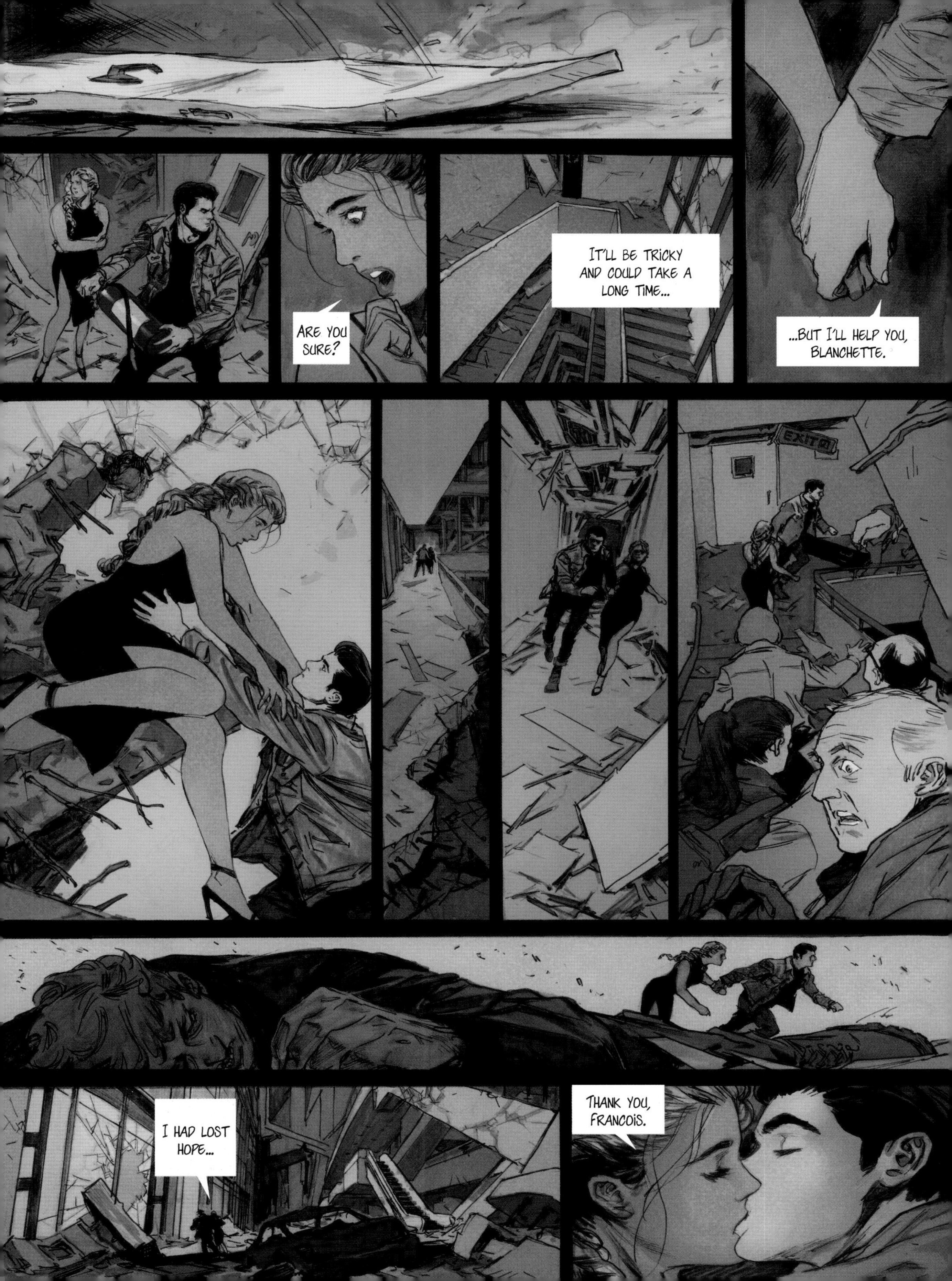

ARE YOU SURE?
IT'LL BE TRICKY AND COULD TAKE A LONG TIME...
...BUT I'LL HELP YOU, BLANCHETTE.
EXIT
I HAD LOST HOPE...
THANK YOU, FRANCOIS.

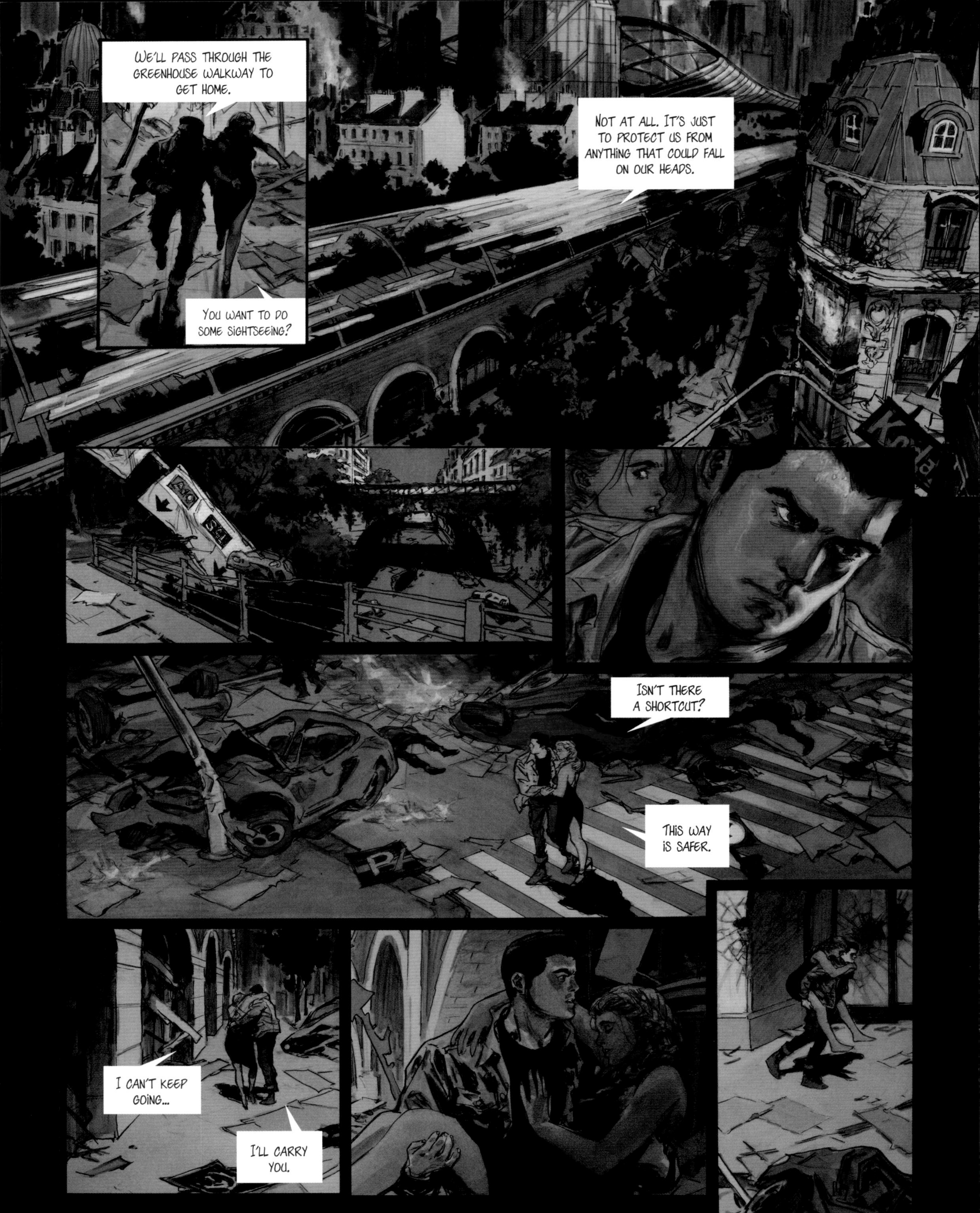

WE'LL PASS THROUGH THE GREENHOUSE WALKWAY TO GET HOME.
YOU WANT TO DO SOME SIGHTSEEING?
NOT AT ALL. IT'S JUST TO PROTECT US FROM ANYTHING THAT COULD FALL ON OUR HEADS.
ISN'T THERE A SHORTCUT?
THIS WAY IS SAFER.
I CAN'T KEEP GOING...
I'LL CARRY YOU.

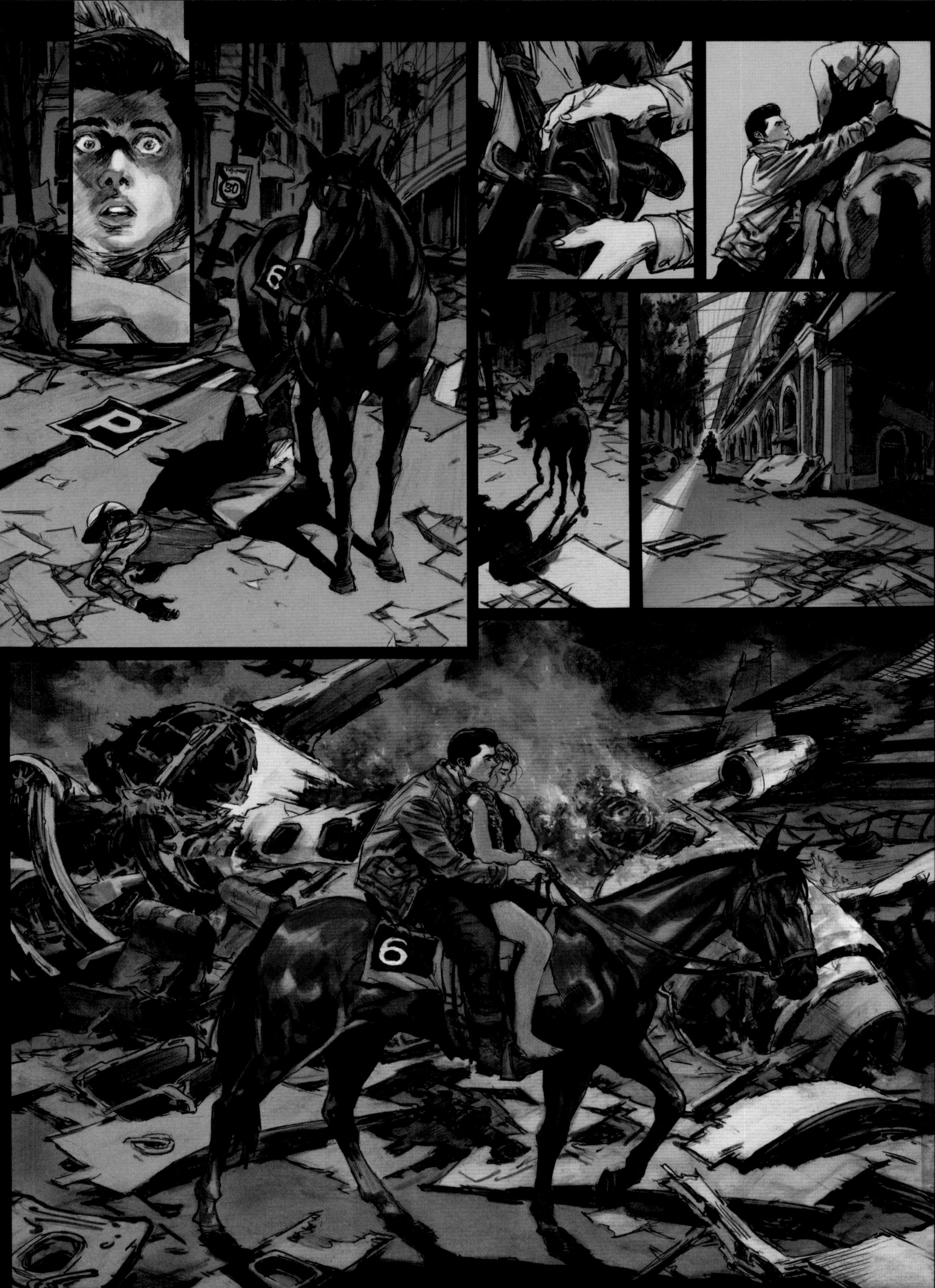

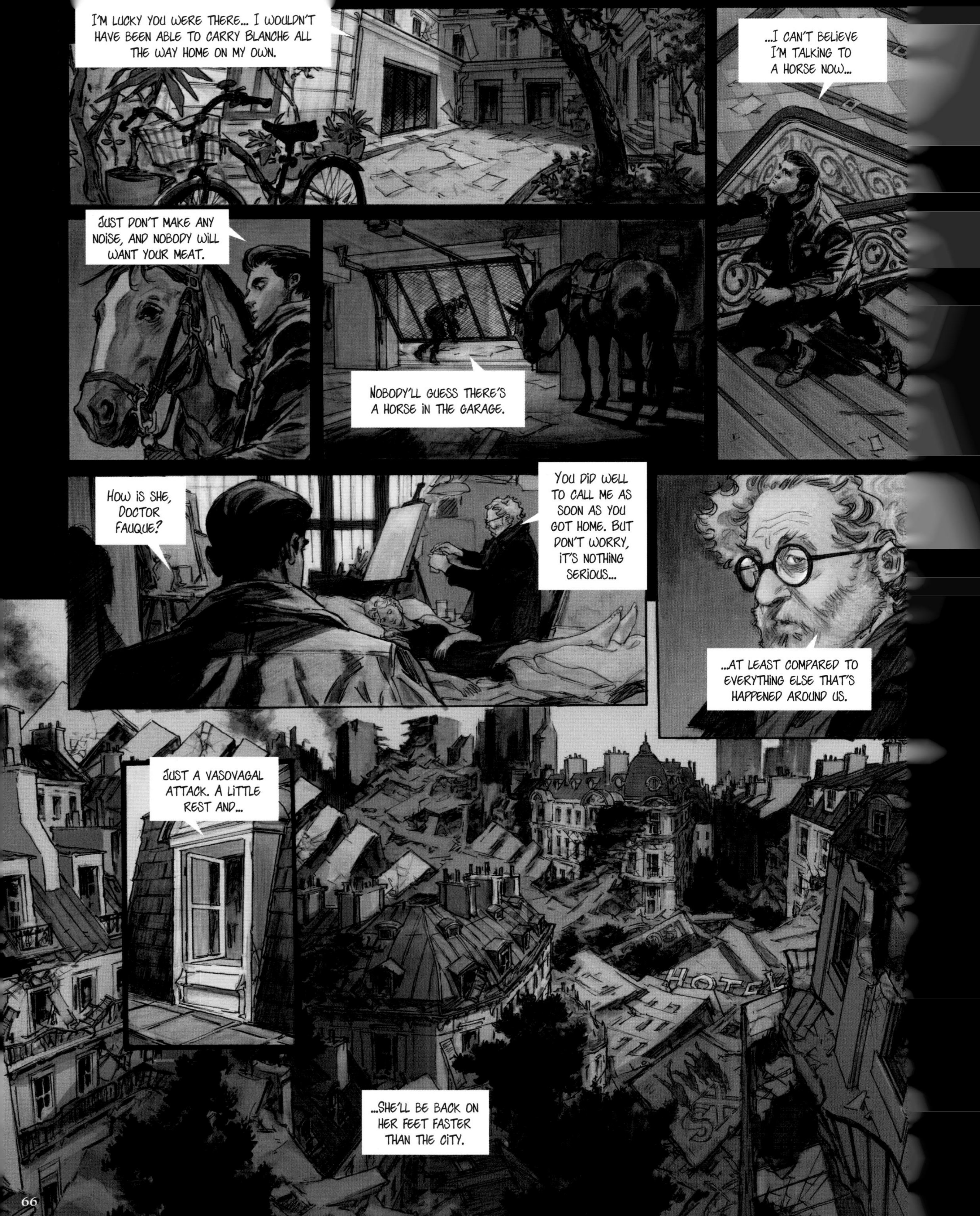

I'M LUCKY YOU WERE THERE... I WOULDN'T HAVE BEEN ABLE TO CARRY BLANCHE ALL THE WAY HOME ON MY OWN.
...I CAN'T BELIEVE I'M TALKING TO A HORSE NOW...
JUST DON'T MAKE ANY NOISE, AND NOBODY WILL WANT YOUR MEAT.
NOBODY'LL GUESS THERE'S A HORSE IN THE GARAGE.
HOW IS SHE, DOCTOR FAUQUE?
YOU DID WELL TO CALL ME AS SOON AS YOU GOT HOME. BUT DON'T WORRY, IT'S NOTHING SERIOUS...
...AT LEAST COMPARED TO EVERYTHING ELSE THAT'S HAPPENED AROUND US.
JUST A VASOVAGAL ATTACK. A LITTLE REST AND...
...SHE'LL BE BACK ON HER FEET FASTER THAN THE CITY.

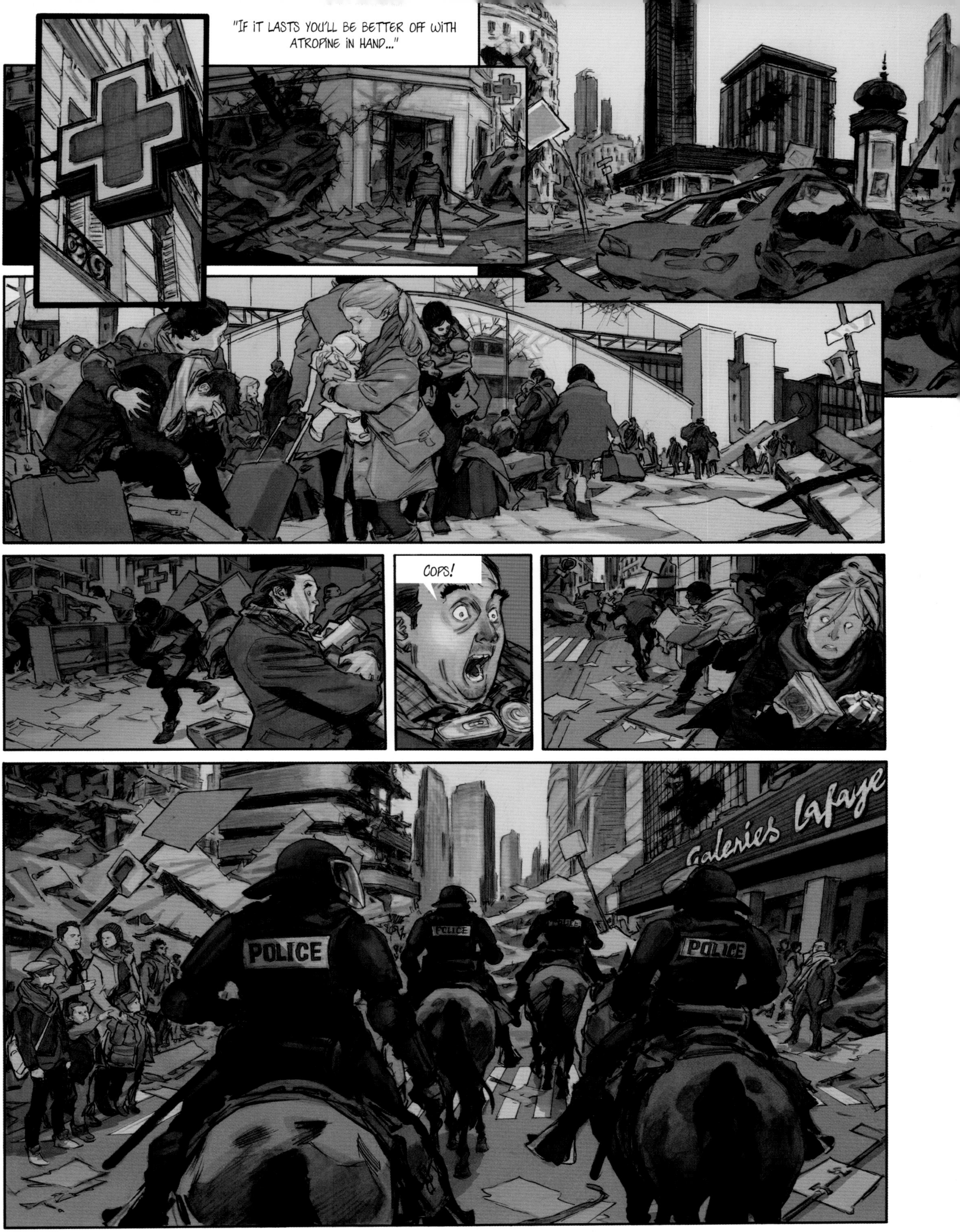

"IF IT LASTS YOU'LL BE BETTER OFF WITH ATROPINE IN HAND..."
COPS!
POLICE
POLICE
POLICE
Galeries Lafaye

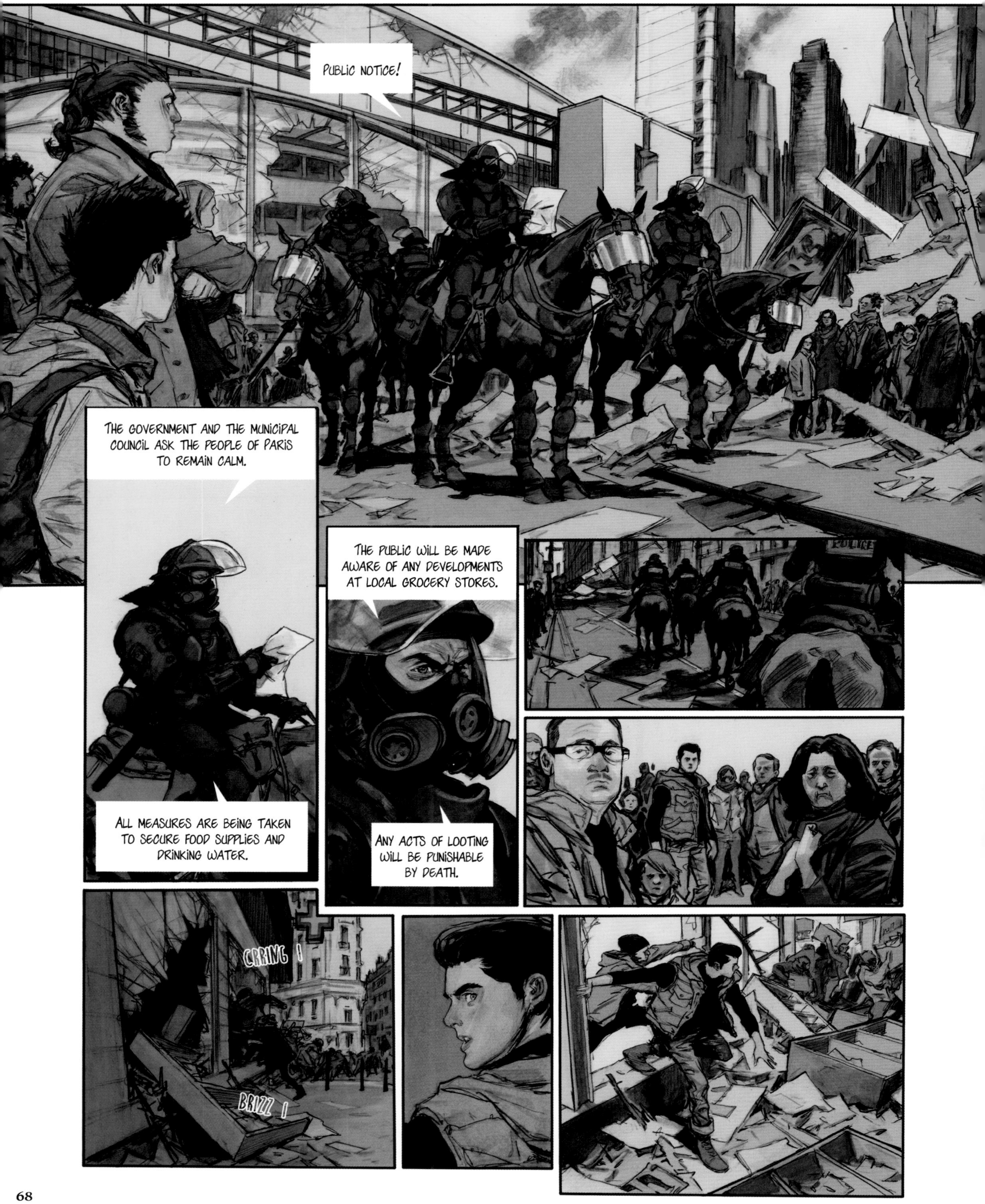
PUBLIC NOTICE!
THE GOVERNMENT AND THE MUNICIPAL COUNCIL ASK THE PEOPLE OF PARIS TO REMAIN CALM.
ALL MEASURES ARE BEING TAKEN TO SECURE FOOD SUPPLIES AND DRINKING WATER.
THE PUBLIC WILL BE MADE AWARE OF ANY DEVELOPMENTS AT LOCAL GROCERY STORES.
ANY ACTS OF LOOTING WILL BE PUNISHABLE BY DEATH.
POLICE
CRRING !
BRIZZ !

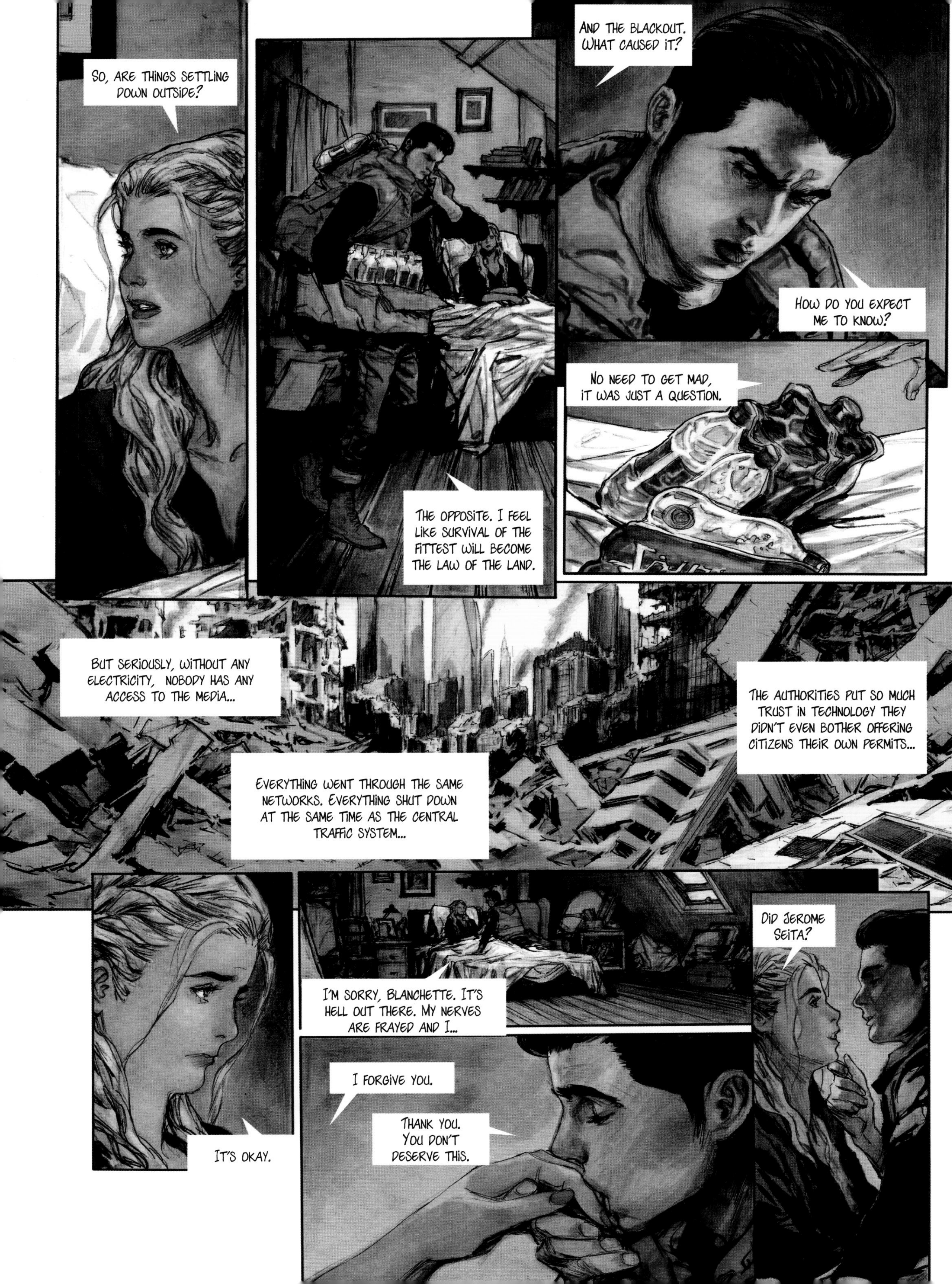

SO, ARE THINGS SETTLING DOWN OUTSIDE?
THE OPPOSITE. I FEEL LIKE SURVIVAL OF THE FITTEST WILL BECOME THE LAW OF THE LAND.
AND THE BLACKOUT. WHAT CAUSED IT?
HOW DO YOU EXPECT ME TO KNOW?
NO NEED TO GET MAD, IT WAS JUST A QUESTION.
BUT SERIOUSLY, WITHOUT ANY ELECTRICITY, NOBODY HAS ANY ACCESS TO THE MEDIA...
EVERYTHING WENT THROUGH THE SAME NETWORKS. EVERYTHING SHUT DOWN AT THE SAME TIME AS THE CENTRAL TRAFFIC SYSTEM...
THE AUTHORITIES PUT SO MUCH TRUST IN TECHNOLOGY THEY DIDN'T EVEN BOTHER OFFERING CITIZENS THEIR OWN PERMITS...
IT'S OKAY.
I'M SORRY, BLANCHETTE. IT'S HELL OUT THERE. MY NERVES ARE FRAYED AND I...
I FORGIVE YOU.
THANK YOU. YOU DON'T DESERVE THIS.
DID JEROME SEITA?

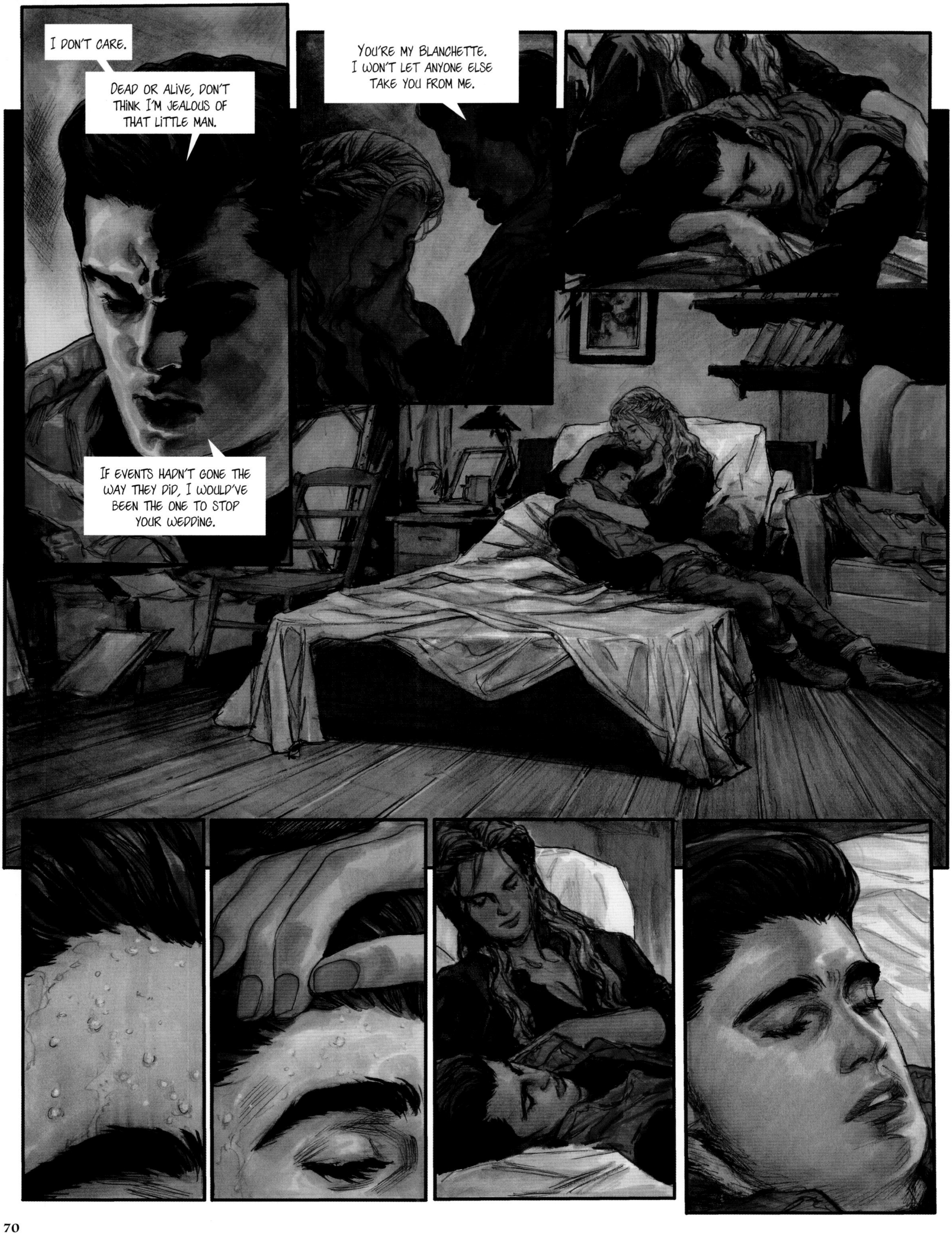
I DON'T CARE.
DEAD OR ALIVE, DON'T THINK I'M JEALOUS OF THAT LITTLE MAN.
IF EVENTS HADN'T GONE THE WAY THEY DID, I WOULD'VE BEEN THE ONE TO STOP YOUR WEDDING.
YOU'RE MY BLANCHETTE. I WON'T LET ANYONE ELSE TAKE YOU FROM ME.

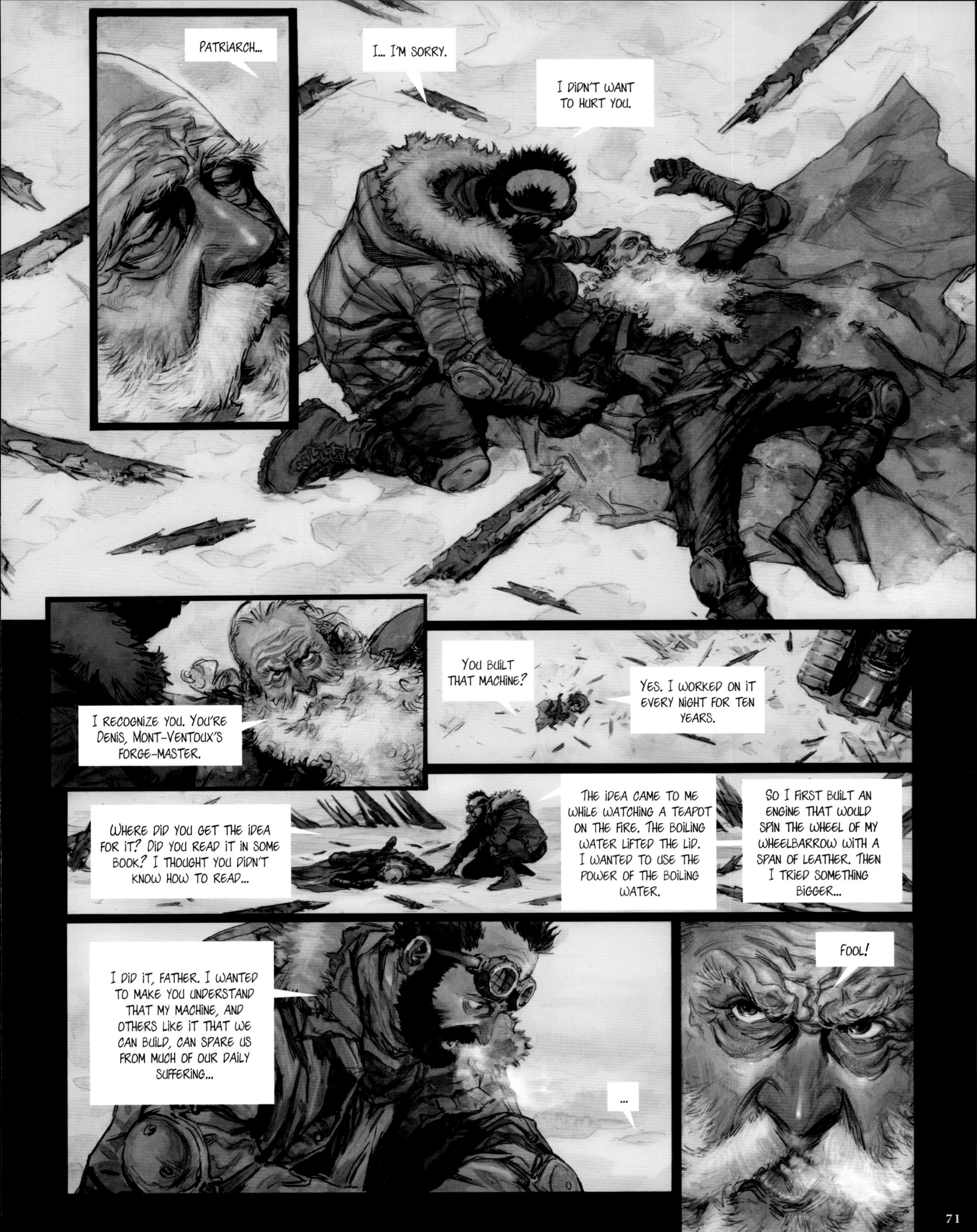
PATRIARCH...
I... I'M SORRY.
I DIDN'T WANT TO HURT YOU.
I RECOGNIZE YOU. YOU'RE DENIS, MONT-VENTOUX'S FORGE-MASTER.
YOU BUILT THAT MACHINE?
YES. I WORKED ON IT EVERY NIGHT FOR TEN YEARS.
WHERE DID YOU GET THE IDEA FOR IT? DID YOU READ IT IN SOME BOOK? I THOUGHT YOU DIDN'T KNOW HOW TO READ...
THE IDEA CAME TO ME WHILE WATCHING A TEAPOT ON THE FIRE. THE BOILING WATER LIFTED THE LID. I WANTED TO USE THE POWER OF THE BOILING WATER.
SO I FIRST BUILT AN ENGINE THAT WOULD SPIN THE WHEEL OF MY WHEELBARROW WITH A SPAN OF LEATHER. THEN I TRIED SOMETHING BIGGER...
I DID IT, FATHER. I WANTED TO MAKE YOU UNDERSTAND THAT MY MACHINE, AND OTHERS LIKE IT THAT WE CAN BUILD, CAN SPARE US FROM MUCH OF OUR DAILY SUFFERING...
...
FOOL!

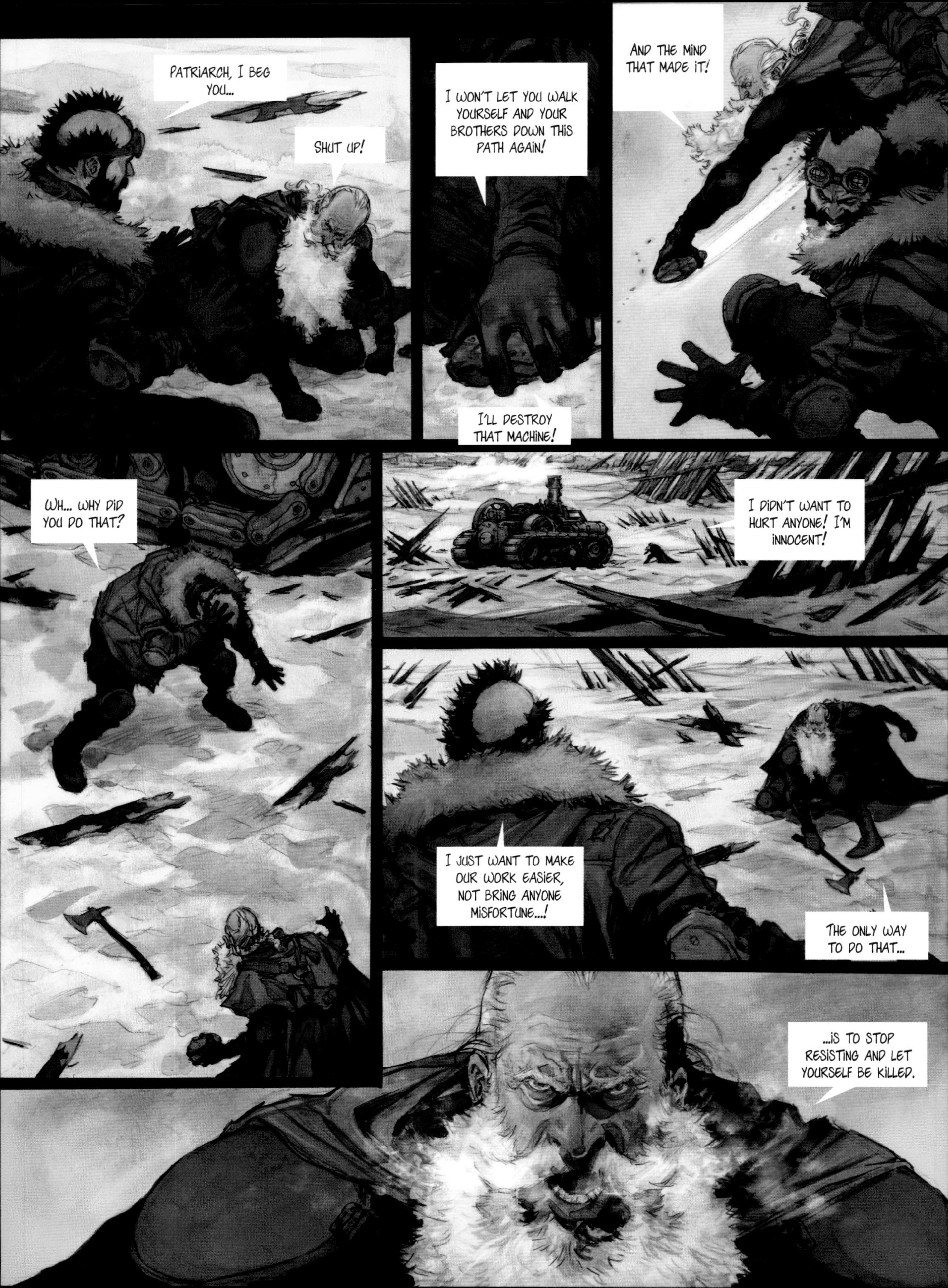
PATRIARCH, I BEG YOU...
SHUT UP!
I WON'T LET YOU WALK YOURSELF AND YOUR BROTHERS DOWN THIS PATH AGAIN!
I'LL DESTROY THAT MACHINE!
AND THE MIND THAT MADE IT!
WH... WHY DID YOU DO THAT?
I DIDN'T WANT TO HURT ANYONE! I'M INNOCENT!
I JUST WANT TO MAKE OUR WORK EASIER, NOT BRING ANYONE MISFORTUNE...!
THE ONLY WAY TO DO THAT...
...IS TO STOP RESISTING AND LET YOURSELF BE KILLED.

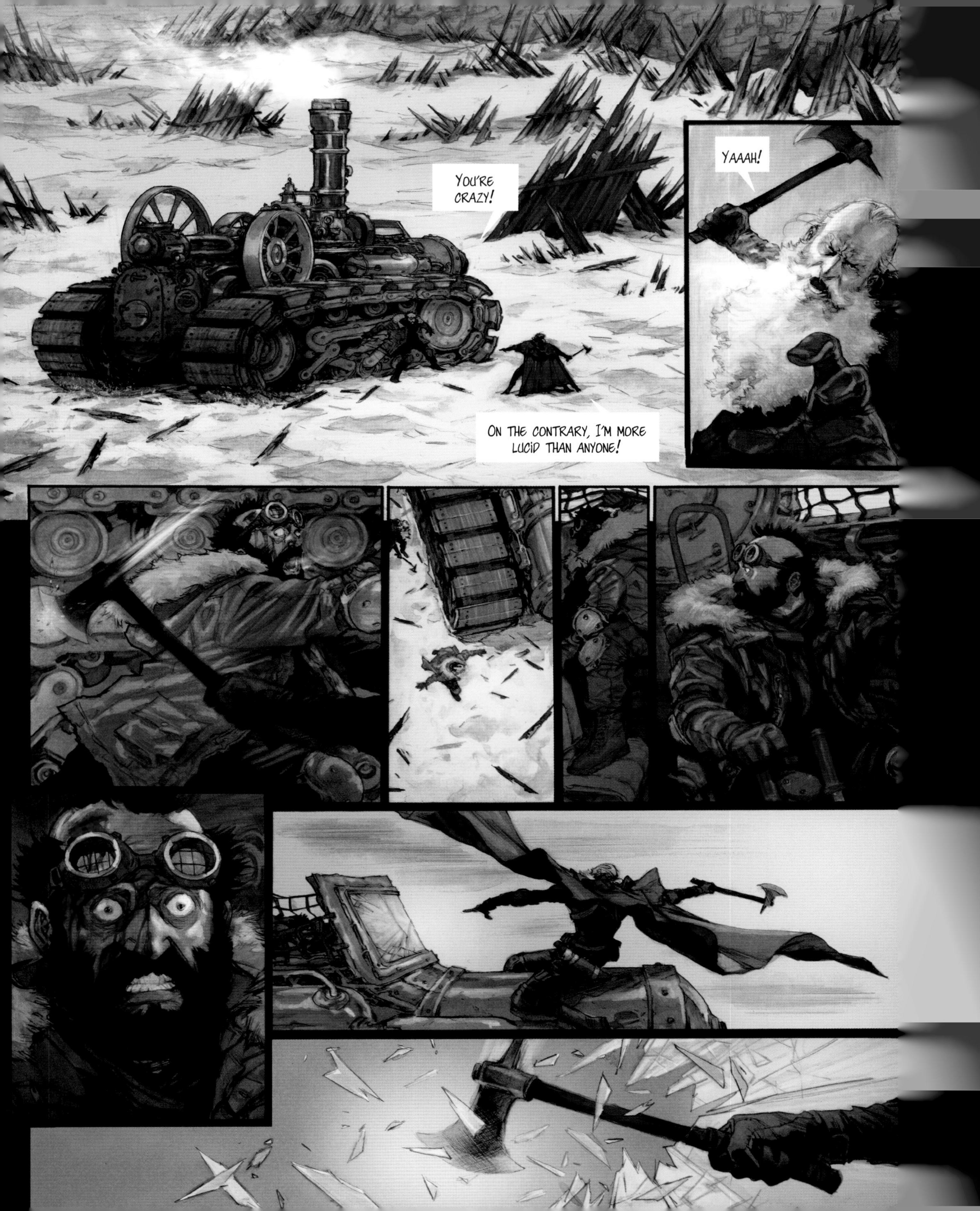
YOU'RE CRAZY!
ON THE CONTRARY, I'M MORE LUCID THAN ANYONE!
YAAAH!

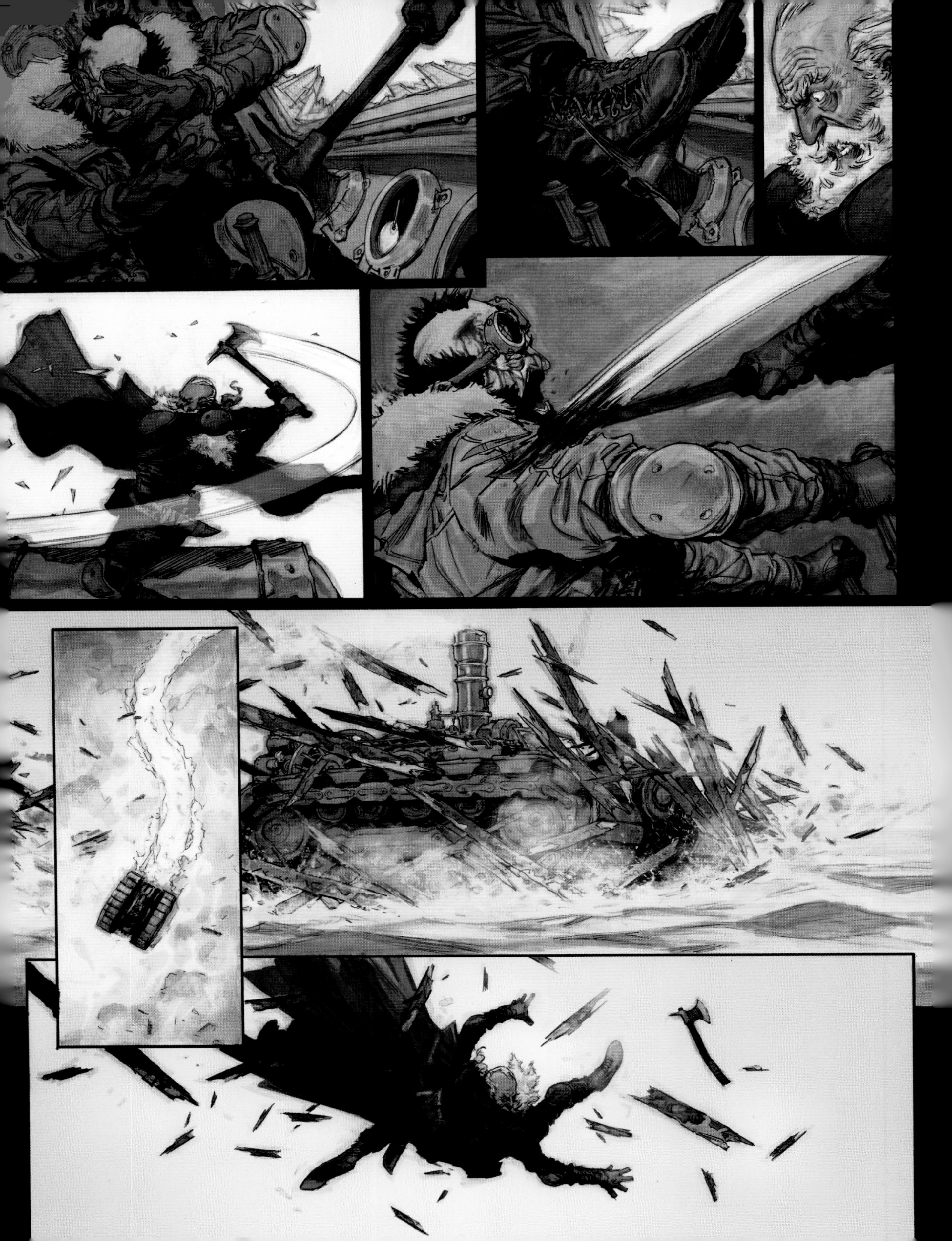

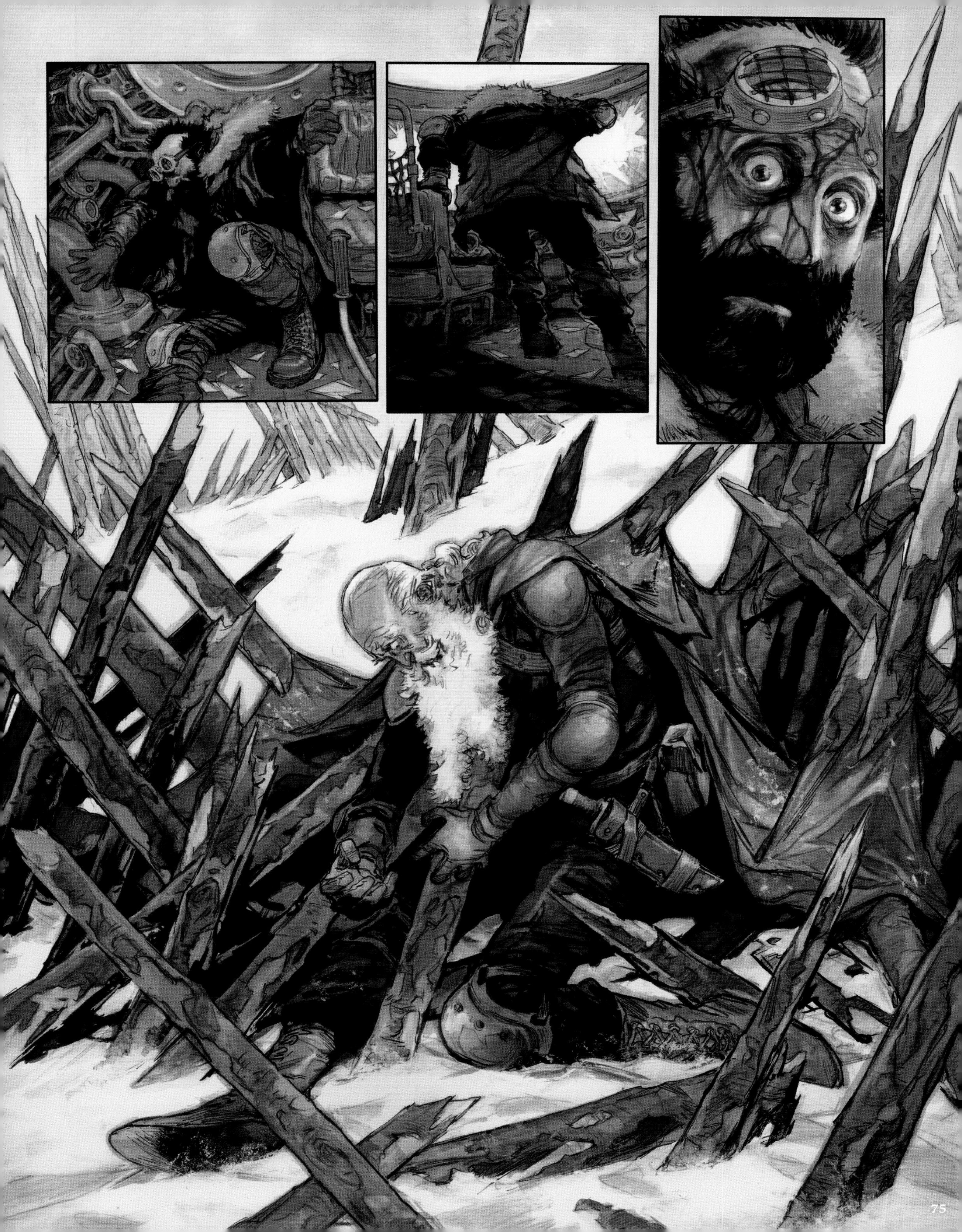

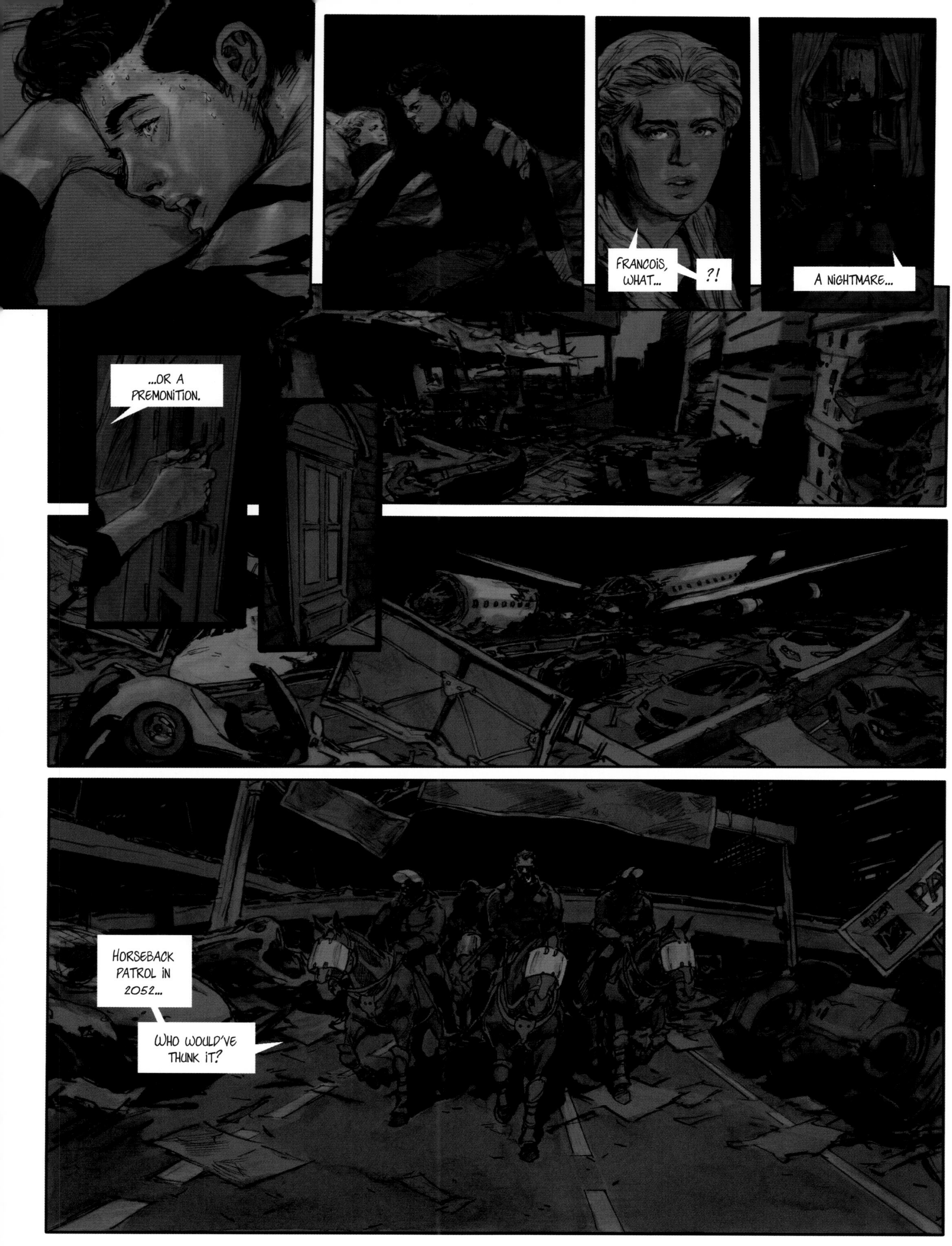
FRANCOIS, WHAT...
?!
A NIGHTMARE...
...OR A PREMONITION.
HORSEBACK PATROL IN 2052...
WHO WOULD'VE THUNK IT?

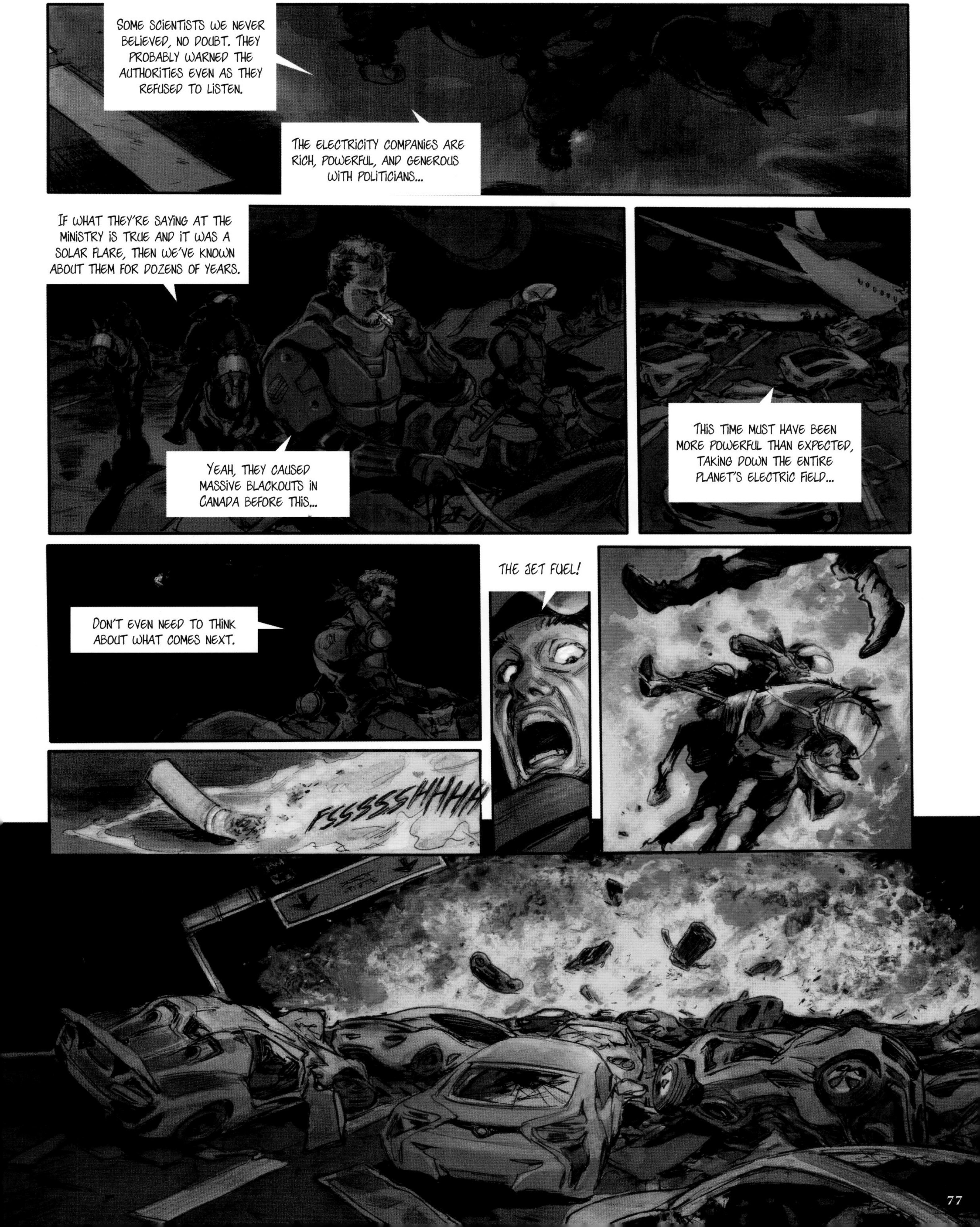
SOME SCIENTISTS WE NEVER BELIEVED, NO DOUBT. THEY PROBABLY WARNED THE AUTHORITIES EVEN AS THEY REFUSED TO LISTEN.
THE ELECTRICITY COMPANIES ARE RICH, POWERFUL, AND GENEROUS WITH POLITICIANS...
IF WHAT THEY'RE SAYING AT THE MINISTRY IS TRUE AND IT WAS A SOLAR FLARE, THEN WE'VE KNOWN ABOUT THEM FOR DOZENS OF YEARS.
YEAH, THEY CAUSED MASSIVE BLACKOUTS IN CANADA BEFORE THIS...
THIS TIME MUST HAVE BEEN MORE POWERFUL THAN EXPECTED, TAKING DOWN THE ENTIRE PLANET'S ELECTRIC FIELD...
DON'T EVEN NEED TO THINK ABOUT WHAT COMES NEXT.
THE JET FUEL!
FSSSSSHHHH

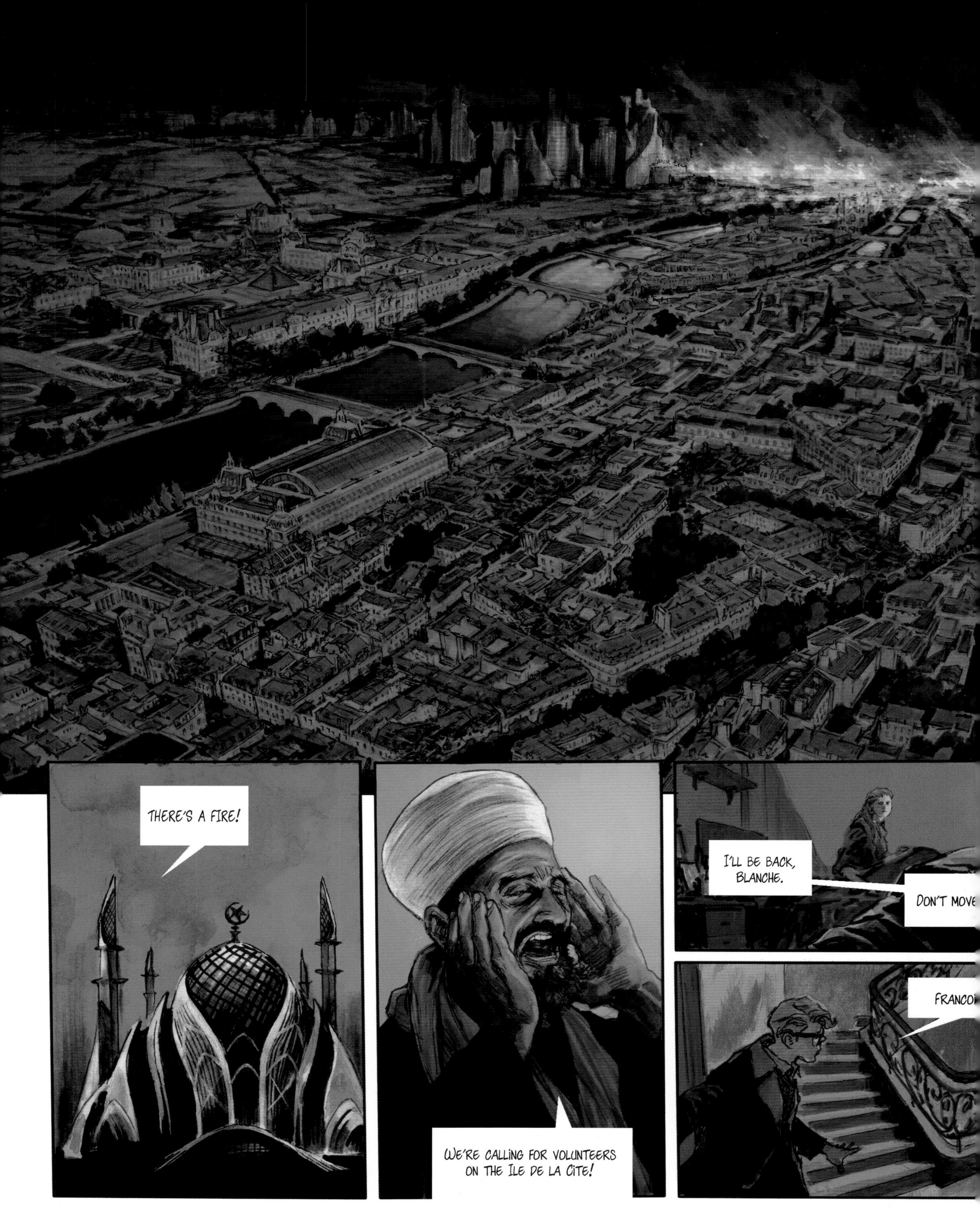
THERE'S A FIRE!
WE'RE CALLING FOR VOLUNTEERS ON THE ILE DE LA CITE!
I'LL BE BACK, BLANCHE.
DON'T MOVE
FRANCO

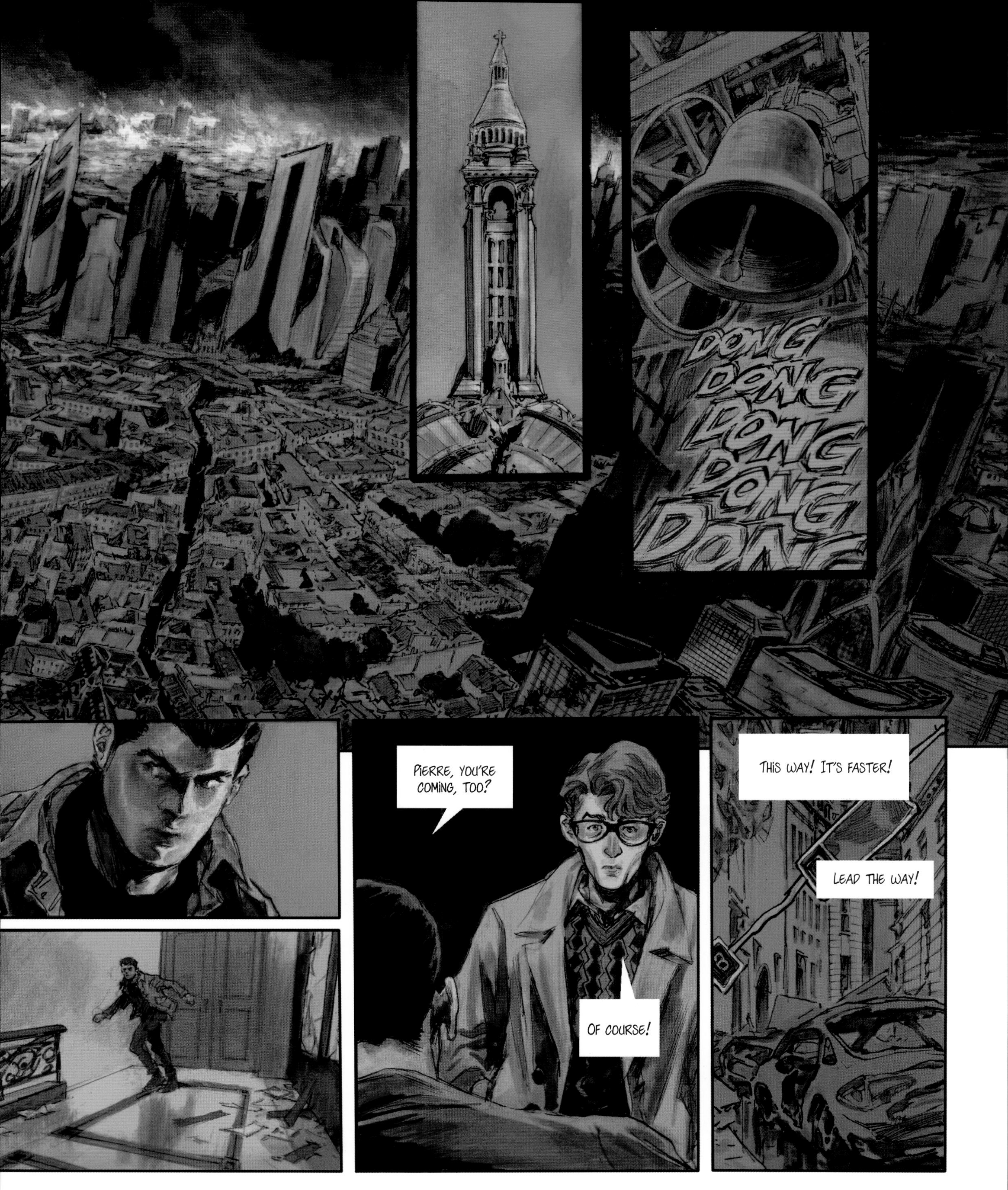
DONG
DONG
DONG
DONG
DONG
DONG
PIERRE, YOU'RE COMING, TOO?
OF COURSE!
THIS WAY! IT'S FASTER!
LEAD THE WAY!

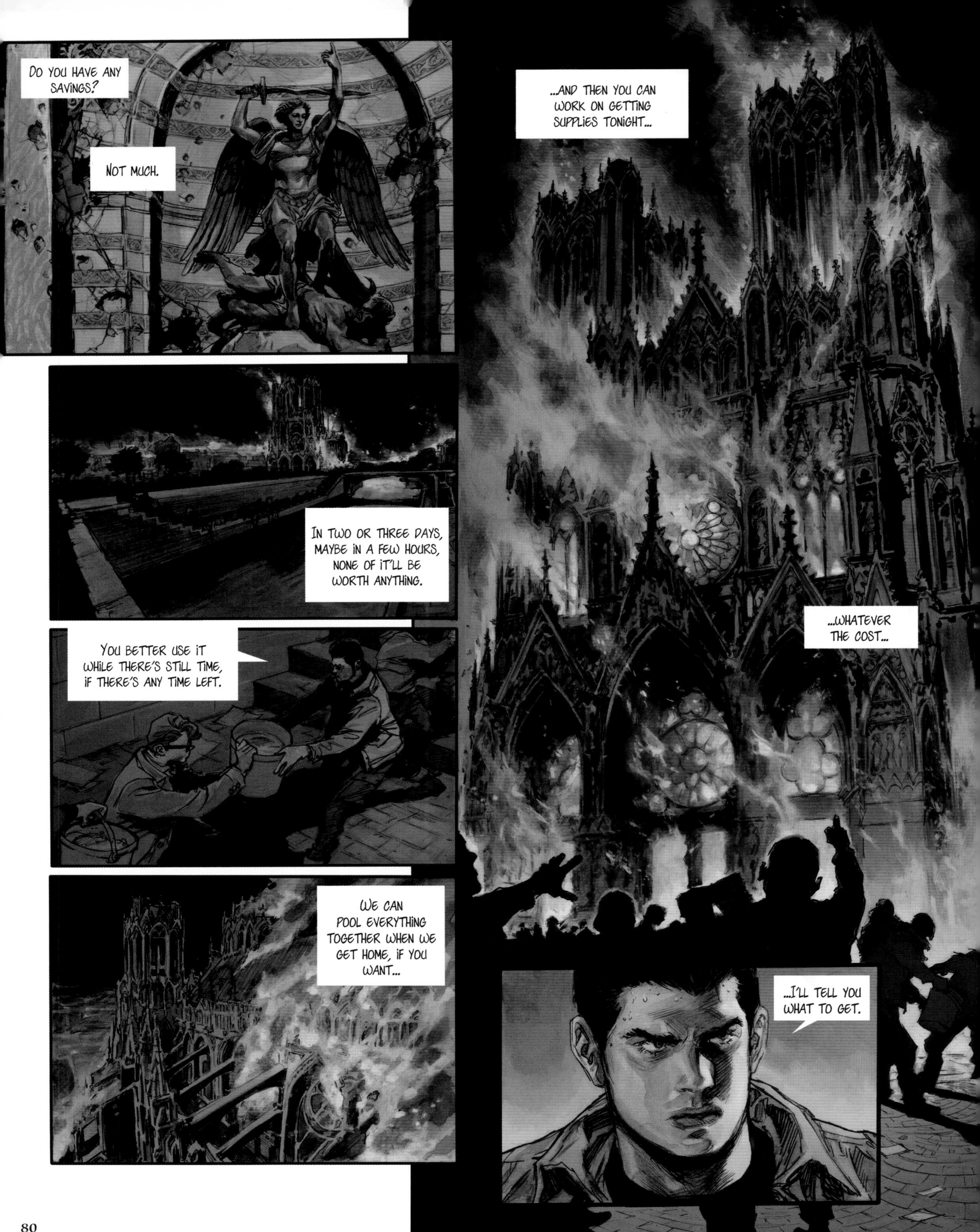
DO YOU HAVE ANY SAVINGS?
NOT MUCH.
IN TWO OR THREE DAYS, MAYBE IN A FEW HOURS, NONE OF IT'LL BE WORTH ANYTHING.
YOU BETTER USE IT WHILE THERE'S STILL TIME, IF THERE'S ANY TIME LEFT.
WE CAN POOL EVERYTHING TOGETHER WHEN WE GET HOME, IF YOU WANT...
...AND THEN YOU CAN WORK ON GETTING SUPPLIES TONIGHT...
...WHATEVER THE COST...
...I'LL TELL YOU WHAT TO GET.

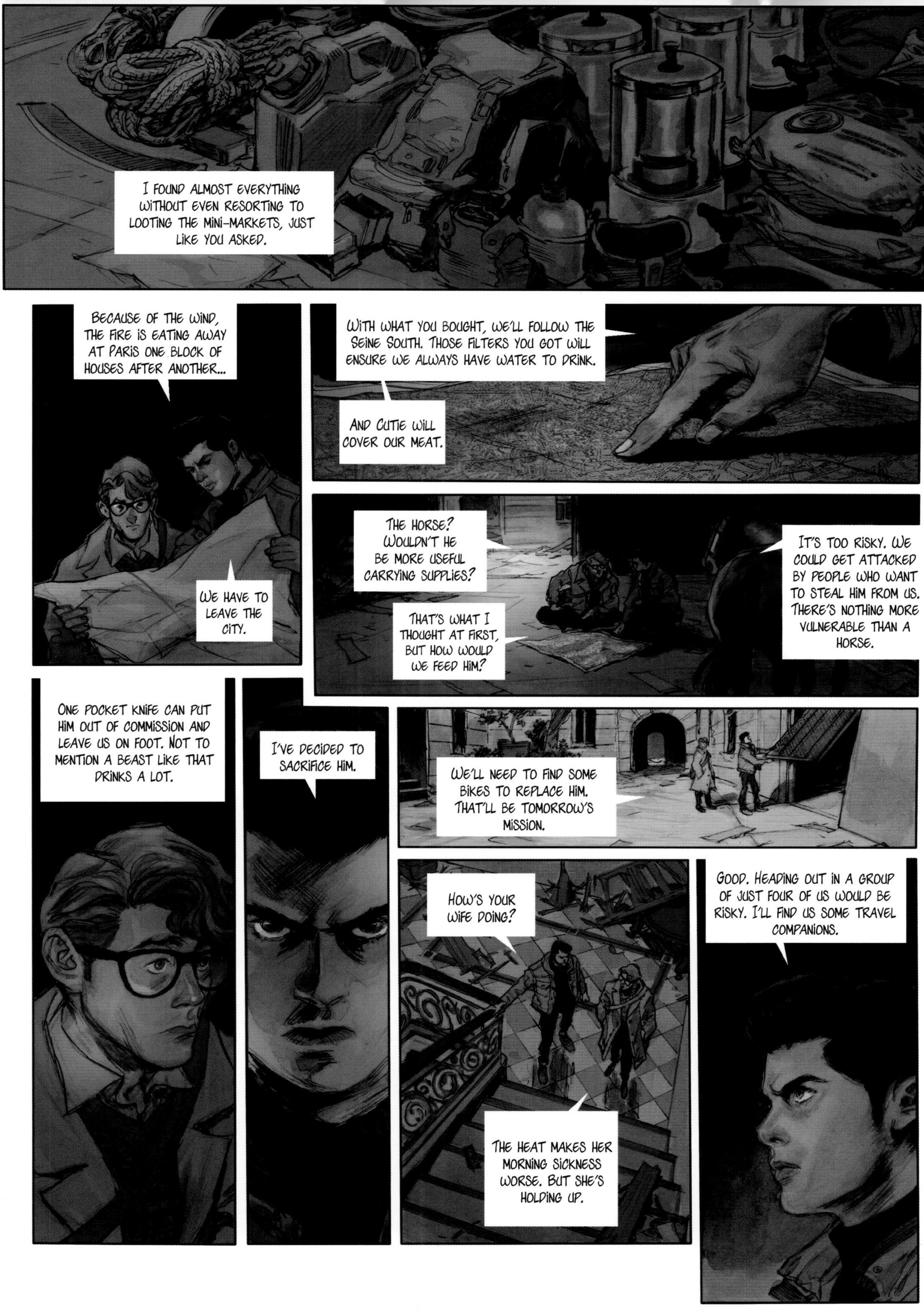
I FOUND ALMOST EVERYTHING WITHOUT EVEN RESORTING TO LOOTING THE MINI-MARKETS, JUST LIKE YOU ASKED.
BECAUSE OF THE WIND, THE FIRE IS EATING AWAY AT PARIS ONE BLOCK OF HOUSES AFTER ANOTHER...
WE HAVE TO LEAVE THE CITY.
WITH WHAT YOU BOUGHT, WE'LL FOLLOW THE SEINE SOUTH. THOSE FILTERS YOU GOT WILL ENSURE WE ALWAYS HAVE WATER TO DRINK.
AND CUTIE WILL COVER OUR MEAT.
THE HORSE? WOULDN'T HE BE MORE USEFUL CARRYING SUPPLIES?
THAT'S WHAT I THOUGHT AT FIRST, BUT HOW WOULD WE FEED HIM?
IT'S TOO RISKY. WE COULD GET ATTACKED BY PEOPLE WHO WANT TO STEAL HIM FROM US. THERE'S NOTHING MORE VULNERABLE THAN A HORSE.
ONE POCKET KNIFE CAN PUT HIM OUT OF COMMISSION AND LEAVE US ON FOOT. NOT TO MENTION A BEAST LIKE THAT DRINKS A LOT.
I'VE DECIDED TO SACRIFICE HIM.
WE'LL NEED TO FIND SOME BIKES TO REPLACE HIM. THAT'LL BE TOMORROW'S MISSION.
HOW'S YOUR WIFE DOING?
THE HEAT MAKES HER MORNING SICKNESS WORSE. BUT SHE'S HOLDING UP.
GOOD. HEADING OUT IN A GROUP OF JUST FOUR OF US WOULD BE RISKY. I'LL FIND US SOME TRAVEL COMPANIONS.

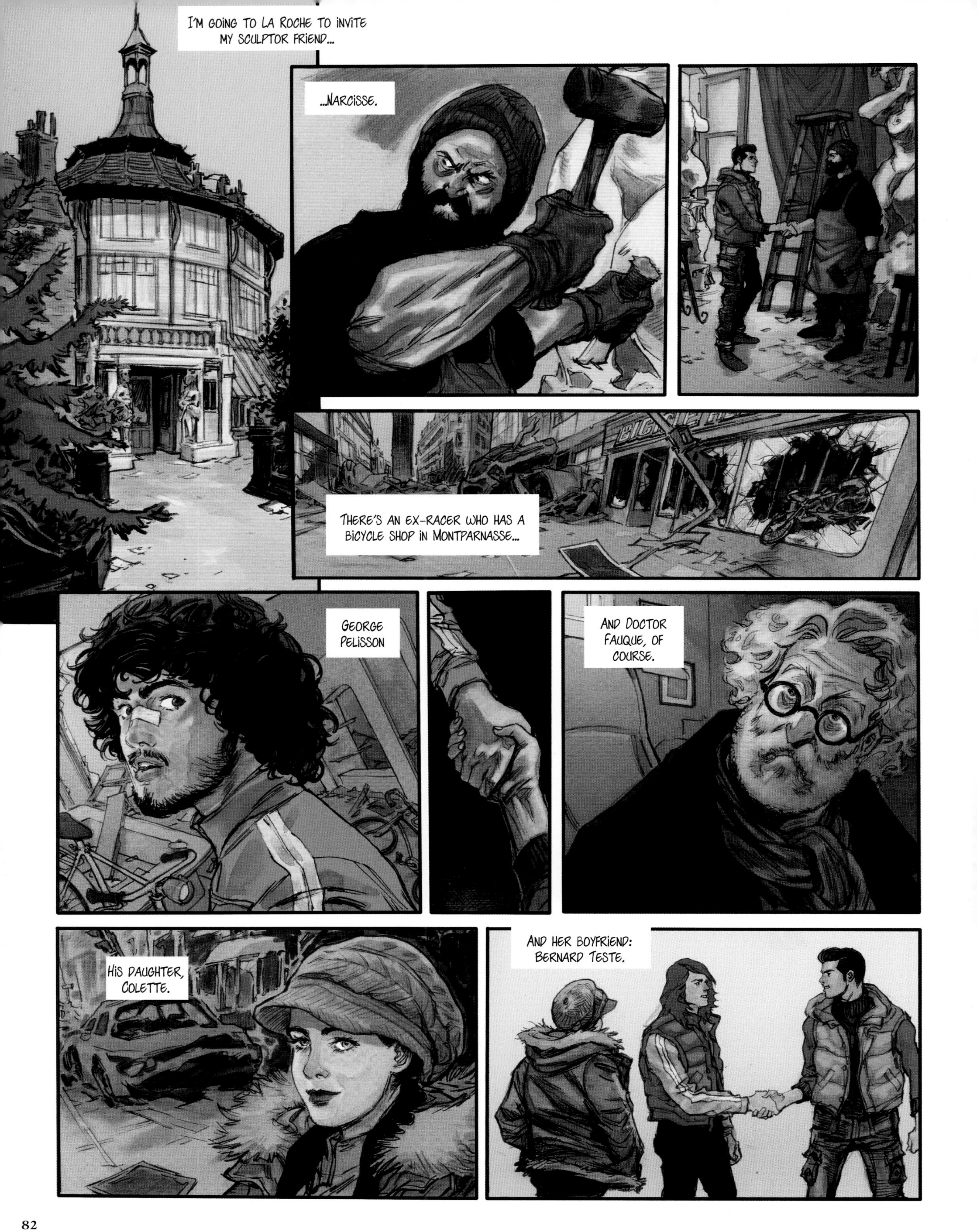
I'M GOING TO LA ROCHE TO INVITE MY SCULPTOR FRIEND...
...NARCISSE.
THERE'S AN EX-RACER WHO HAS A BICYCLE SHOP IN MONTPARNASSE...
GEORGE PELISSON
AND DOCTOR FAUQUE, OF COURSE.
HIS DAUGHTER, COLETTE.
AND HER BOYFRIEND: BERNARD TESTE.

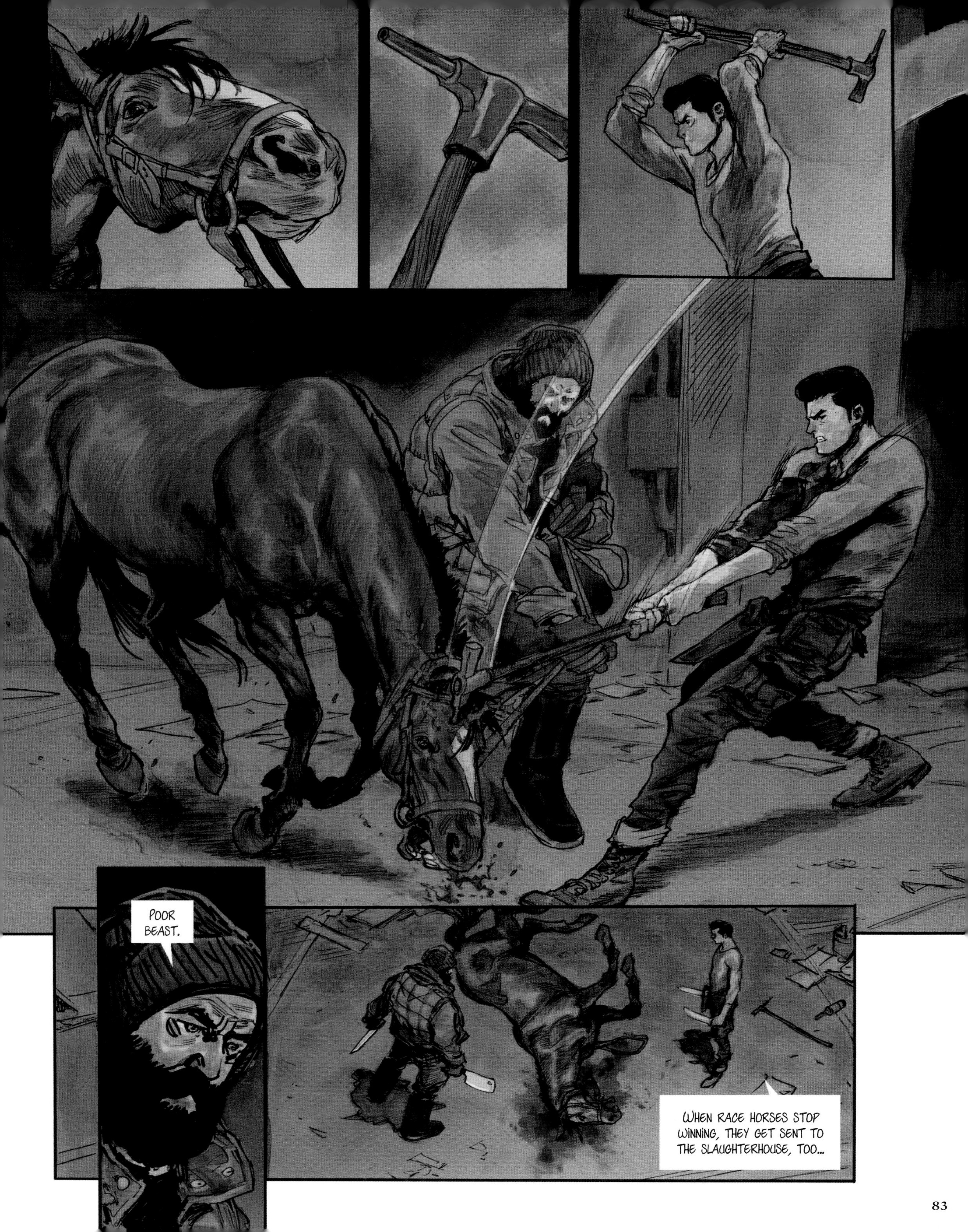
POOR BEAST.
WHEN RACE HORSES STOP WINNING, THEY GET SENT TO THE SLAUGHTERHOUSE, TOO...

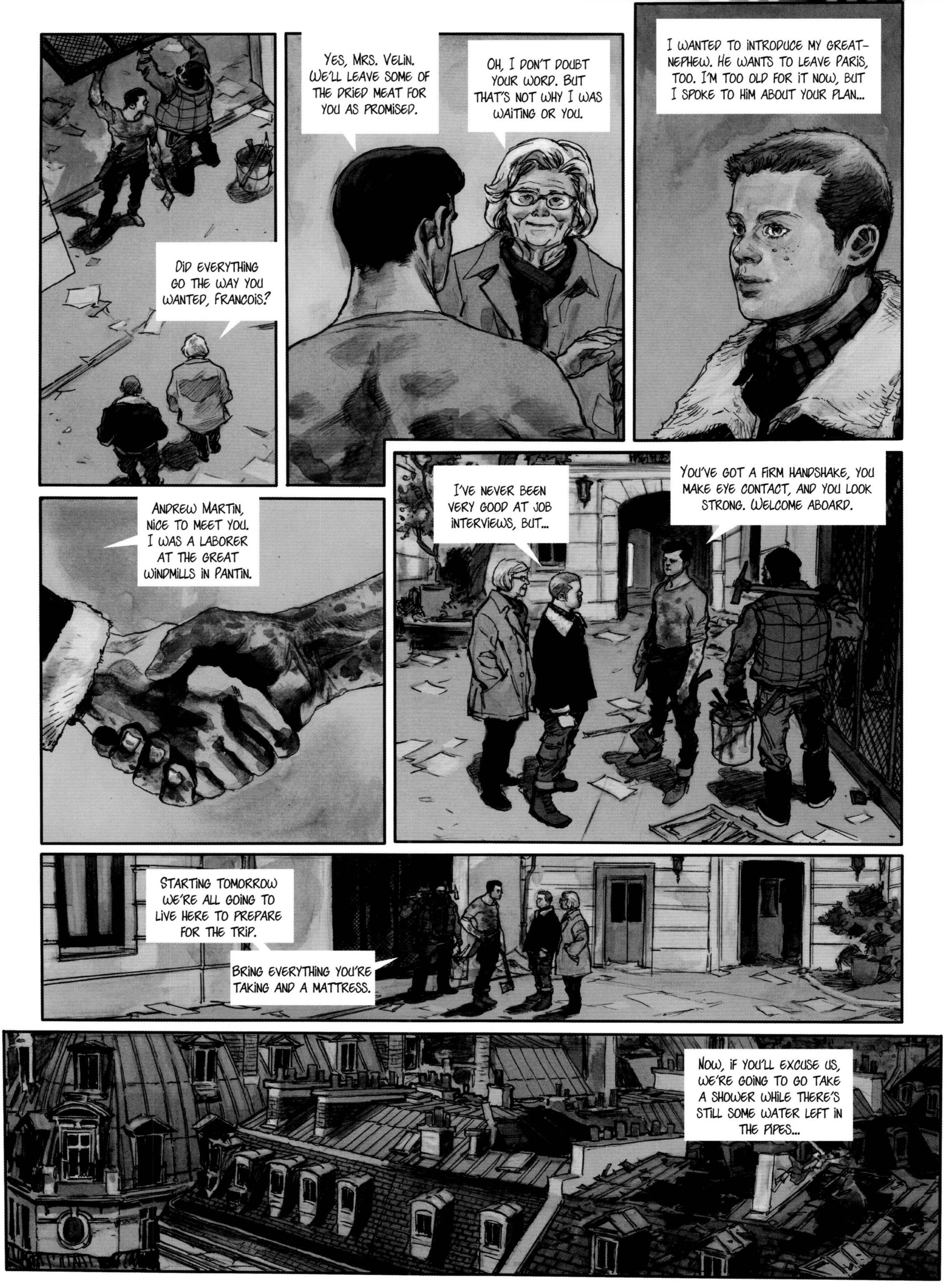
Did everything go the way you wanted, Francois?
Yes, Mrs. Velin. We'll leave some of the dried meat for you as promised.
Oh, I don't doubt your word. But that's not why I was waiting or you.
I wanted to introduce my great-nephew. He wants to leave Paris, too. I'm too old for it now, but I spoke to him about your plan...
Andrew Martin, nice to meet you. I was a laborer at the great windmills in Pantin.
I've never been very good at job interviews, but...
You've got a firm handshake, you make eye contact, and you look strong. Welcome aboard.
Starting tomorrow we're all going to live here to prepare for the trip.
Bring everything you're taking and a mattress.
Now, if you'll excuse us, we're going to go take a shower while there's still some water left in the pipes...

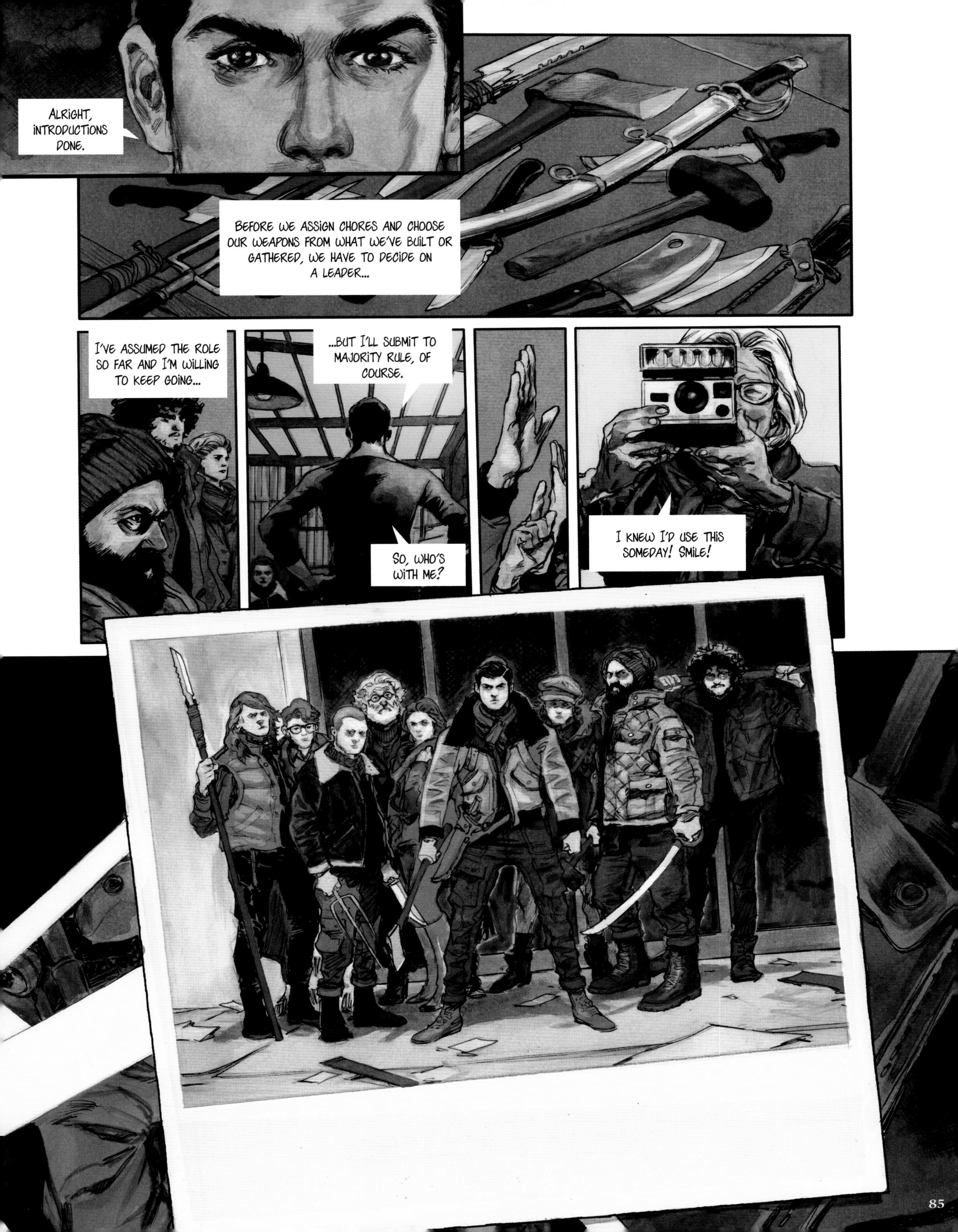
ALRIGHT, INTRODUCTIONS DONE.
BEFORE WE ASSIGN CHORES AND CHOOSE OUR WEAPONS FROM WHAT WE'VE BUILT OR GATHERED, WE HAVE TO DECIDE ON A LEADER...
I'VE ASSUMED THE ROLE SO FAR AND I'M WILLING TO KEEP GOING...
...BUT I'LL SUBMIT TO MAJORITY RULE, OF COURSE.
SO, WHO'S WITH ME?
I KNEW I'D USE THIS SOMEDAY! SMILE!

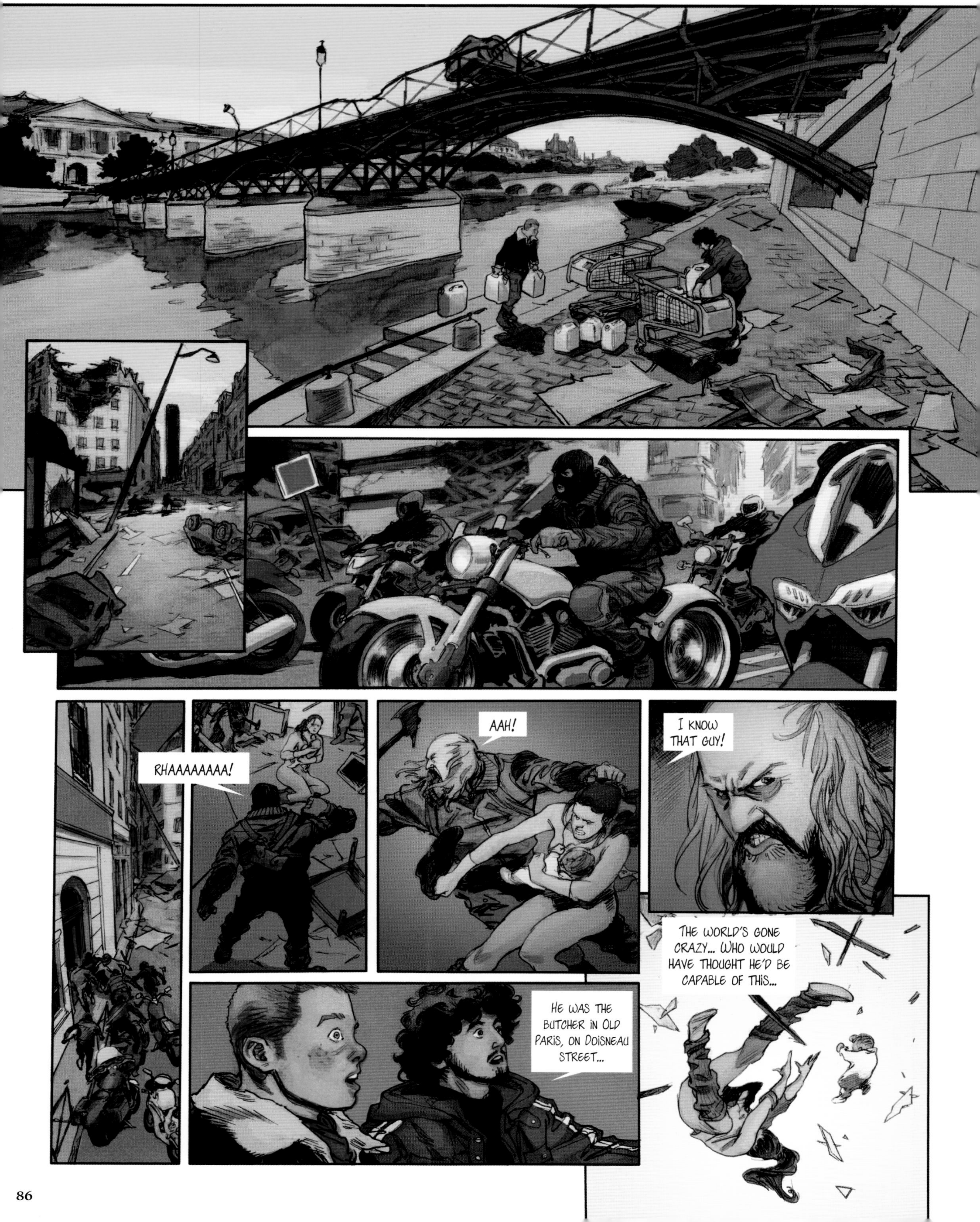
RHAAAAAAAA!
AAH!
I KNOW THAT GUY!
THE WORLD'S GONE CRAZY... WHO WOULD HAVE THOUGHT HE'D BE CAPABLE OF THIS...
HE WAS THE BUTCHER IN OLD PARIS, ON DOISNEAU STREET...

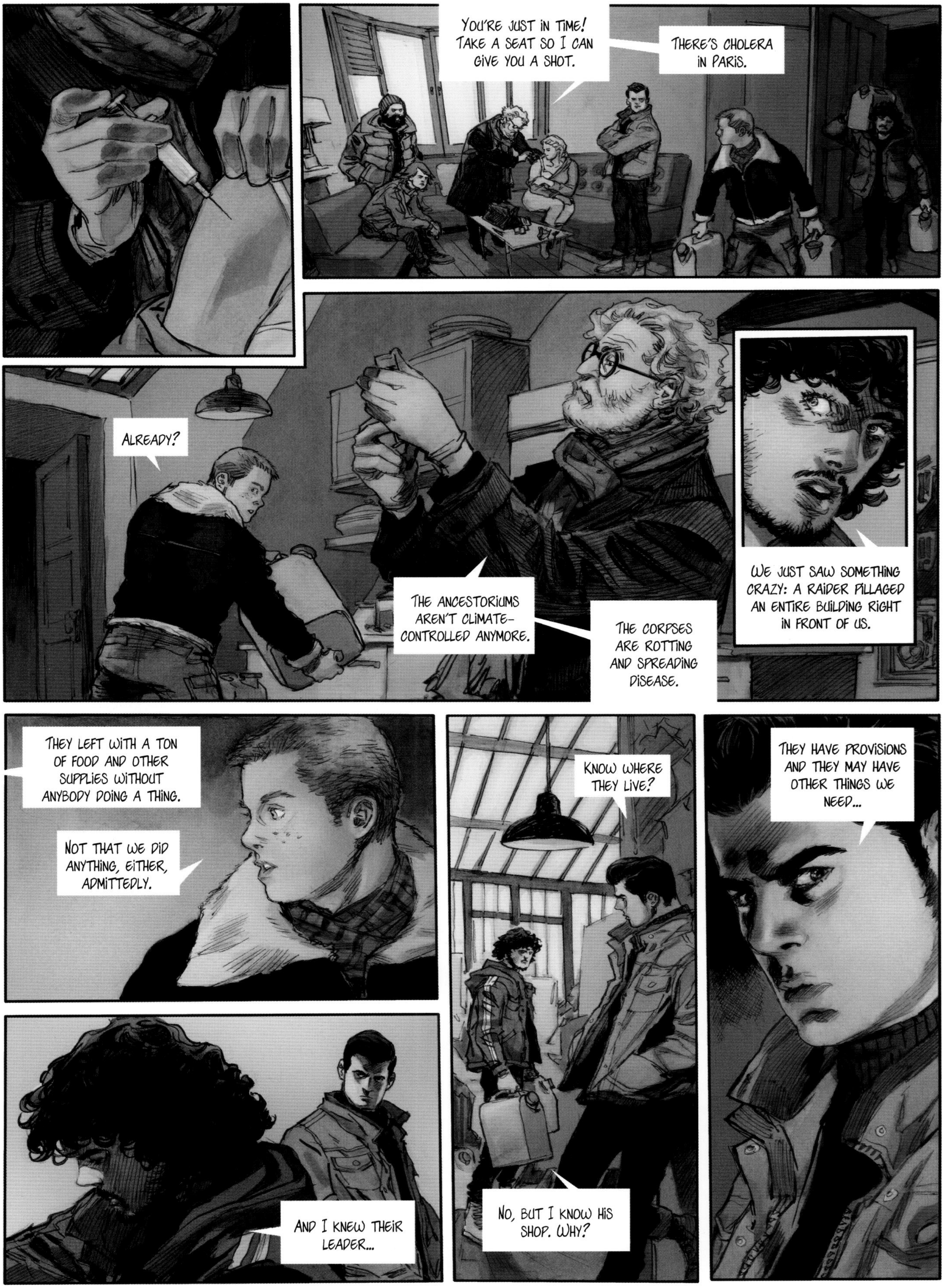
YOU'RE JUST IN TIME! TAKE A SEAT SO I CAN GIVE YOU A SHOT.
THERE'S CHOLERA IN PARIS.
ALREADY?
THE ANCESTORIUMS AREN'T CLIMATE-CONTROLLED ANYMORE.
THE CORPSES ARE ROTTING AND SPREADING DISEASE.
WE JUST SAW SOMETHING CRAZY: A RAIDER PILLAGED AN ENTIRE BUILDING RIGHT IN FRONT OF US.
THEY LEFT WITH A TON OF FOOD AND OTHER SUPPLIES WITHOUT ANYBODY DOING A THING.
NOT THAT WE DID ANYTHING, EITHER, ADMITTEDLY.
AND I KNEW THEIR LEADER...
KNOW WHERE THEY LIVE?
NO, BUT I KNOW HIS SHOP. WHY?
THEY HAVE PROVISIONS AND THEY MAY HAVE OTHER THINGS WE NEED...

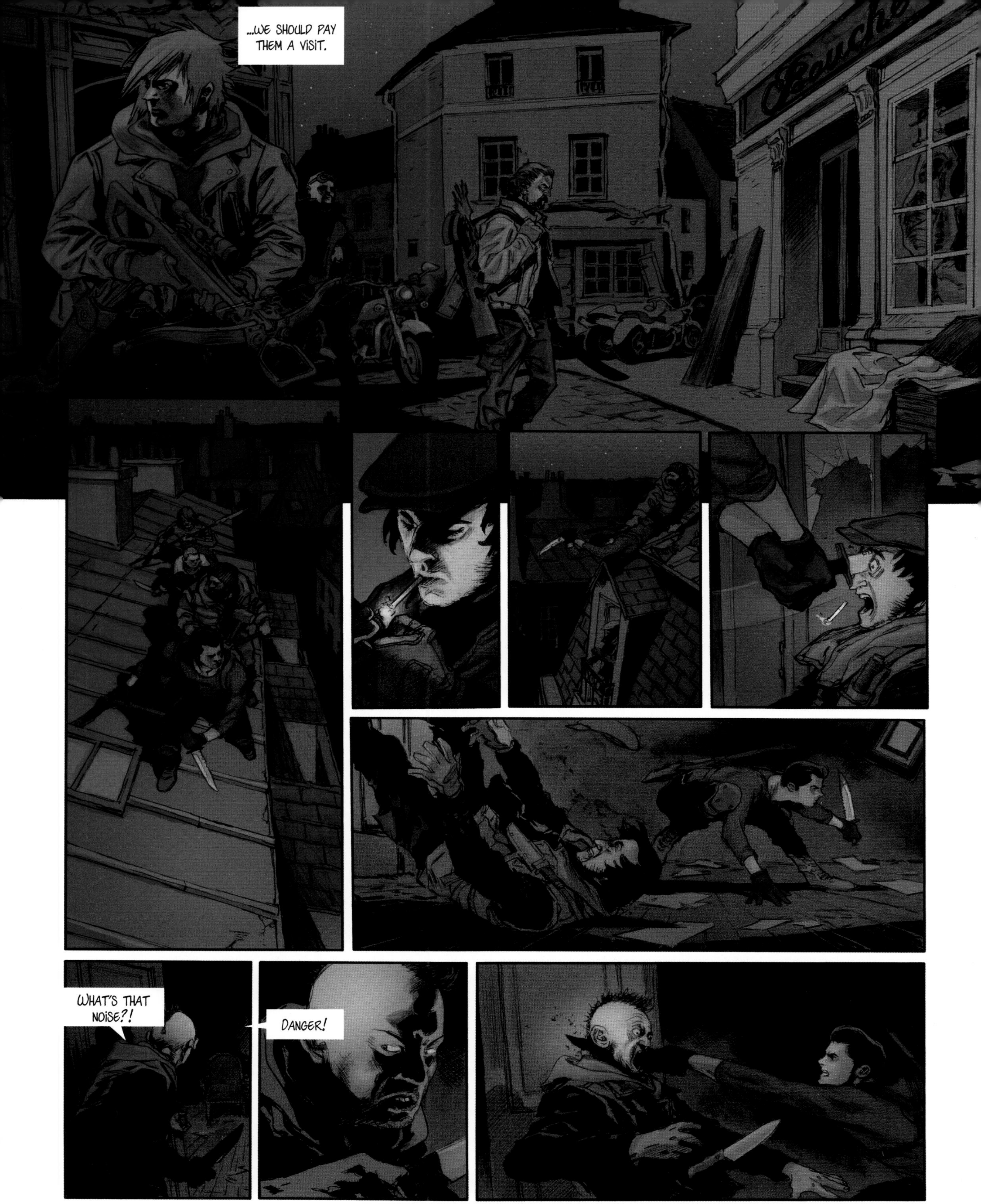
...WE SHOULD PAY THEM A VISIT.
WHAT'S THAT NOISE?!
DANGER!

INTRUDERS!

KILL THEM!

IT TAKES A DEAD MAN...

...TO KNOW ONE.

AHH!

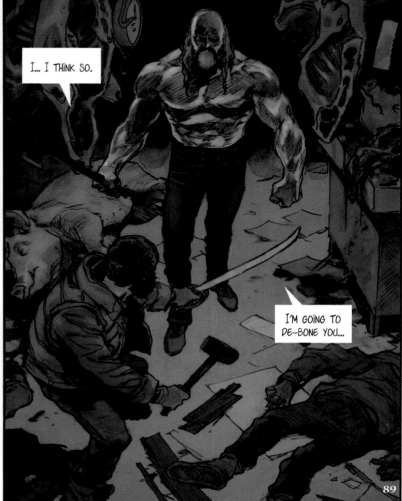

I... I THINK SO.

I'M GOING TO DE-BONE YOU...

AHRR!

NARCISSE, DID YOU FIND THE BUTCHER?

89

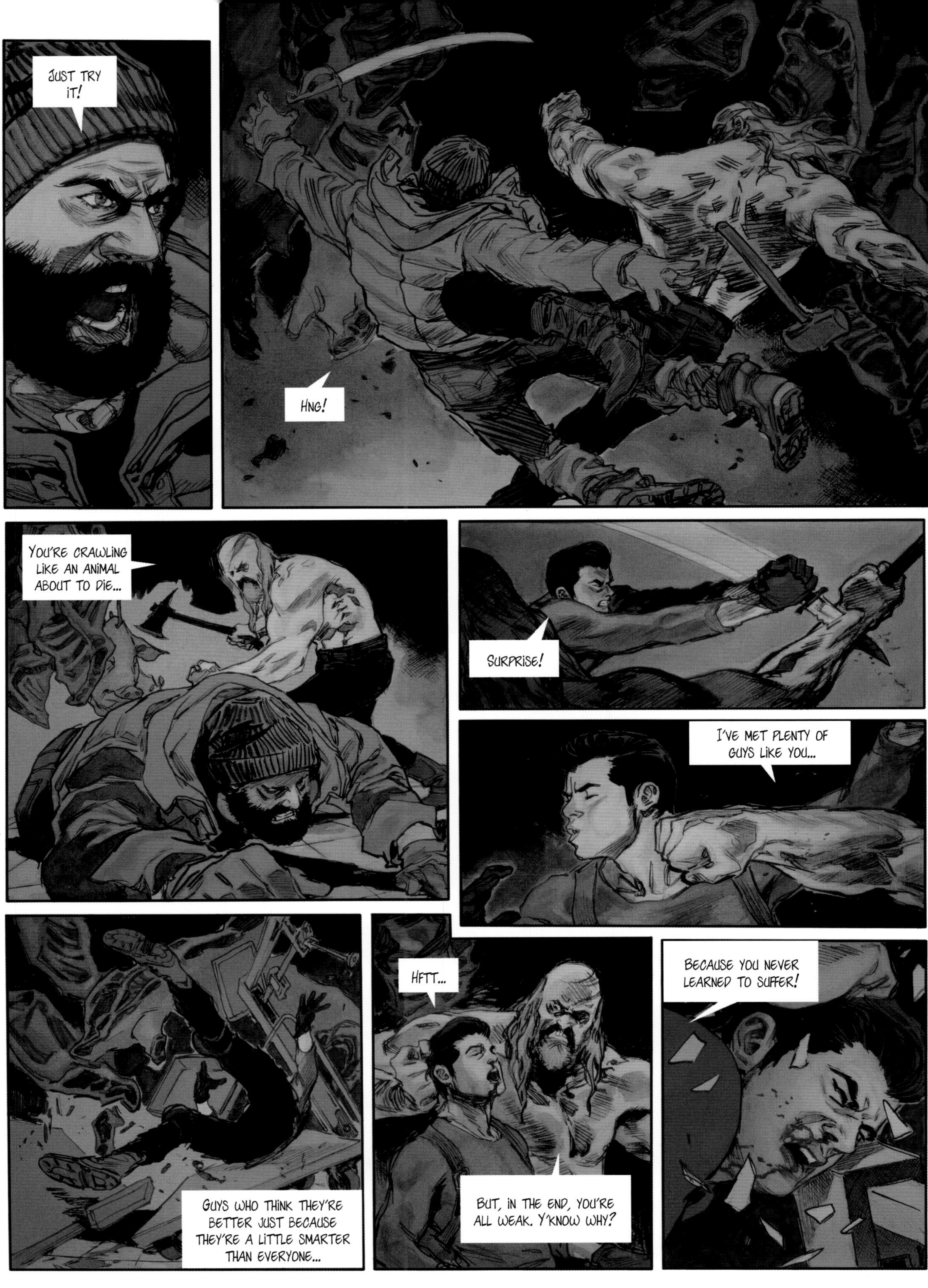
JUST TRY IT!
HNG!
YOU'RE CRAWLING LIKE AN ANIMAL ABOUT TO DIE...
SURPRISE!
I'VE MET PLENTY OF GUYS LIKE YOU...
GUYS WHO THINK THEY'RE BETTER JUST BECAUSE THEY'RE A LITTLE SMARTER THAN EVERYONE...
HFTT...
BUT, IN THE END, YOU'RE ALL WEAK. Y'KNOW WHY?
BECAUSE YOU NEVER LEARNED TO SUFFER!

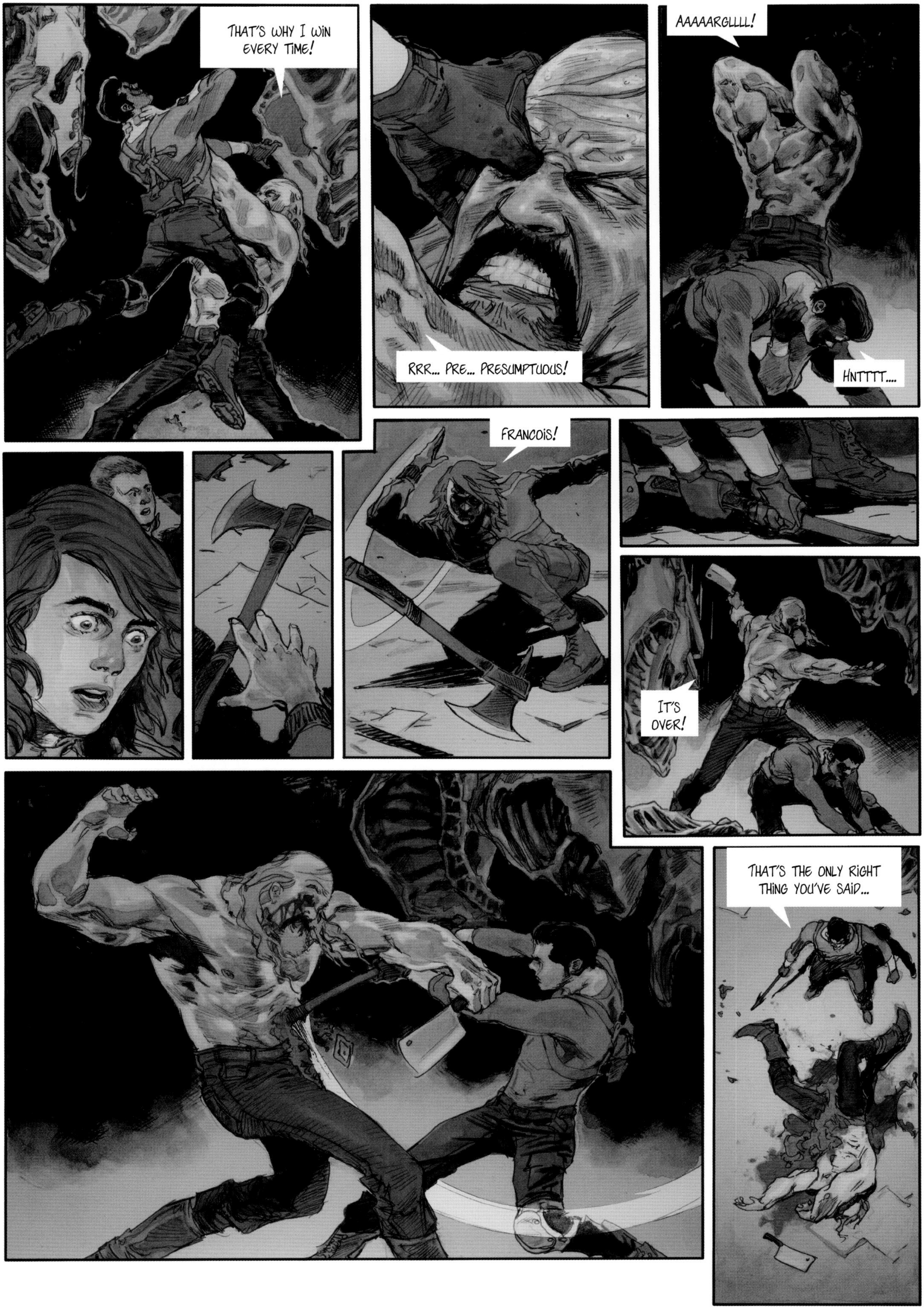
THAT'S WHY I WIN EVERY TIME!
RRR... PRE... PRESUMPTUOUS!
AAAAARGLLLL!
HNTTTT....
FRANCOIS!
IT'S OVER!
THAT'S THE ONLY RIGHT THING YOU'VE SAID...

THERE ARE THREE SURVIVORS.

IN DIFFERENT STATES.

WHAT'LL WE DO WITH THEM?

I SAY WE KEEP THEM HERE UNTIL WE CLEAR EVERYTHING OUT. THEN WE GIVE THEM A CHANCE TO RUN.

IF WE LET THEM GO, THEY MIGHT FOLLOW OUR TRAIL.

I KNOW IT'S NO LAUGHING MATTER TO KILL DEFENSELESS PEOPLE, BUT OUR FIRST PRIORITY IS TO MAKE SURE WE'RE SAFE.

WE'RE LIVING IN EXTRAORDINARY CIRCUMSTANCES THAT DEMAND EXTRAORDINARY MEASURES. THE PEOPLE THAT MAKE IT OUT OF THIS HELL WILL BE FEW. IF WE WANT TO BE AMONG THEM, WE NEED TO FORGET PITY.

NONE OF THEM LEAVE HERE ALIVE.

I COULD DO THIS MYSELF WITH NO REMORSE...

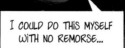

...BUT IN OUR LONG-TERM INTEREST, EACH OF YOU NEEDS TO GET USED TO LISTENING TO ME WITHOUT QUESTIONS, NO MATTER WHAT I ASK YOU TO DO.

ARGH!

PLEASE!

RRRH!

AFTER THIS...

I'M READY FOR ANYTHING.

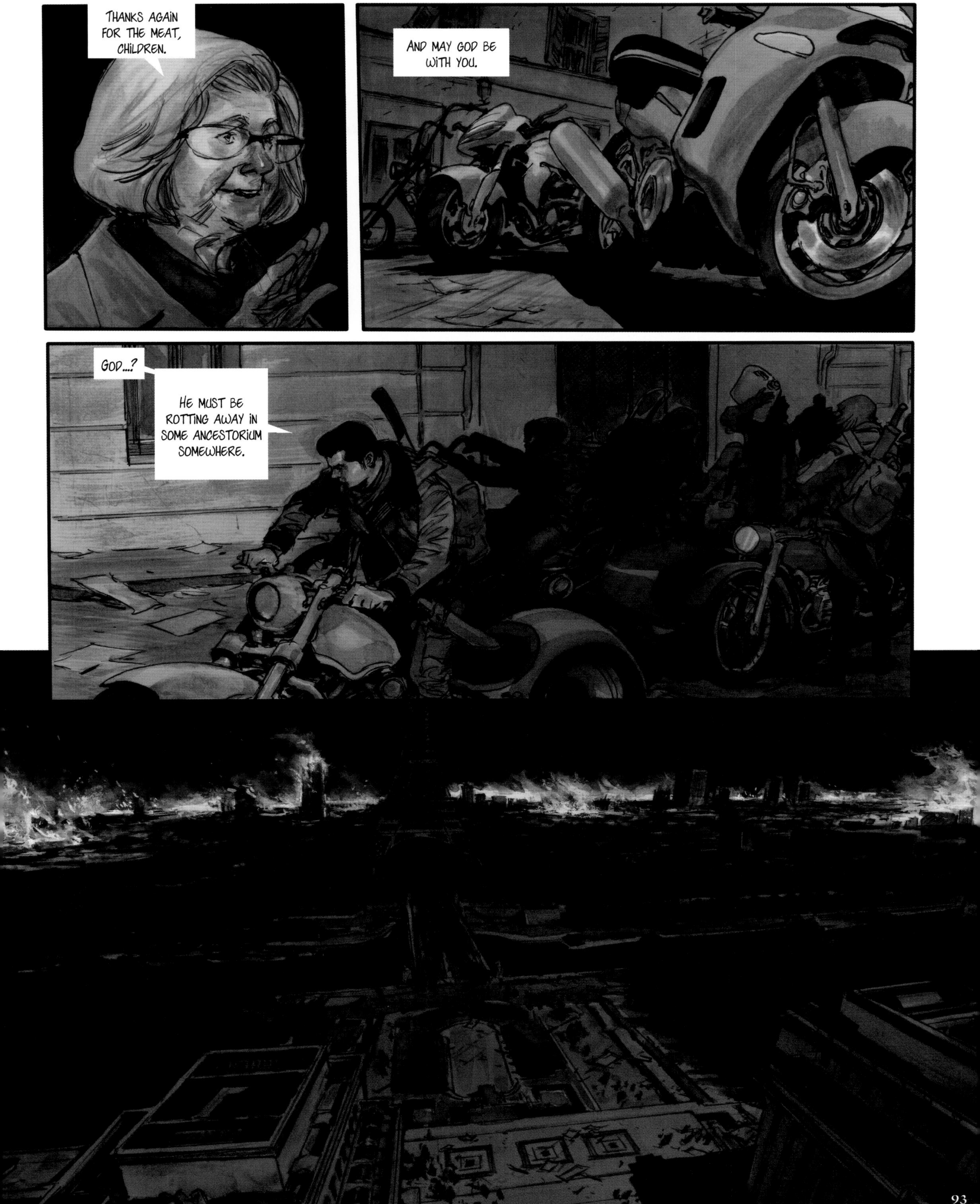
THANKS AGAIN FOR THE MEAT, CHILDREN.
AND MAY GOD BE WITH YOU.
GOD...?
HE MUST BE ROTTING AWAY IN SOME ANCESTORIUM SOMEWHERE.

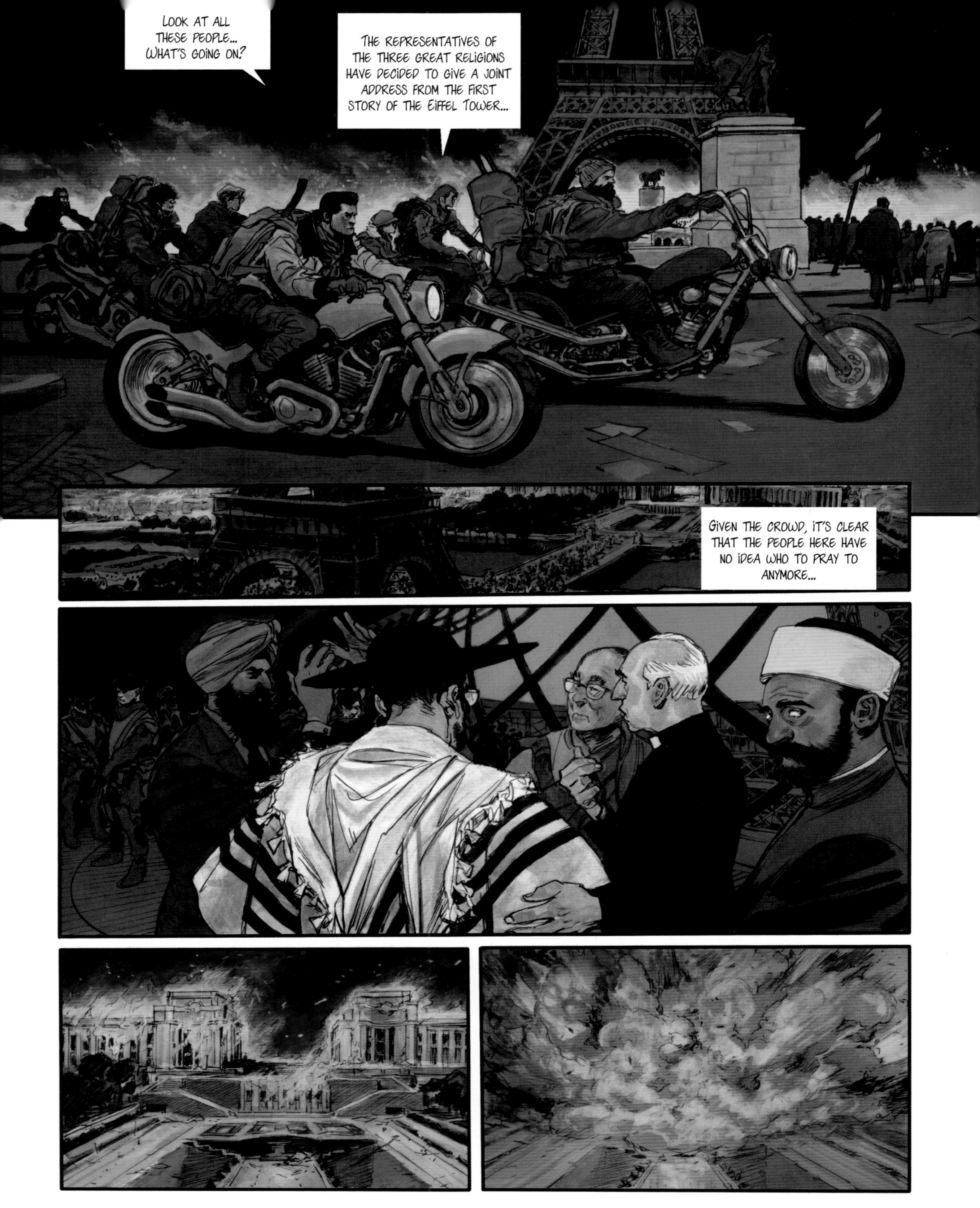

LOOK AT ALL THESE PEOPLE... WHAT'S GOING ON?
THE REPRESENTATIVES OF THE THREE GREAT RELIGIONS HAVE DECIDED TO GIVE A JOINT ADDRESS FROM THE FIRST STORY OF THE EIFFEL TOWER...
GIVEN THE CROWD, IT'S CLEAR THAT THE PEOPLE HERE HAVE NO IDEA WHO TO PRAY TO ANYMORE...

THE UNDERGROUND MUNITIONS DEPOT IN THE CHAILLOT BARRACKS...

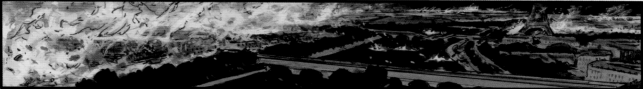

95

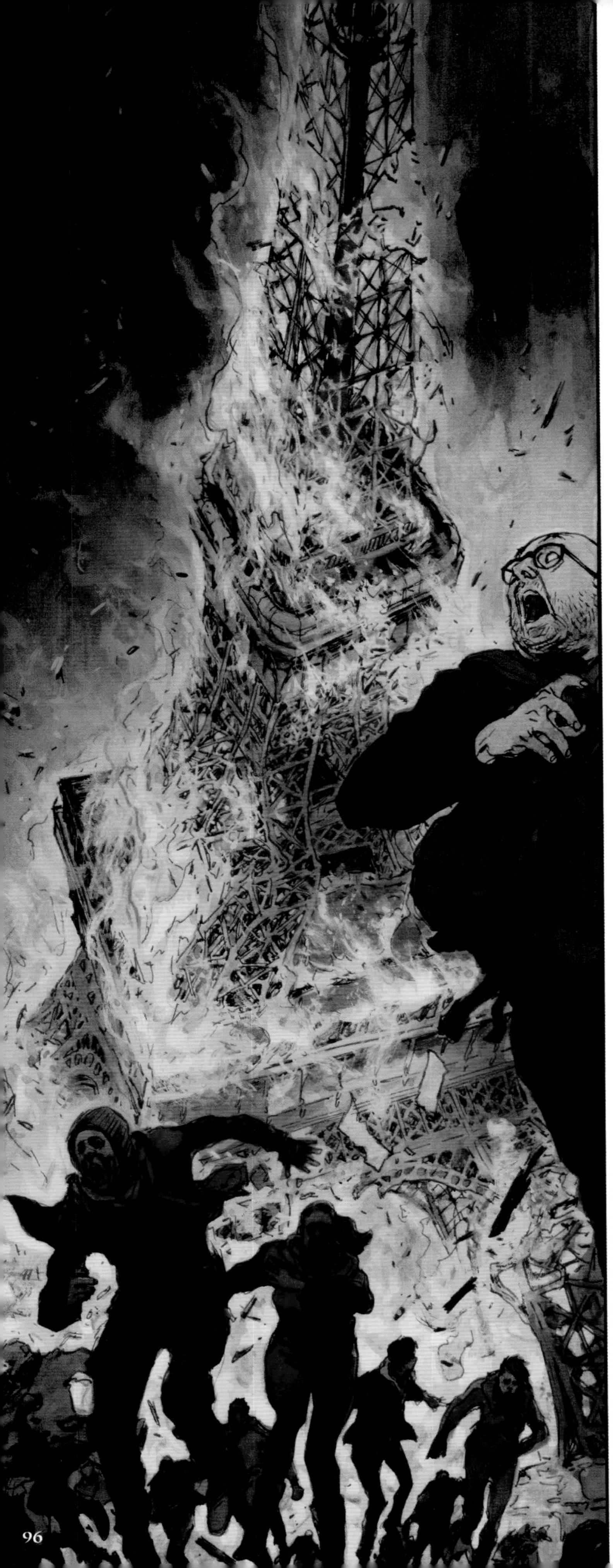

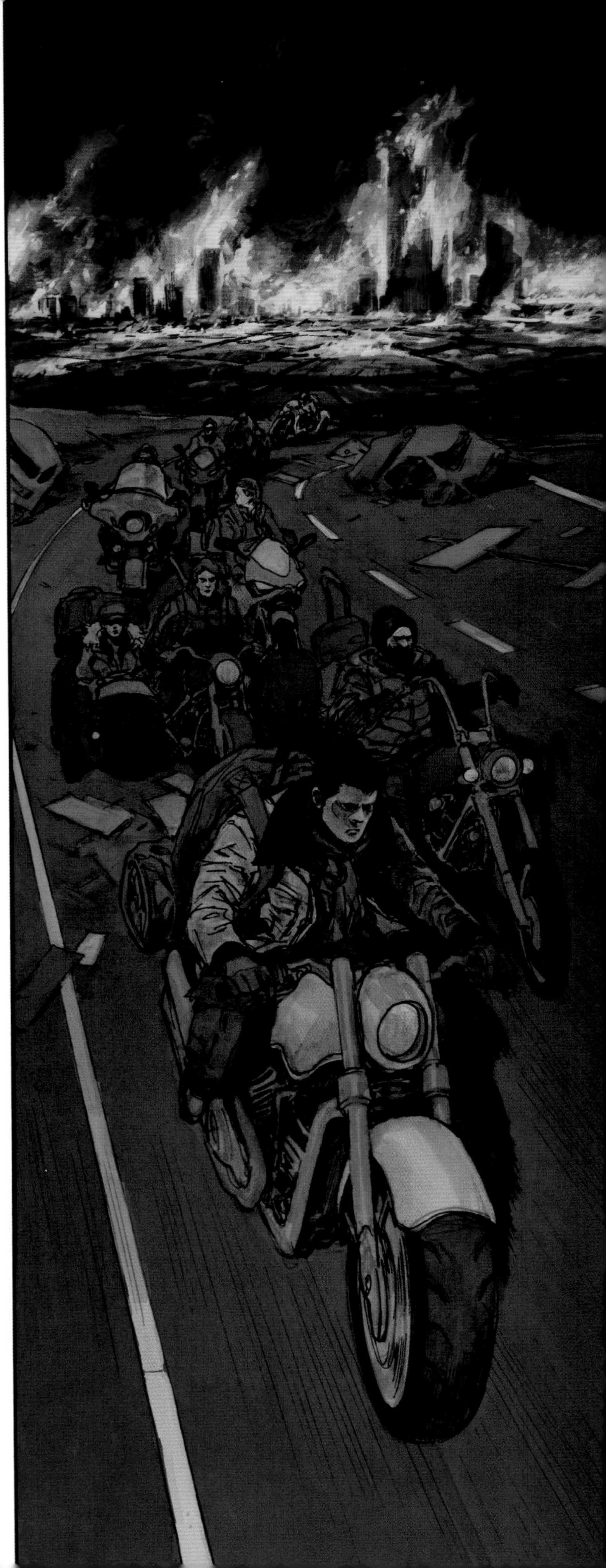

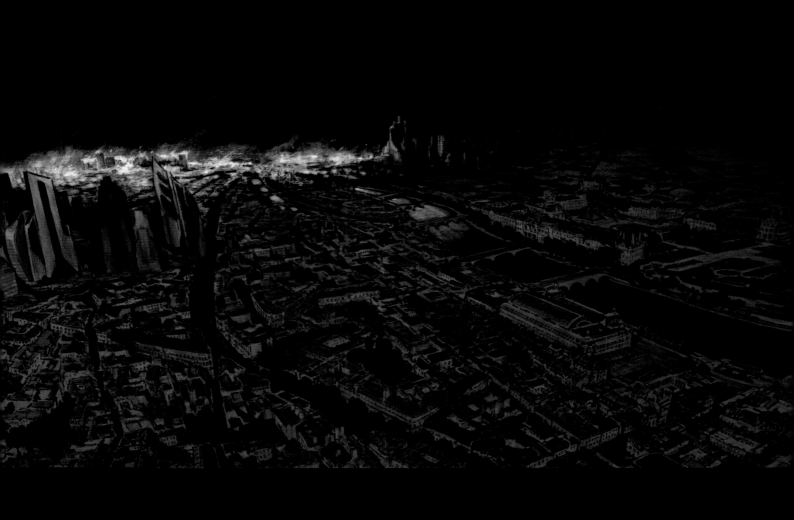

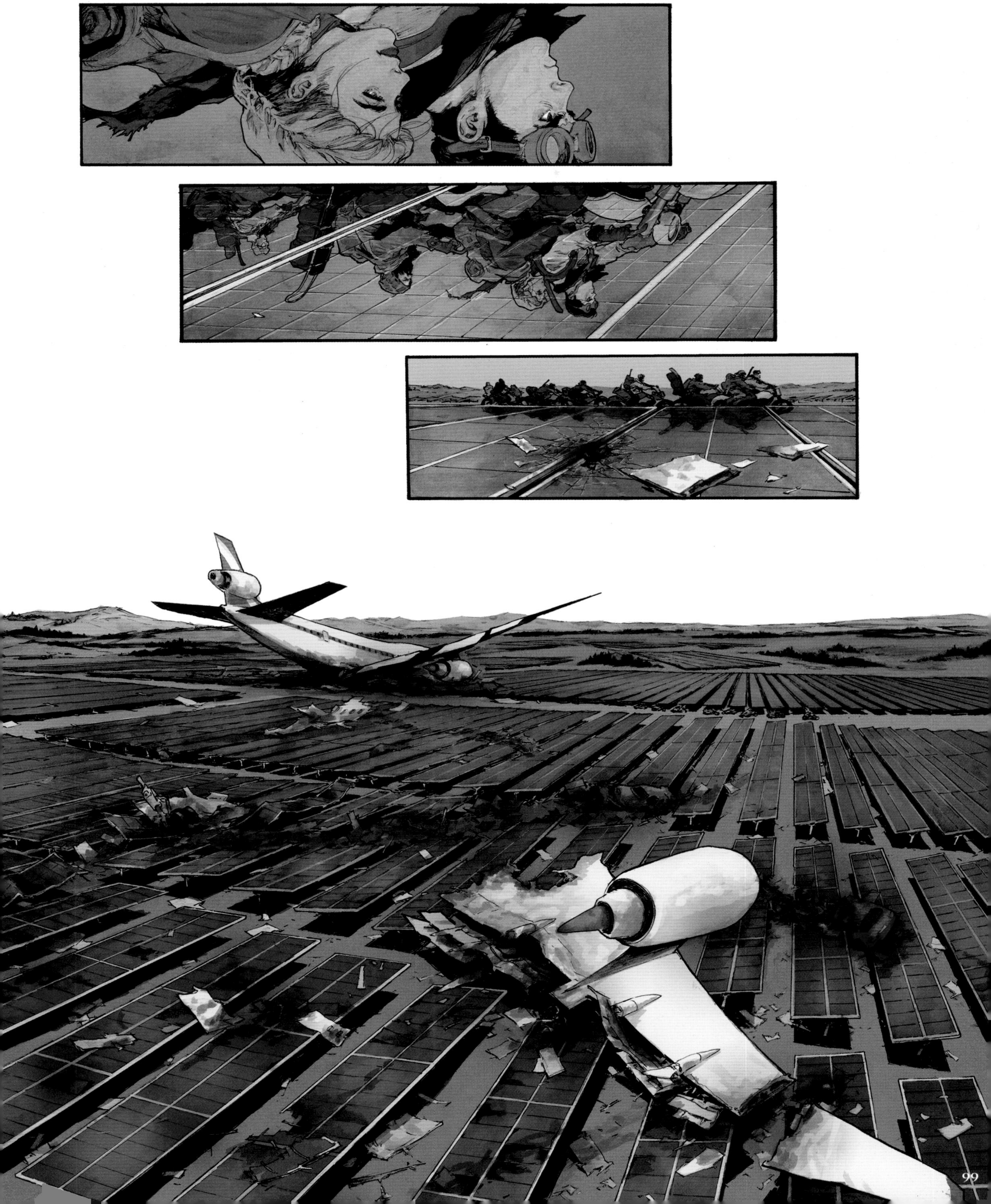

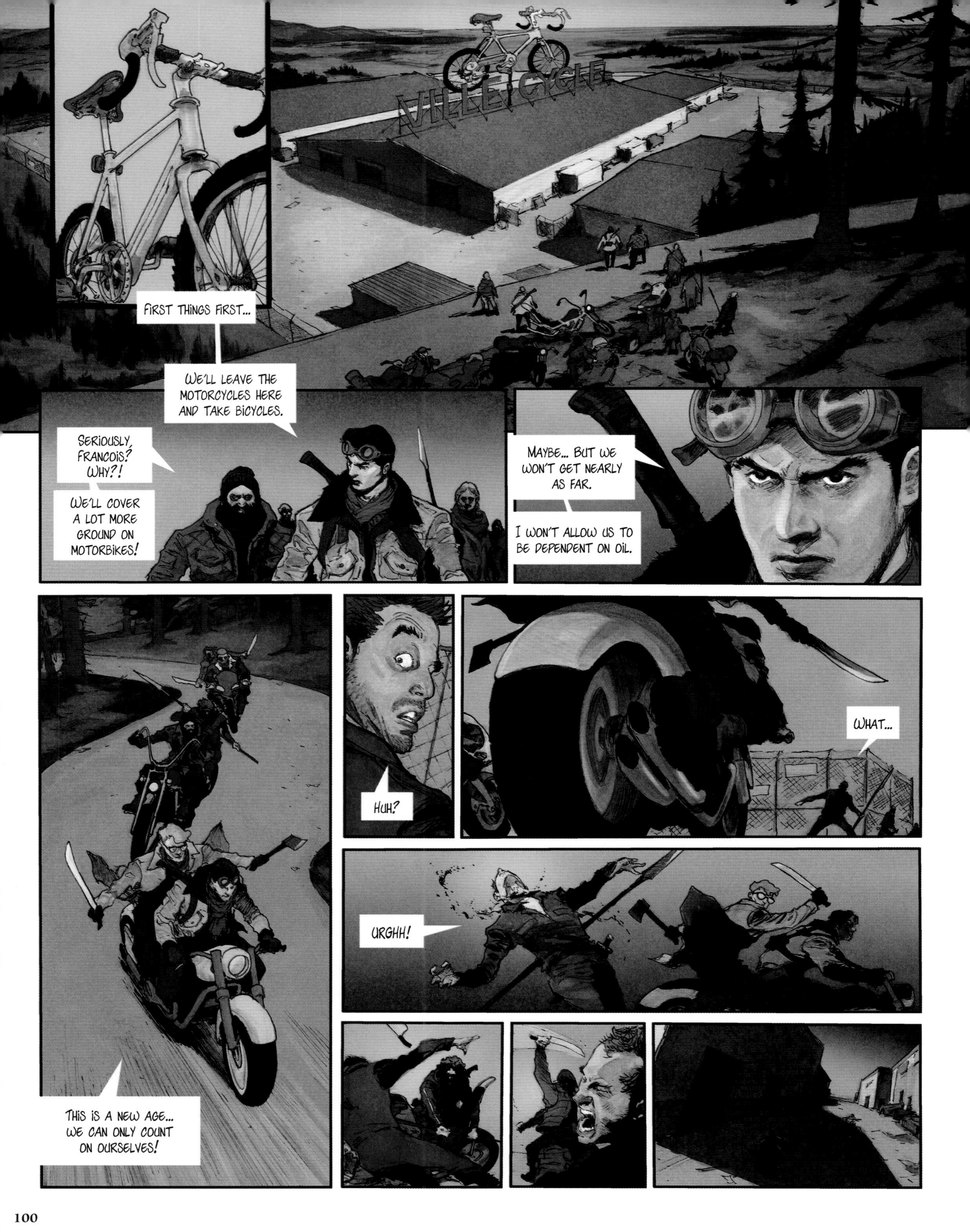
VILLE CYCLE
FIRST THINGS FIRST...
WE'LL LEAVE THE MOTORCYCLES HERE AND TAKE BICYCLES.
SERIOUSLY, FRANCOIS? WHY?!
WE'LL COVER A LOT MORE GROUND ON MOTORBIKES!
MAYBE... BUT WE WON'T GET NEARLY AS FAR.
I WON'T ALLOW US TO BE DEPENDENT ON OIL.
THIS IS A NEW AGE... WE CAN ONLY COUNT ON OURSELVES!
HUH?
WHAT...
URGHH!

PIERRE, GRAB THE TRUCK WITH THE MOST FUEL IN IT.

GEORGE AND BERNARD, START GATHERING THE BIKES!

MOVE IT!

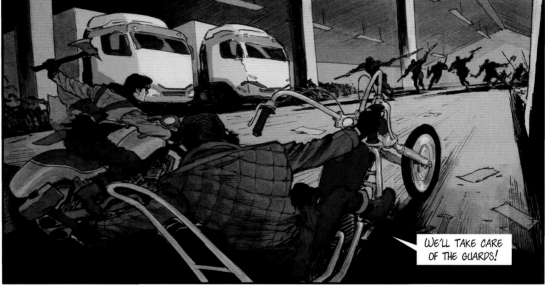

WE'LL TAKE CARE OF THE GUARDS!

GEORGE, LOAD EVERYTHING INTO THIS ONE!

HURRY!

LET'S GO!

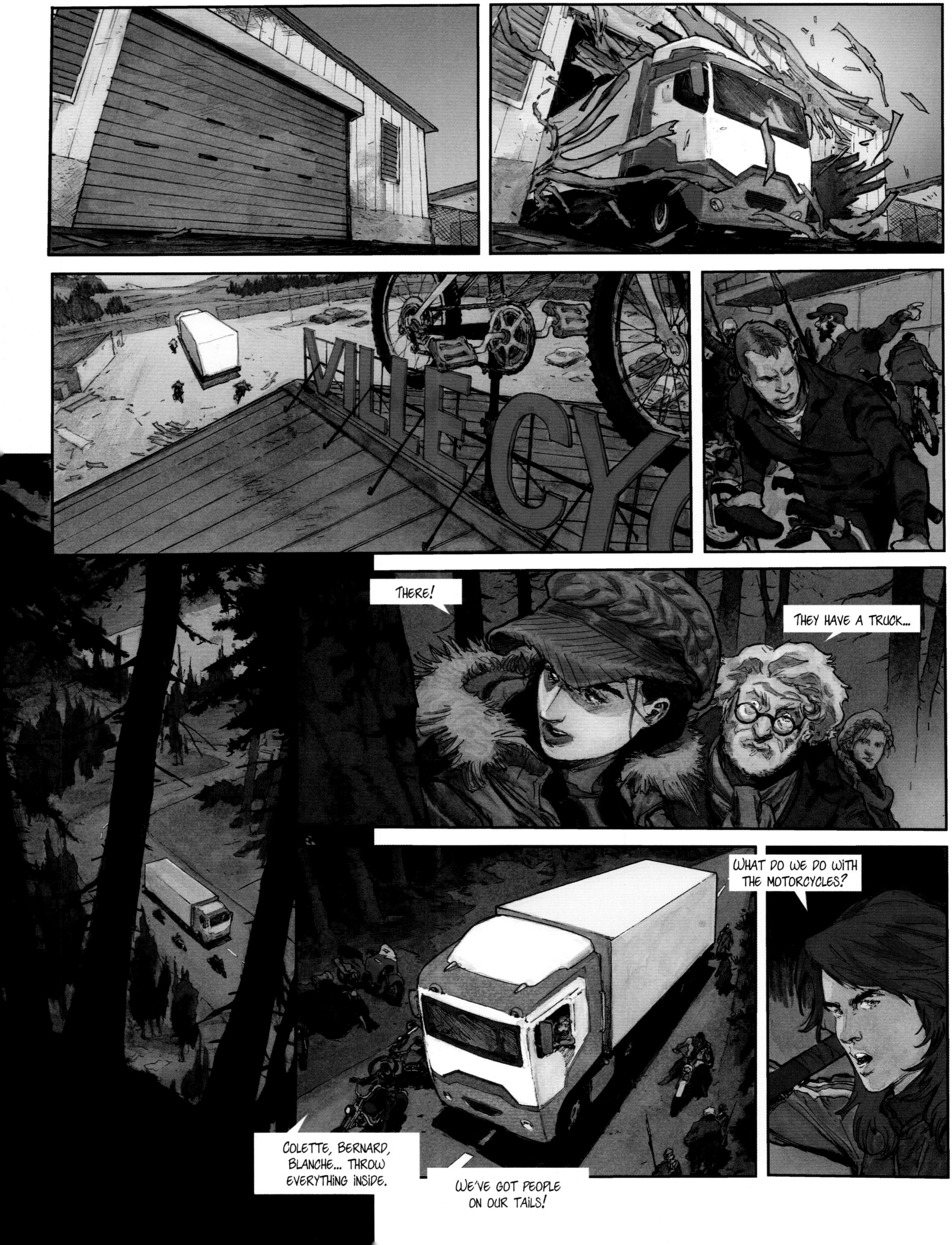
VILLE CY
THERE!
THEY HAVE A TRUCK...
WHAT DO WE DO WITH THE MOTORCYCLES?
COLETTE, BERNARD, BLANCHE... THROW EVERYTHING INSIDE.
WE'VE GOT PEOPLE ON OUR TAILS!

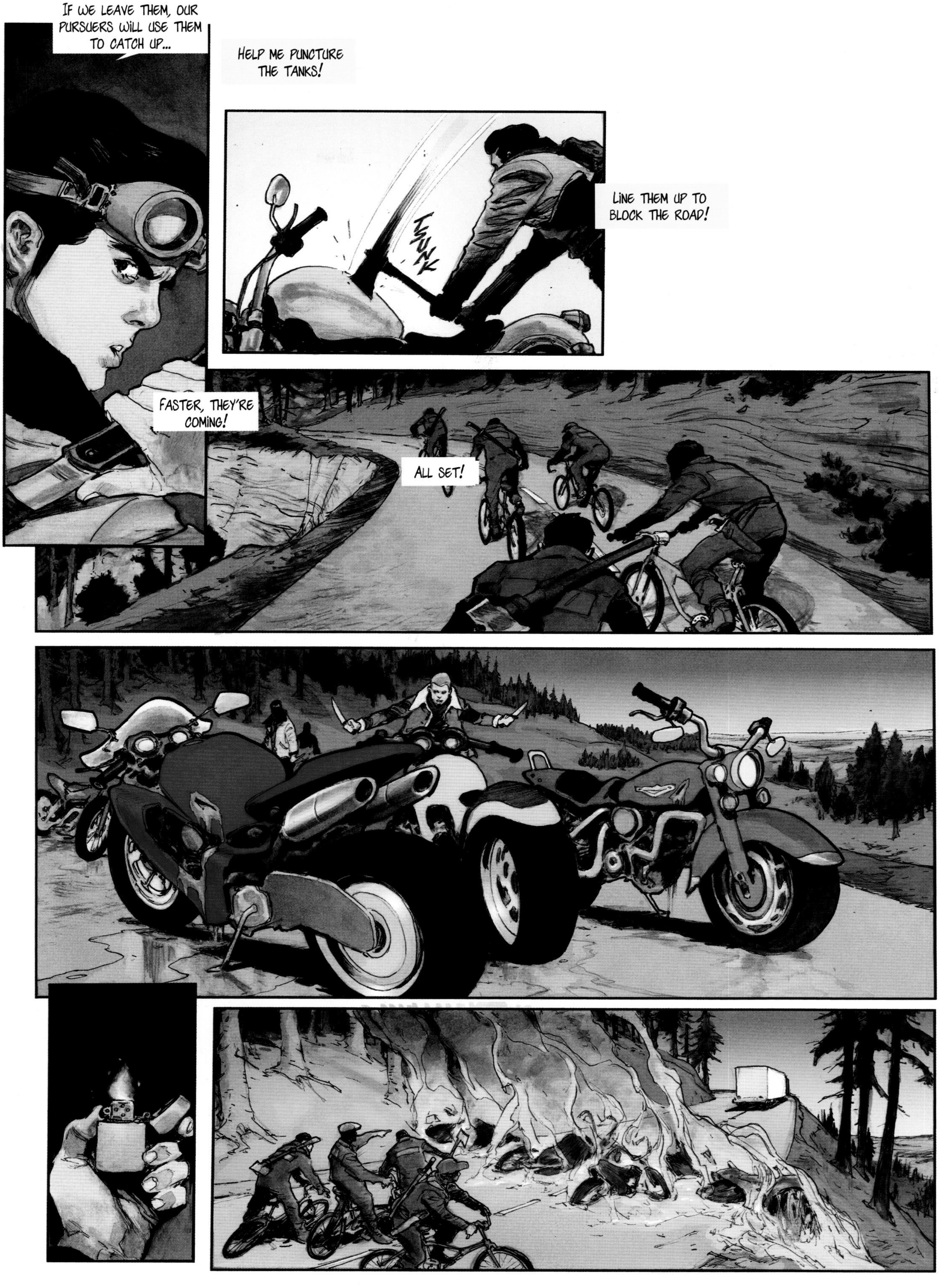
If we leave them, our pursuers will use them to catch up...
Help me puncture the tanks!
Line them up to block the road!
Faster, they're coming!
All set!

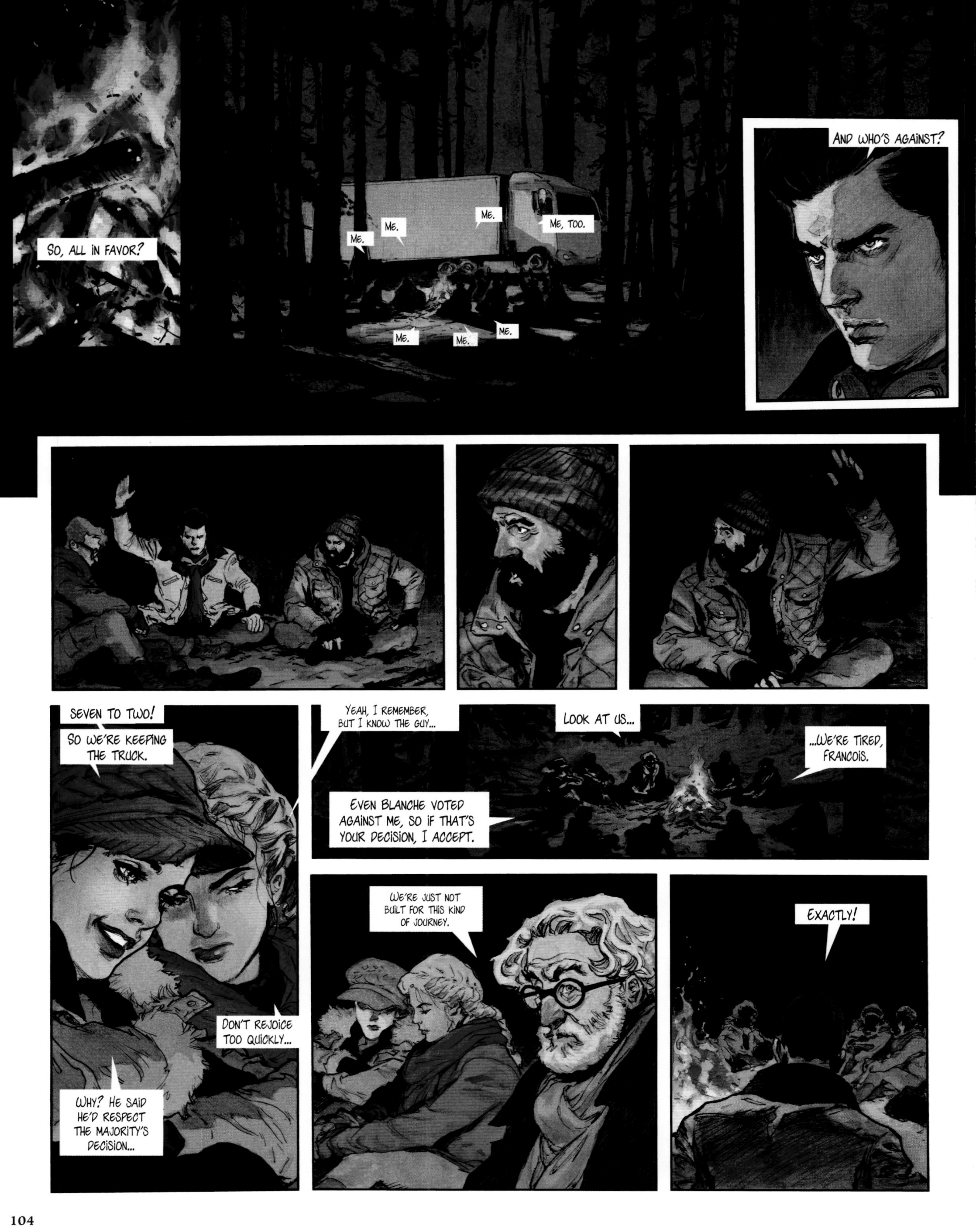
SO, ALL IN FAVOR?
ME.
ME.
ME.
ME, TOO.
ME.
ME.
ME.
AND WHO'S AGAINST?
SEVEN TO TWO!
SO WE'RE KEEPING THE TRUCK.
DON'T REJOICE TOO QUICKLY...
WHY? HE SAID HE'D RESPECT THE MAJORITY'S DECISION...
YEAH, I REMEMBER, BUT I KNOW THE GUY...
LOOK AT US...
...WE'RE TIRED, FRANCOIS.
EVEN BLANCHE VOTED AGAINST ME, SO IF THAT'S YOUR DECISION, I ACCEPT.
WE'RE JUST NOT BUILT FOR THIS KIND OF JOURNEY.
EXACTLY!

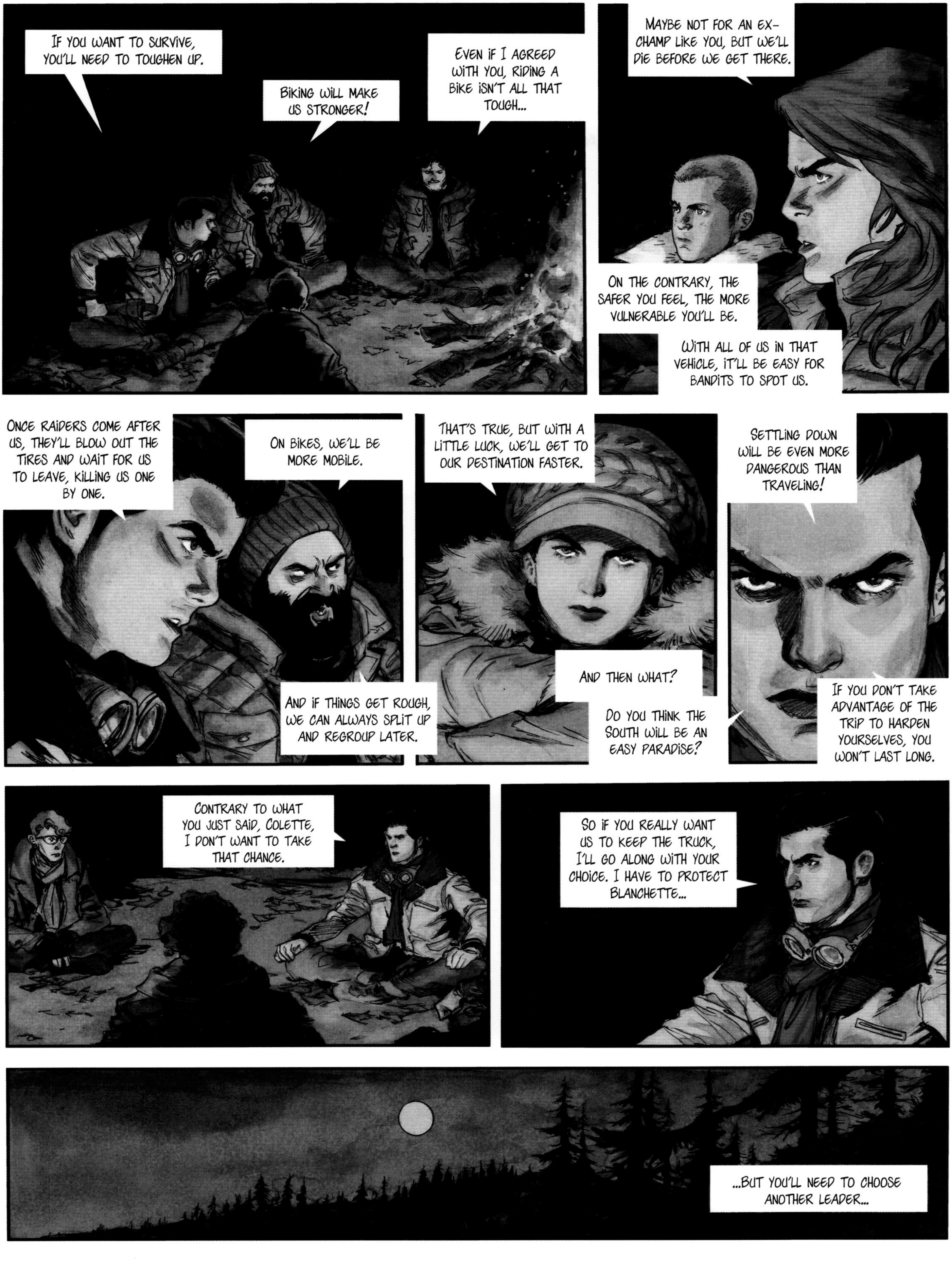
If you want to survive, you'll need to toughen up.
Biking will make us stronger!
Even if I agreed with you, riding a bike isn't all that tough...
Maybe not for an ex-champ like you, but we'll die before we get there.
On the contrary, the safer you feel, the more vulnerable you'll be.
With all of us in that vehicle, it'll be easy for bandits to spot us.
Once raiders come after us, they'll blow out the tires and wait for us to leave, killing us one by one.
On bikes, we'll be more mobile.
And if things get rough, we can always split up and regroup later.
That's true, but with a little luck, we'll get to our destination faster.
And then what?
Do you think the South will be an easy paradise?
Settling down will be even more dangerous than traveling!
If you don't take advantage of the trip to harden yourselves, you won't last long.
Contrary to what you just said, Colette, I don't want to take that chance.
So if you really want us to keep the truck, I'll go along with your choice. I have to protect Blanchette...
...but you'll need to choose another leader...

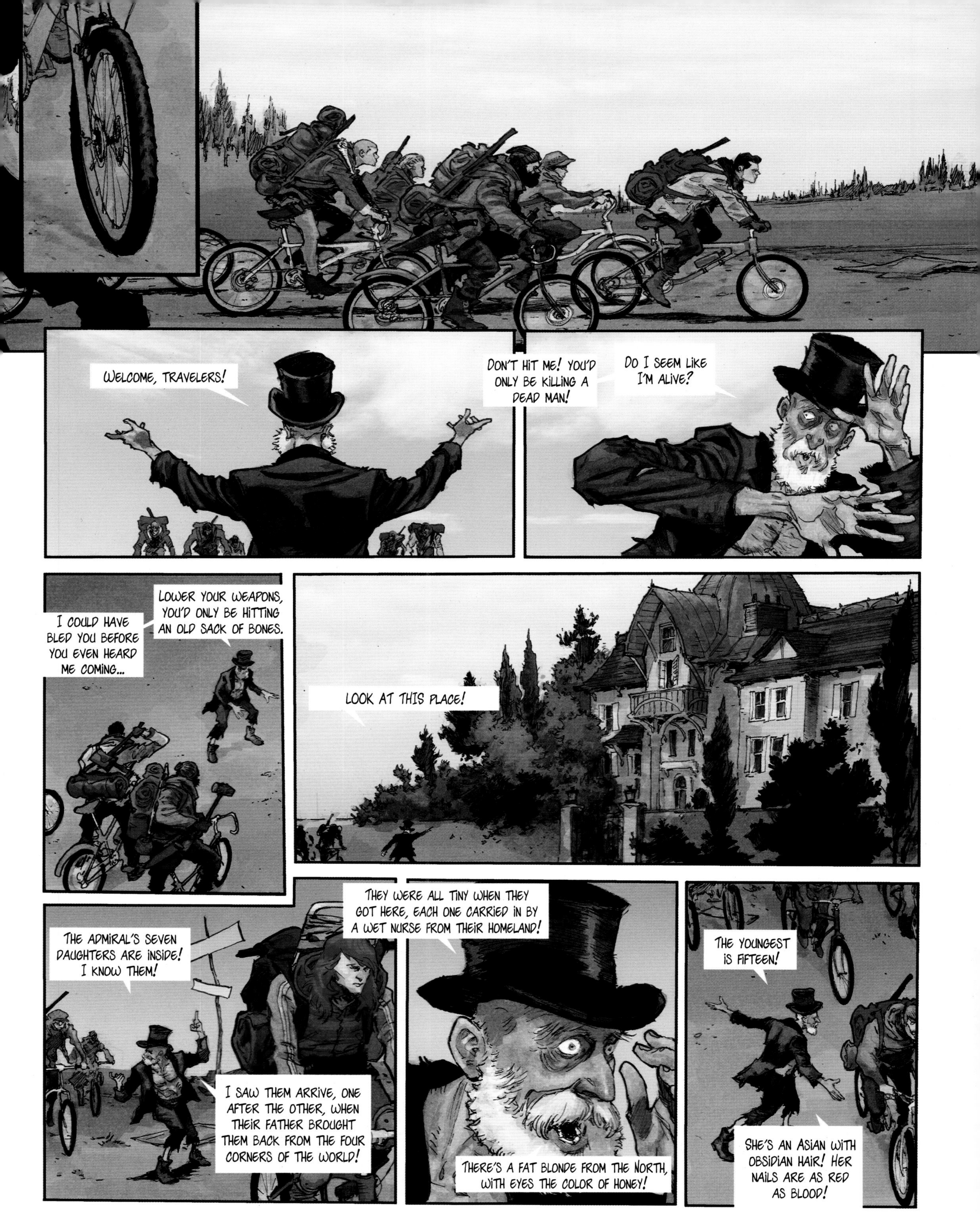
WELCOME, TRAVELERS!
DON'T HIT ME! YOU'D ONLY BE KILLING A DEAD MAN!
DO I SEEM LIKE I'M ALIVE?
I COULD HAVE BLED YOU BEFORE YOU EVEN HEARD ME COMING...
LOWER YOUR WEAPONS, YOU'D ONLY BE HITTING AN OLD SACK OF BONES.
LOOK AT THIS PLACE!
THE ADMIRAL'S SEVEN DAUGHTERS ARE INSIDE! I KNOW THEM!
I SAW THEM ARRIVE, ONE AFTER THE OTHER, WHEN THEIR FATHER BROUGHT THEM BACK FROM THE FOUR CORNERS OF THE WORLD!
THEY WERE ALL TINY WHEN THEY GOT HERE, EACH ONE CARRIED IN BY A WET NURSE FROM THEIR HOMELAND!
THERE'S A FAT BLONDE FROM THE NORTH, WITH EYES THE COLOR OF HONEY!
THE YOUNGEST IS FIFTEEN!
SHE'S AN ASIAN WITH OBSIDIAN HAIR! HER NAILS ARE AS RED AS BLOOD!

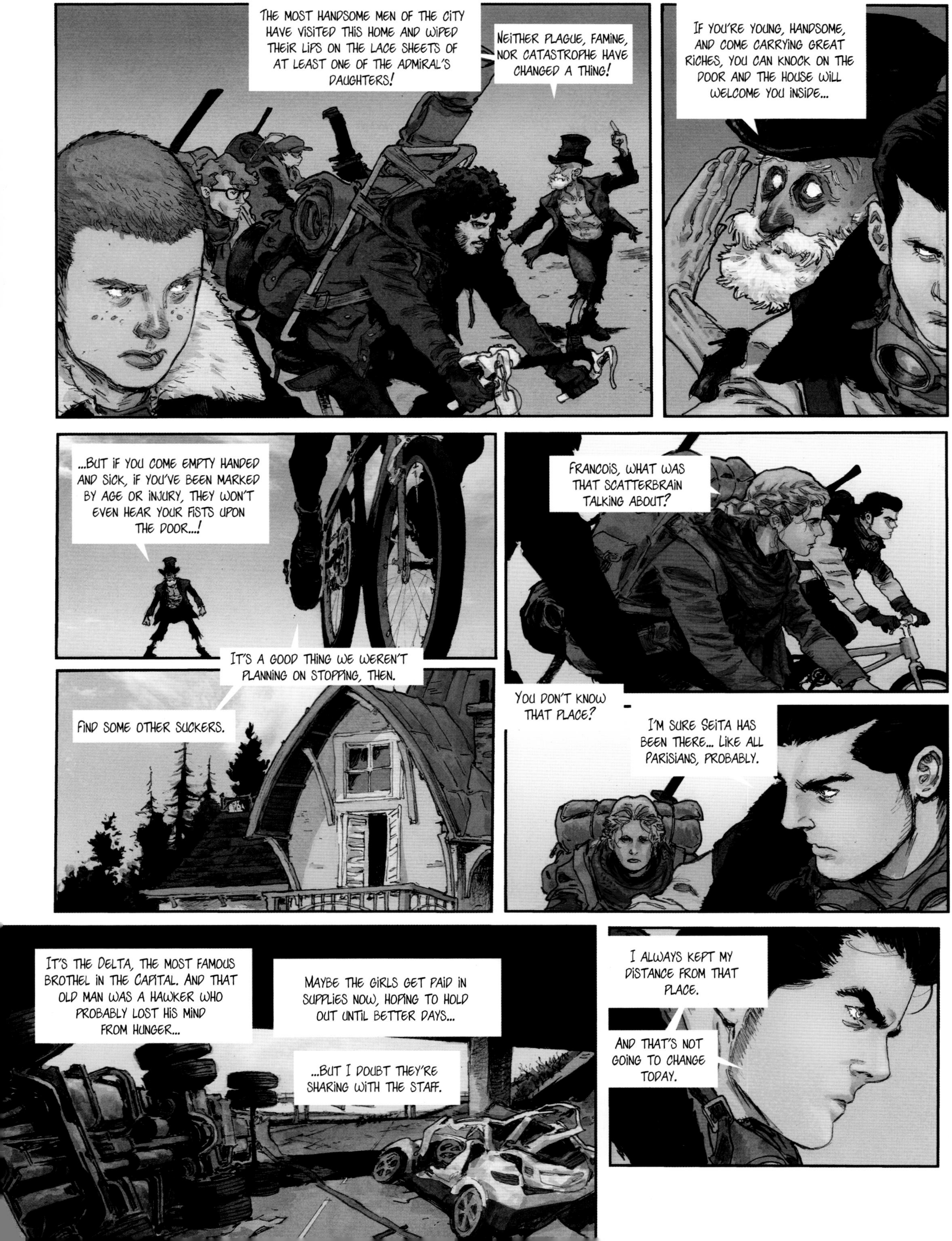
THE MOST HANDSOME MEN OF THE CITY HAVE VISITED THIS HOME AND WIPED THEIR LIPS ON THE LACE SHEETS OF AT LEAST ONE OF THE ADMIRAL'S DAUGHTERS!
NEITHER PLAGUE, FAMINE, NOR CATASTROPHE HAVE CHANGED A THING!
IF YOU'RE YOUNG, HANDSOME, AND COME CARRYING GREAT RICHES, YOU CAN KNOCK ON THE DOOR AND THE HOUSE WILL WELCOME YOU INSIDE...
...BUT IF YOU COME EMPTY HANDED AND SICK, IF YOU'VE BEEN MARKED BY AGE OR INJURY, THEY WON'T EVEN HEAR YOUR FISTS UPON THE DOOR...!
IT'S A GOOD THING WE WEREN'T PLANNING ON STOPPING, THEN.
FIND SOME OTHER SUCKERS.
FRANCOIS, WHAT WAS THAT SCATTERBRAIN TALKING ABOUT?
YOU DON'T KNOW THAT PLACE?
I'M SURE SEITA HAS BEEN THERE... LIKE ALL PARISIANS, PROBABLY.
IT'S THE DELTA, THE MOST FAMOUS BROTHEL IN THE CAPITAL. AND THAT OLD MAN WAS A HAWKER WHO PROBABLY LOST HIS MIND FROM HUNGER...
MAYBE THE GIRLS GET PAID IN SUPPLIES NOW, HOPING TO HOLD OUT UNTIL BETTER DAYS...
...BUT I DOUBT THEY'RE SHARING WITH THE STAFF.
I ALWAYS KEPT MY DISTANCE FROM THAT PLACE.
AND THAT'S NOT GOING TO CHANGE TODAY.

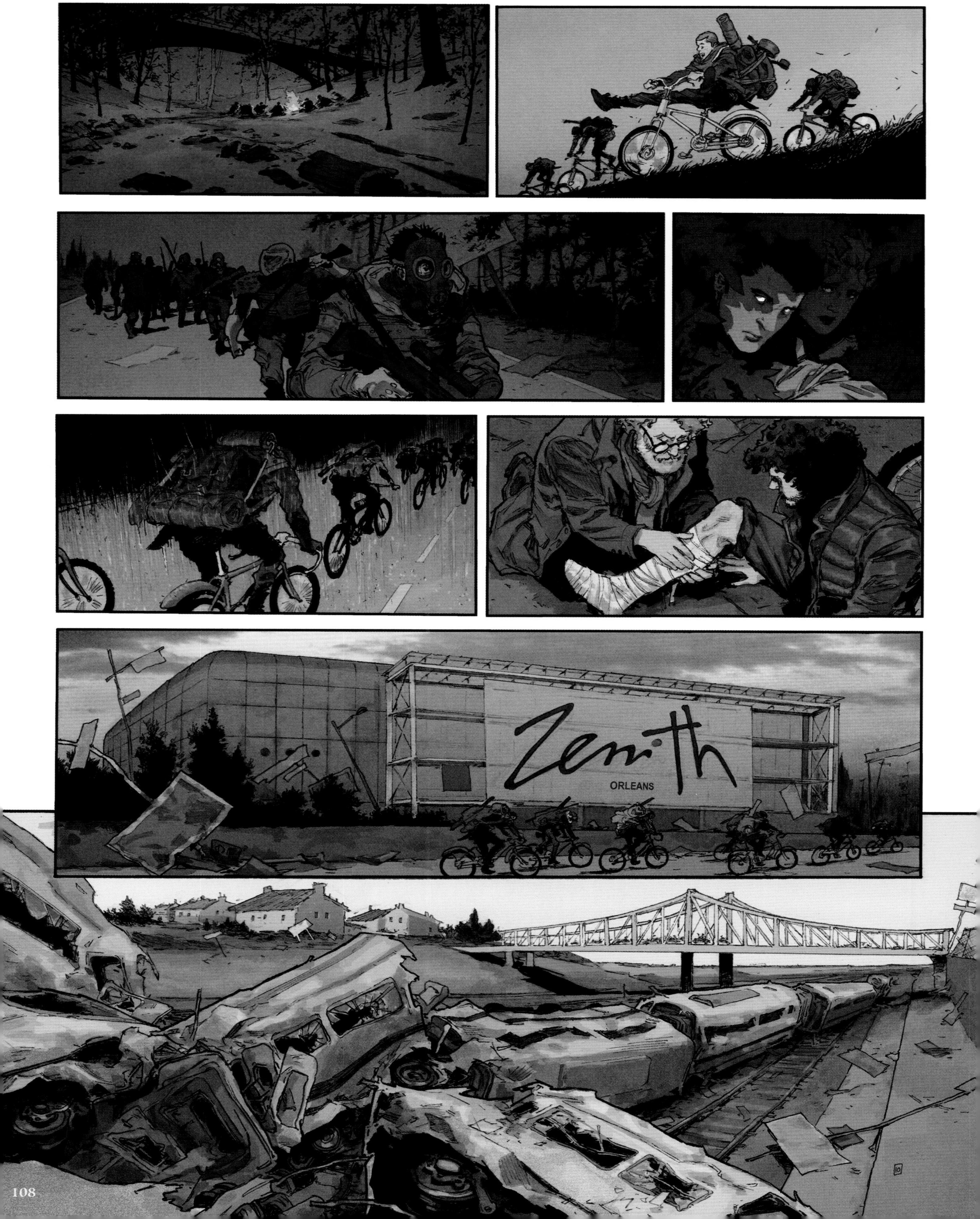
Zenith
ORLEANS

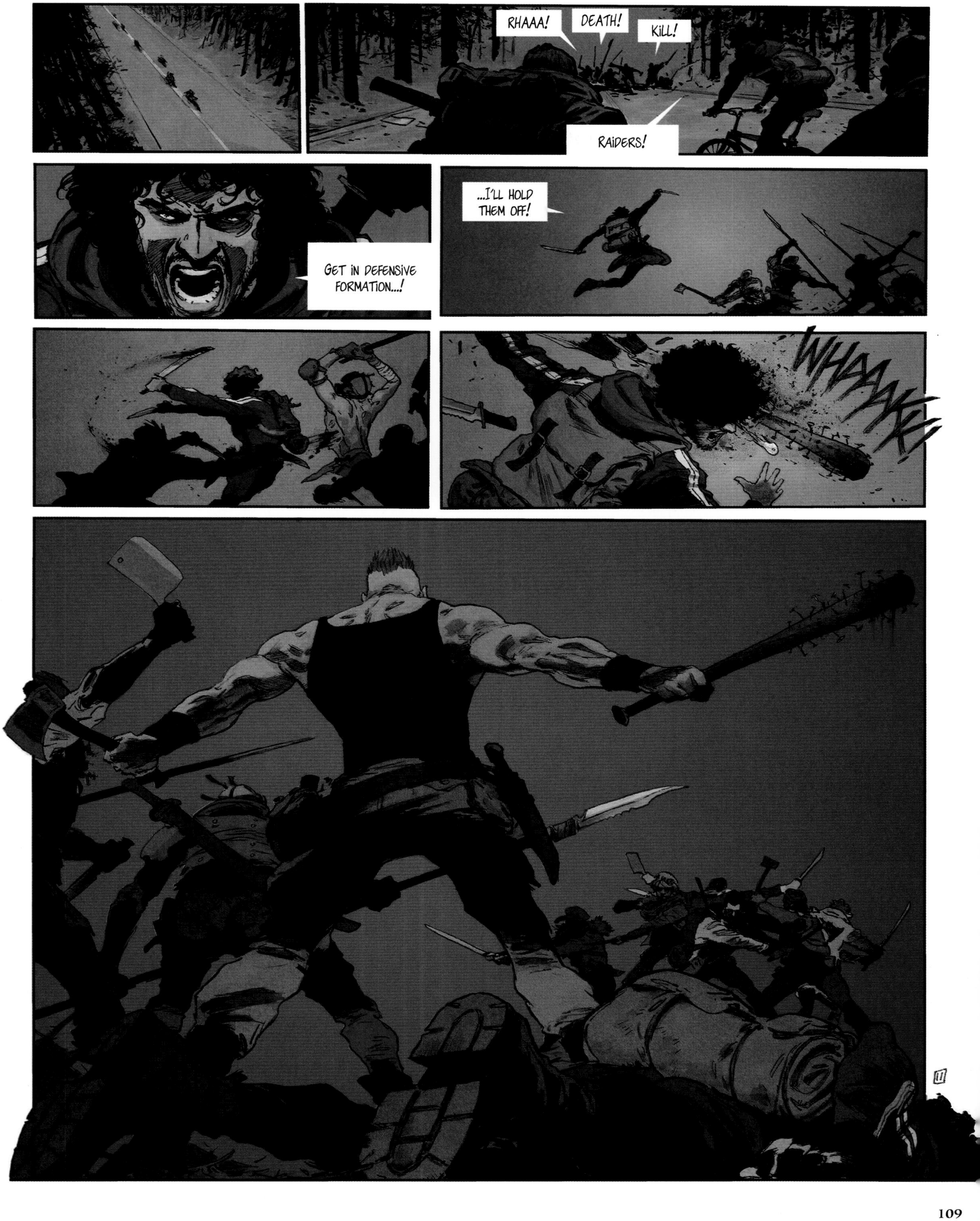
RHAAA!
DEATH!
KILL!
RAIDERS!
GET IN DEFENSIVE FORMATION...!
...I'LL HOLD THEM OFF!
WHAAAK!!

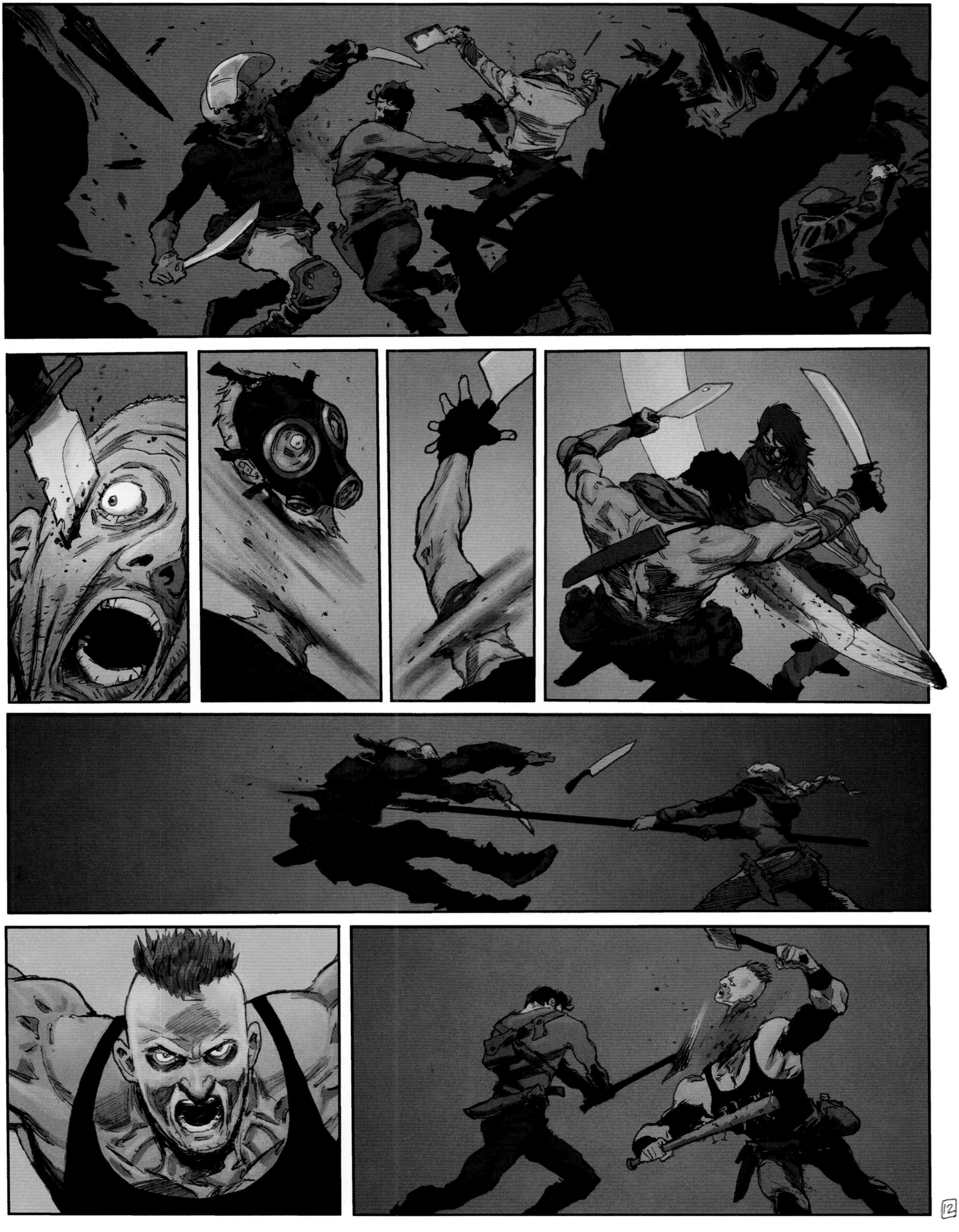

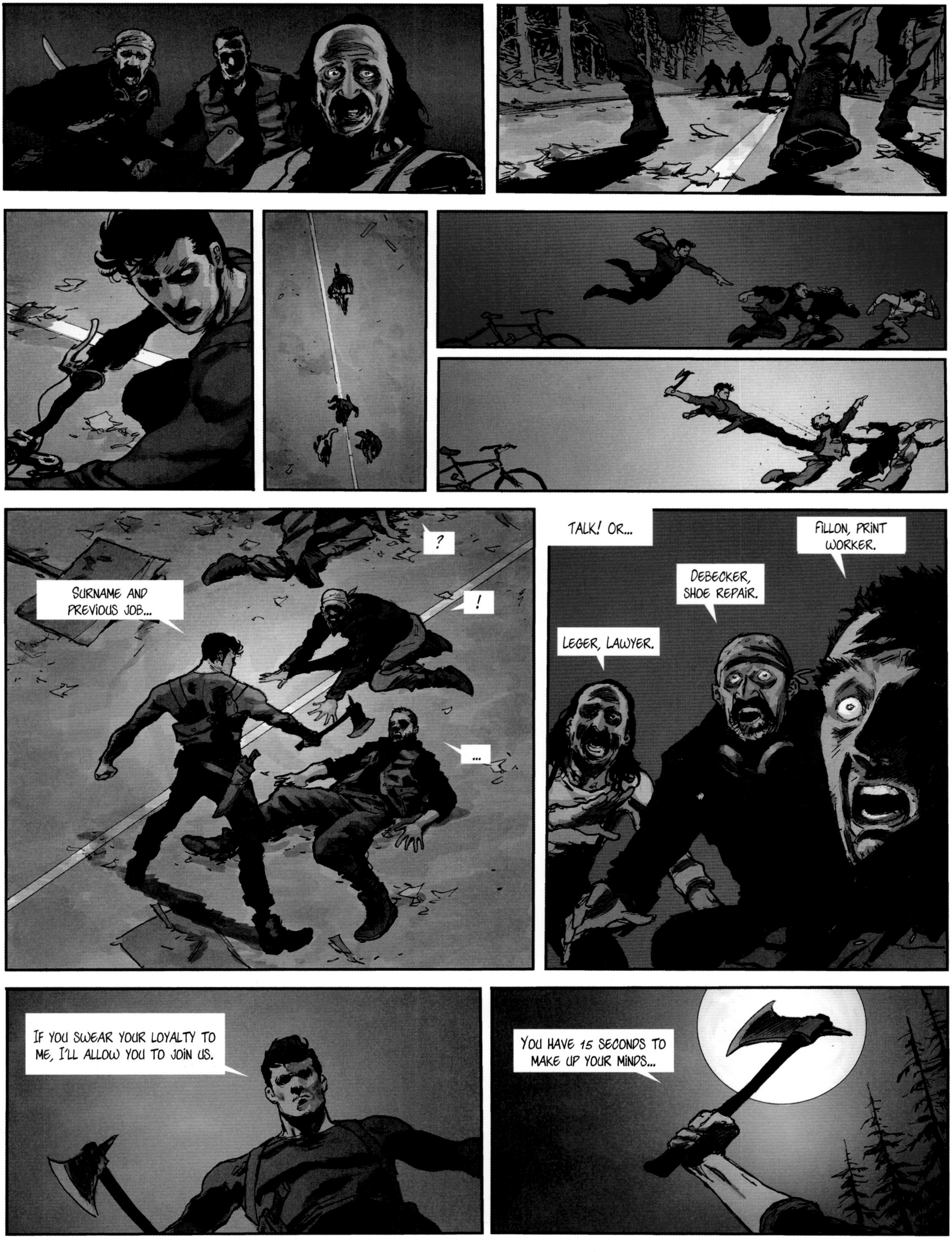
?
Surname and previous job...
!
...
Talk! Or...
Fillon, print worker.
Debecker, shoe repair.
Leger, lawyer.
If you swear your loyalty to me, I'll allow you to join us.
You have 15 seconds to make up your minds...
13

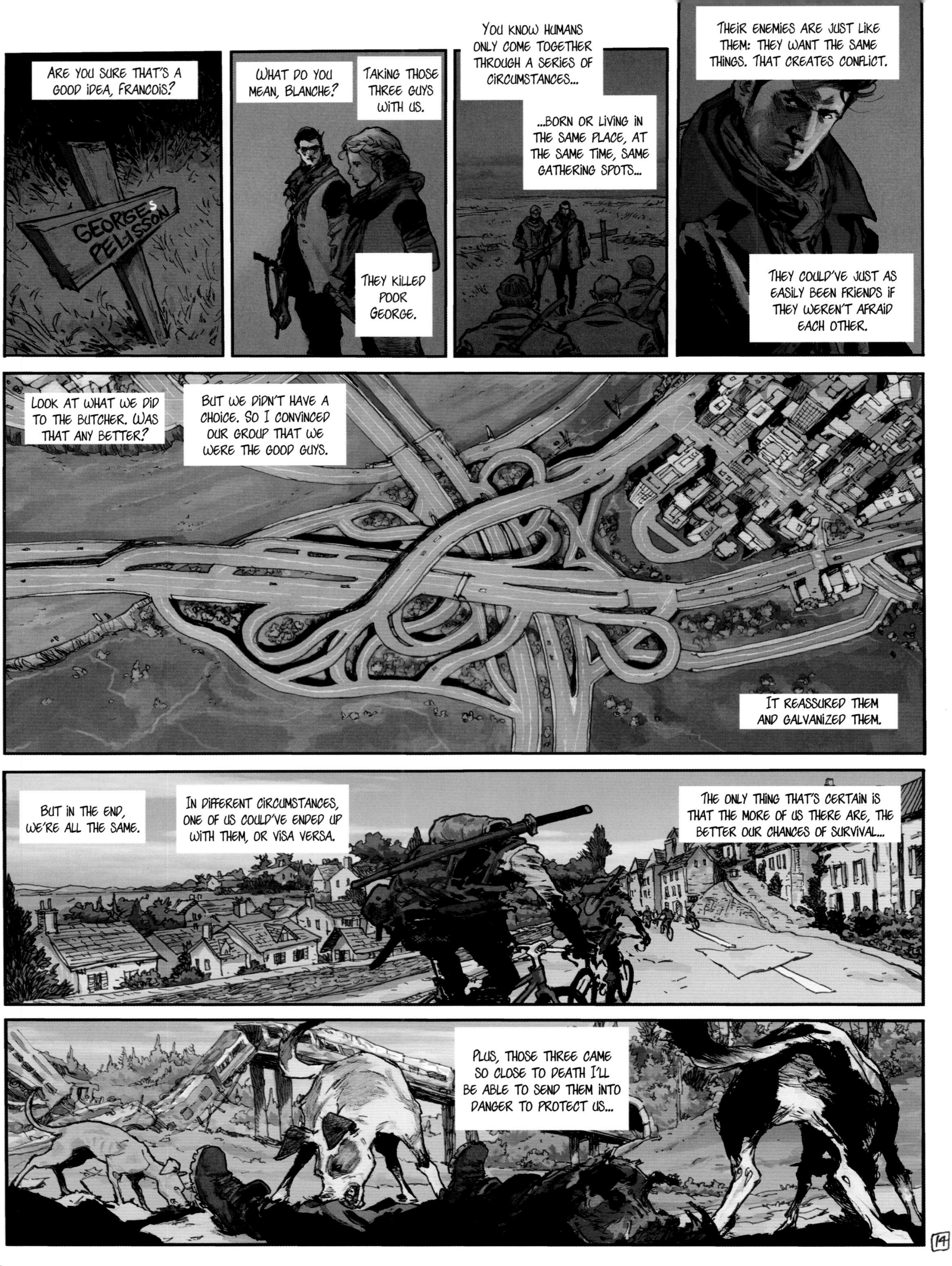

ARE YOU SURE THAT'S A GOOD IDEA, FRANCOIS?
GEORGES PELISSON
WHAT DO YOU MEAN, BLANCHE?
TAKING THOSE THREE GUYS WITH US.
THEY KILLED POOR GEORGE.
YOU KNOW HUMANS ONLY COME TOGETHER THROUGH A SERIES OF CIRCUMSTANCES...
...BORN OR LIVING IN THE SAME PLACE, AT THE SAME TIME, SAME GATHERING SPOTS...
THEIR ENEMIES ARE JUST LIKE THEM: THEY WANT THE SAME THINGS. THAT CREATES CONFLICT.
THEY COULD'VE JUST AS EASILY BEEN FRIENDS IF THEY WEREN'T AFRAID EACH OTHER.
LOOK AT WHAT WE DID TO THE BUTCHER. WAS THAT ANY BETTER?
BUT WE DIDN'T HAVE A CHOICE. SO I CONVINCED OUR GROUP THAT WE WERE THE GOOD GUYS.
IT REASSURED THEM AND GALVANIZED THEM.
BUT IN THE END, WE'RE ALL THE SAME.
IN DIFFERENT CIRCUMSTANCES, ONE OF US COULD'VE ENDED UP WITH THEM, OR VISA VERSA.
THE ONLY THING THAT'S CERTAIN IS THAT THE MORE OF US THERE ARE, THE BETTER OUR CHANCES OF SURVIVAL...
PLUS, THOSE THREE CAME SO CLOSE TO DEATH I'LL BE ABLE TO SEND THEM INTO DANGER TO PROTECT US...
14

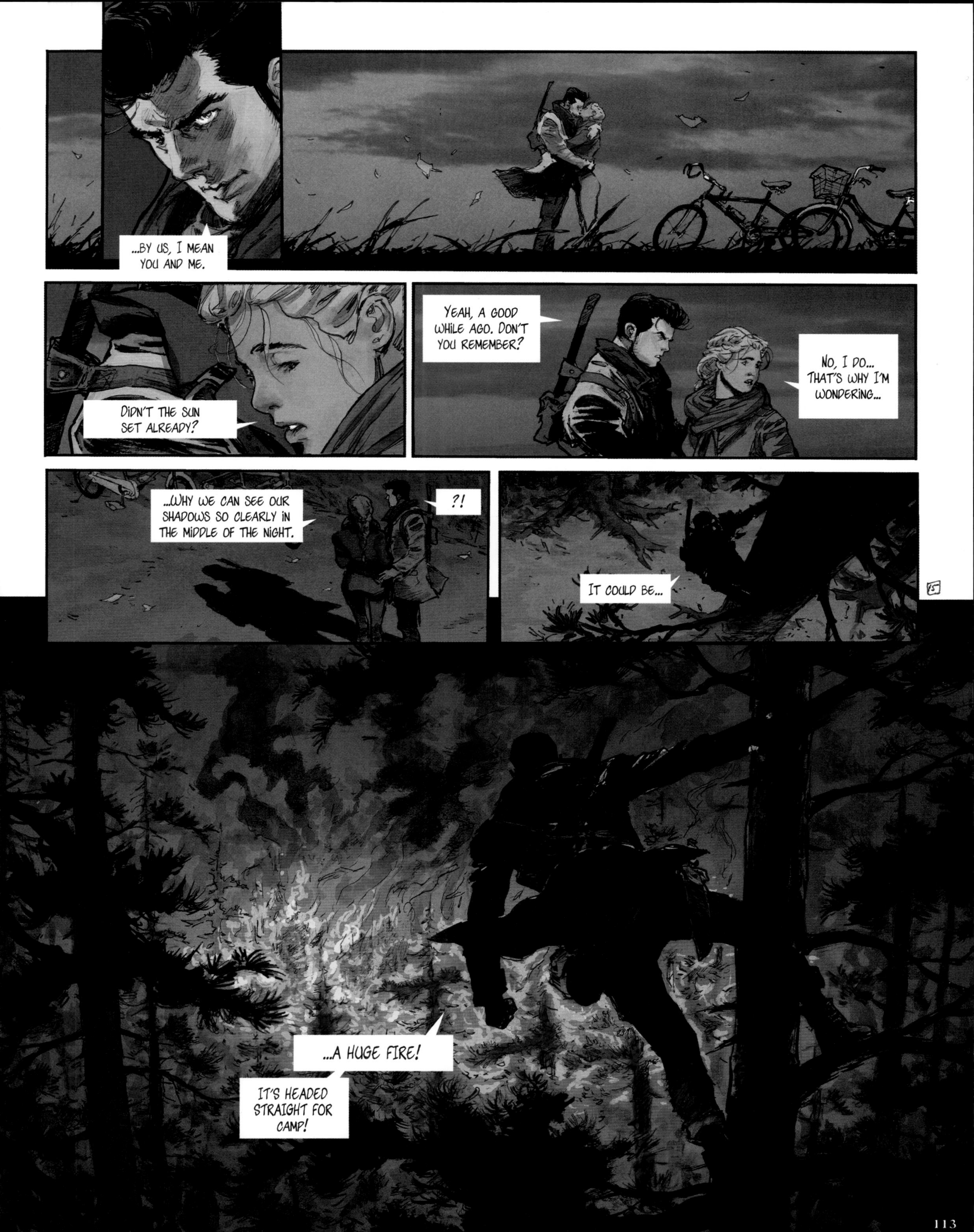
...BY US, I MEAN YOU AND ME.
DIDN'T THE SUN SET ALREADY?
YEAH, A GOOD WHILE AGO. DON'T YOU REMEMBER?
NO, I DO... THAT'S WHY I'M WONDERING...
...WHY WE CAN SEE OUR SHADOWS SO CLEARLY IN THE MIDDLE OF THE NIGHT.
?!
IT COULD BE...
15
...A HUGE FIRE!
IT'S HEADED STRAIGHT FOR CAMP!

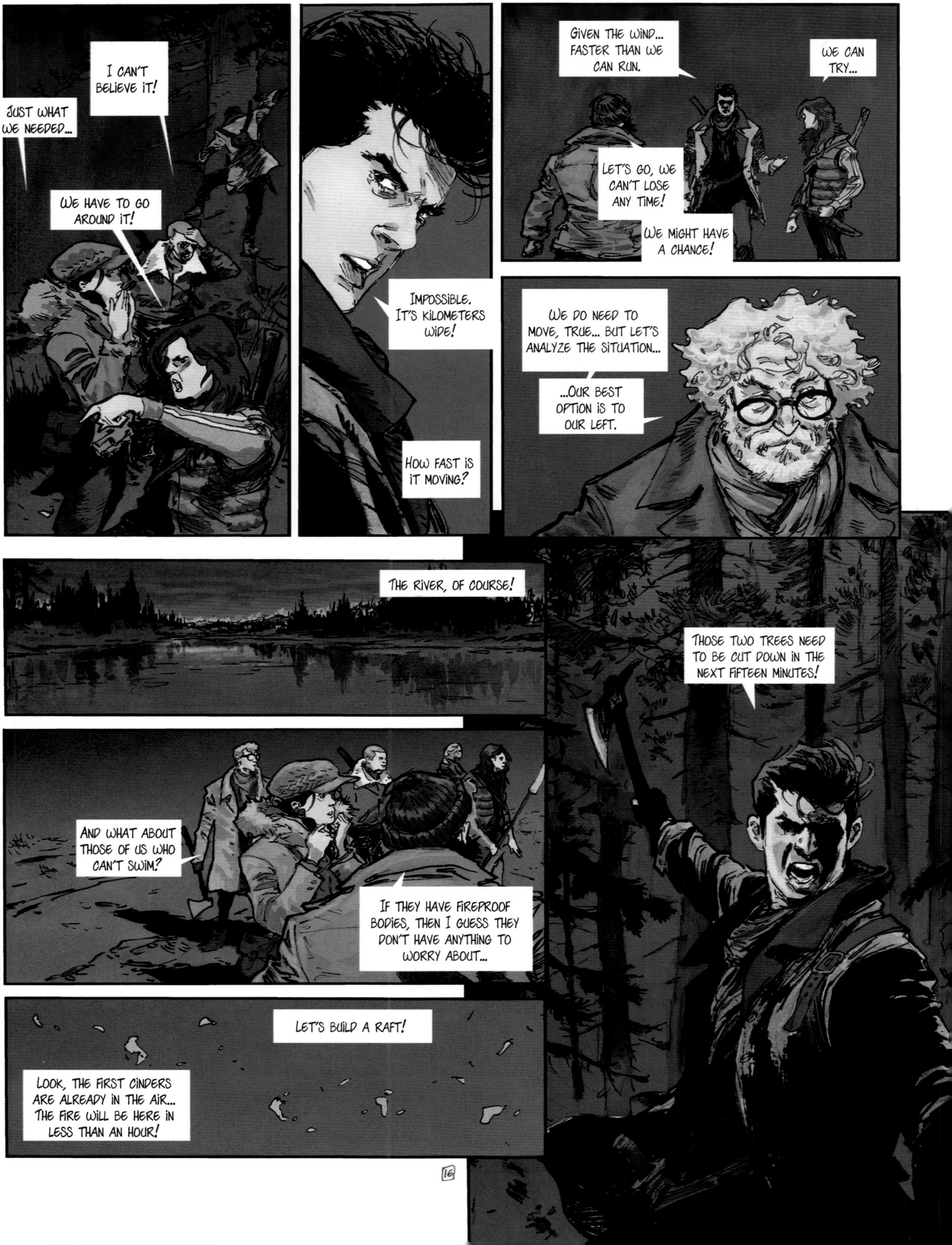
JUST WHAT WE NEEDED...
I CAN'T BELIEVE IT!
WE HAVE TO GO AROUND IT!
IMPOSSIBLE. IT'S KILOMETERS WIDE!
HOW FAST IS IT MOVING?
GIVEN THE WIND... FASTER THAN WE CAN RUN.
WE CAN TRY...
LET'S GO, WE CAN'T LOSE ANY TIME!
WE MIGHT HAVE A CHANCE!
WE DO NEED TO MOVE, TRUE... BUT LET'S ANALYZE THE SITUATION...
...OUR BEST OPTION IS TO OUR LEFT.
THE RIVER, OF COURSE!
AND WHAT ABOUT THOSE OF US WHO CAN'T SWIM?
IF THEY HAVE FIREPROOF BODIES, THEN I GUESS THEY DON'T HAVE ANYTHING TO WORRY ABOUT...
LET'S BUILD A RAFT!
LOOK, THE FIRST CINDERS ARE ALREADY IN THE AIR... THE FIRE WILL BE HERE IN LESS THAN AN HOUR!
THOSE TWO TREES NEED TO BE CUT DOWN IN THE NEXT FIFTEEN MINUTES!
16

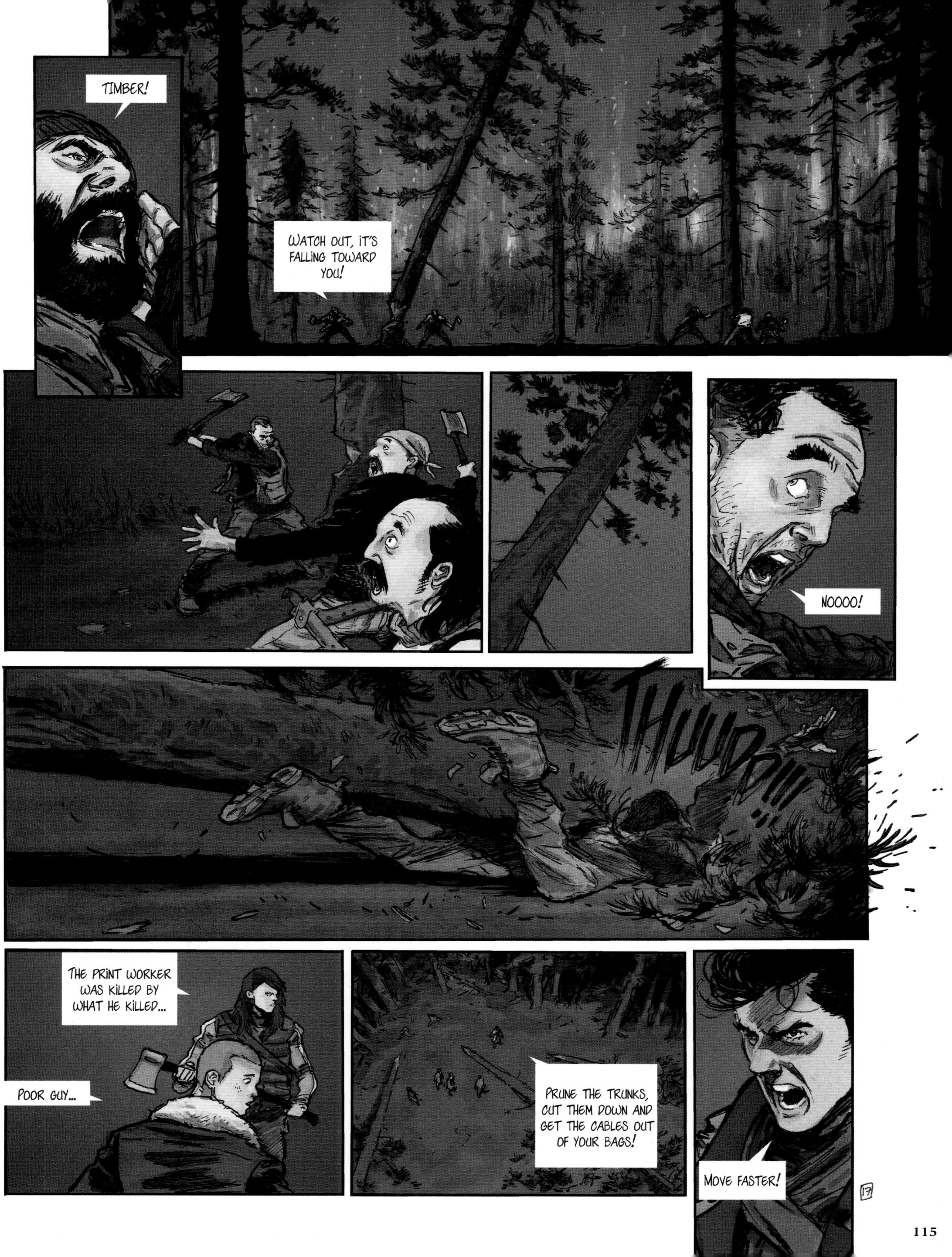
TIMBER!
WATCH OUT, IT'S FALLING TOWARD YOU!
NOOOO!
THUUDD!!!
THE PRINT WORKER WAS KILLED BY WHAT HE KILLED...
POOR GUY...
PRUNE THE TRUNKS, CUT THEM DOWN AND GET THE CABLES OUT OF YOUR BAGS!
MOVE FASTER!
17

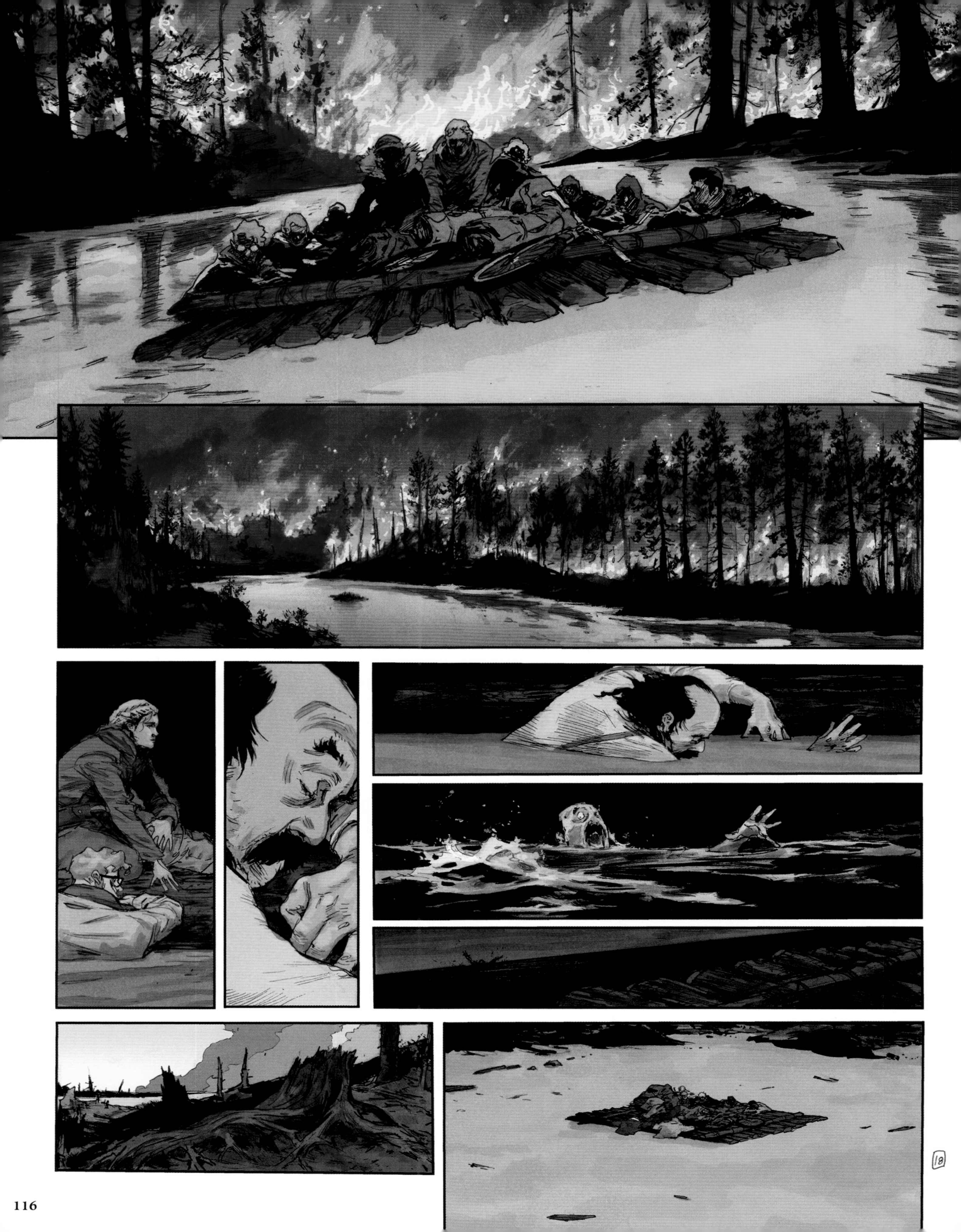

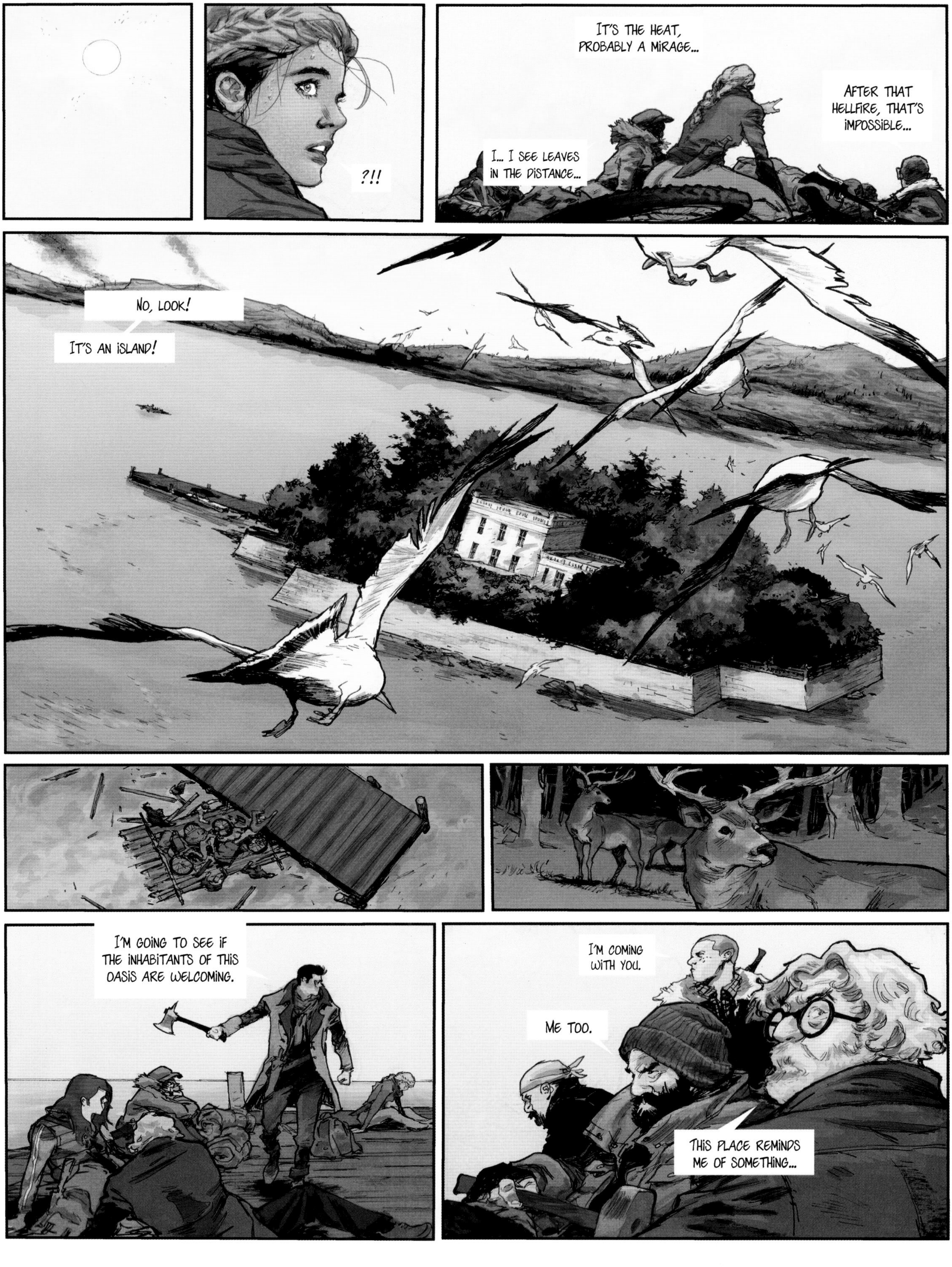
?!!
IT'S THE HEAT, PROBABLY A MIRAGE...
I... I SEE LEAVES IN THE DISTANCE...
AFTER THAT HELLFIRE, THAT'S IMPOSSIBLE...
NO, LOOK!
IT'S AN ISLAND!
I'M GOING TO SEE IF THE INHABITANTS OF THIS OASIS ARE WELCOMING.
I'M COMING WITH YOU.
ME TOO.
THIS PLACE REMINDS ME OF SOMETHING...
19

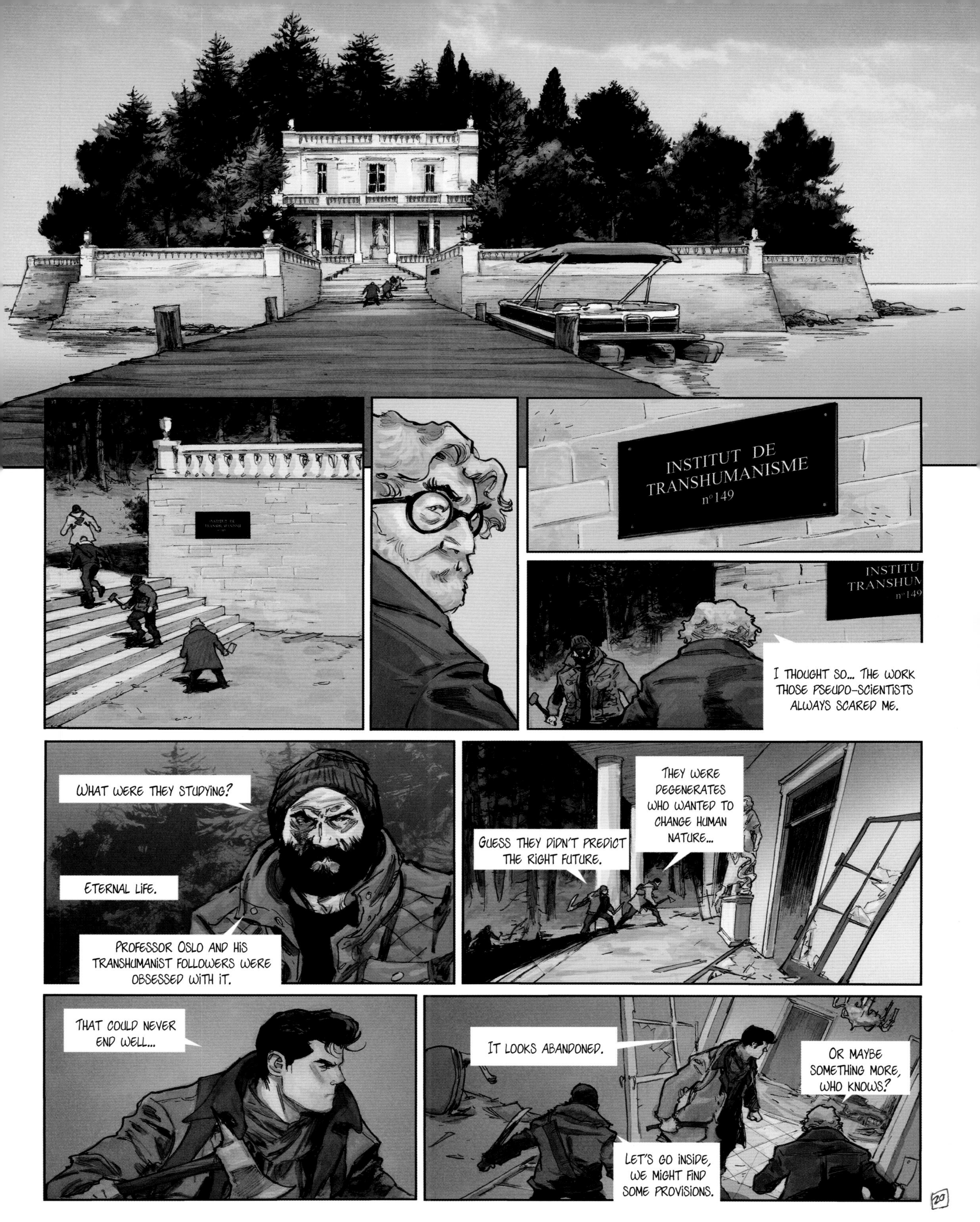
INSTITUT DE
TRANSHUMANISME
n°149
I THOUGHT SO... THE WORK THOSE PSEUDO-SCIENTISTS ALWAYS SCARED ME.
WHAT WERE THEY STUDYING?
ETERNAL LIFE.
PROFESSOR OSLO AND HIS TRANSHUMANIST FOLLOWERS WERE OBSESSED WITH IT.
THEY WERE DEGENERATES WHO WANTED TO CHANGE HUMAN NATURE...
GUESS THEY DIDN'T PREDICT THE RIGHT FUTURE.
THAT COULD NEVER END WELL...
IT LOOKS ABANDONED.
OR MAYBE SOMETHING MORE, WHO KNOWS?
LET'S GO INSIDE, WE MIGHT FIND SOME PROVISIONS.
20

I NEVER LOOKED AT THEIR EXPERIMENTS, BUT I HEARD THAT A GUINEA PIG INFECTED WITH COVID-49 RECOVERED TO FULL HEALTH IN A MATTER OF HOURS...

AN ADULT COW'S FRACTURED HOOF BONES REPAIRED THEMSELVES IN ONE NIGHT....

A CHICKEN'S FEATHERS GREW BACK, A DISEMBOWELED DOG'S STOMACH CLOSED UP, AND DOZENS OF FISH LIVED FOR THREE WEEKS OUT OF WATER.

FROM SOME SORT OF VACCINE?

SECRÉTARIAT

IT'S SIMILAR, BUT IN REALITY, THEY'RE CALLED NANOMACHINES.

MILLIONS OF LITTLE "ROBOTS" BY THE GALLON?

THAT'S ONE WAY TO PUT IT.

IT GIVES A CONSIDERABLE AMOUNT OF ENERGY TO THE ORGANISM THEY INHABIT...

ÉCONOMAT

DIRECTION

...AND THEY DEPLOY AROUND THE MOST THREATENED AREAS, DEPENDING ON THE SERIOUSNESS OF THE THREAT.

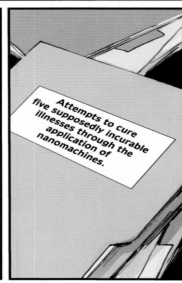

Attempts to cure five supposedly incurable illnesses through the application of the nanomachines.

FRANCOIS, I'D LIKE TO READ THESE FILES.

LET ME KNOW WHEN WE'RE LEAVING.

UNDERSTOOD, DOCTOR.

I won't hide the fact that that my conclusion is rather pessimistic. Not only are the mental patients showing no sign of improvement, but on the contrary they seem to draw on the energy the nanomachines provide to them as if a new source of nurishment for their madness to prey upon.

I chose to stop the study, but the result proved catastrophic. The patients reacted with extreme violence which led three among their number to hallucinate elements of their madness, followed soon after by death.

It seems that the energy they accumulate is suddenly and violently released through their mental illness, which gives it such intensity that it passes into the realm of the unreal.

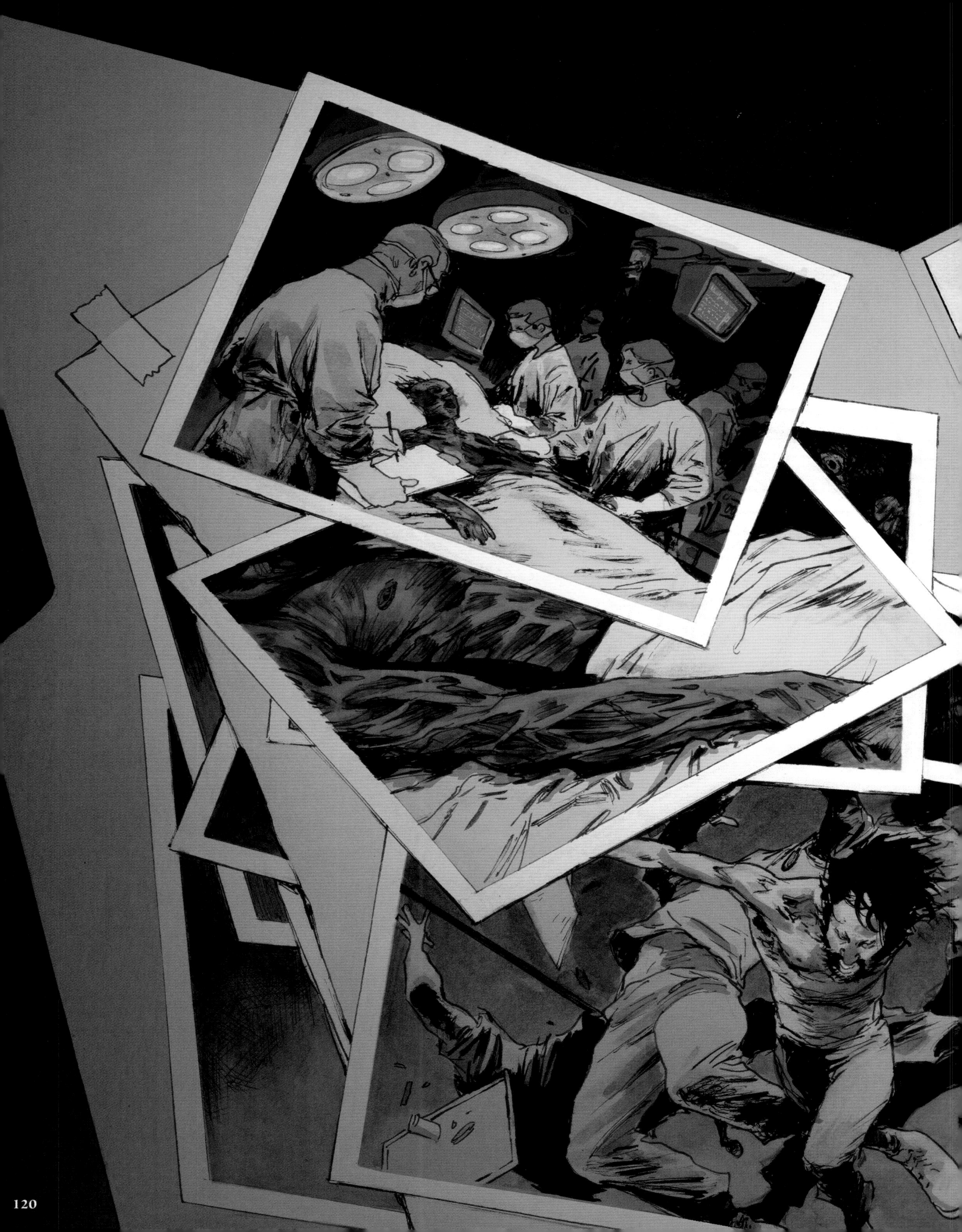

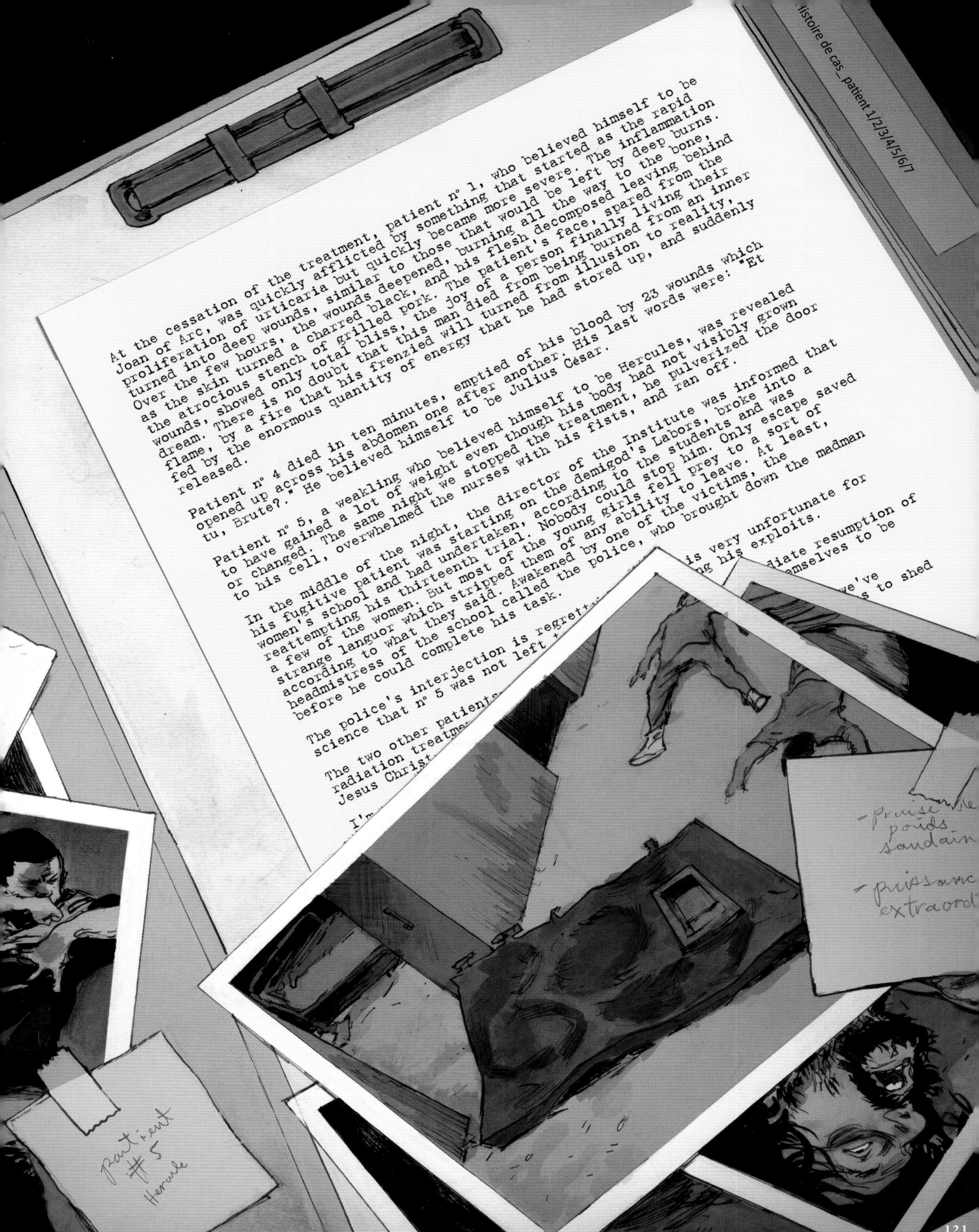
istoire de cas_patient 1/2/3/4/5/6/7
At the cessation of the treatment, patient n° 1, who believed himself to be Joan of Arc, was quickly afflicted by something that started as the rapid proliferation of urticaria but quickly became more severe. The inflammation turned into deep wounds, similar to those that would be left by deep burns. Over the few hours, the wounds deepened, burning all the way to the bone, as the skin turned a charred black, and his flesh decomposed leaving behind the atrocious stench of grilled pork. The patient's face, spared from the wounds, showed only total bliss, the joy of a person finally living their dream. There is no doubt that this man died from being burned from an inner flame, by a fire that his frenzied will turned from illusion to reality, fed by the enormous quantity of energy that he had stored up, and suddenly released.
Patient n° 4 died in ten minutes, emptied of his blood by 23 wounds which opened up across his abdomen one after another. His last words were: "Et tu, Brute?." He believed himself to be Julius César.
Patient n° 5, a weakling who believed himself to be Hercules, was revealed to have gained a lot of weight even though his body had not visibly grown or changed. The same night we stopped the treatment, he pulverized the door to his cell, overwhelmed the nurses with his fists, and ran off.
In the middle of the night, the director of the Institute was informed that his fugitive patient was starting on the demigod's Labors, broke into a women's school and had undertaken, according to the students and was reattempting his thirteenth trial. Nobody could stop him. Only escape saved a few of the women. But most of the young girls fell prey to a sort of strange languor which stripped them of any ability to leave. At least, according to what they said. Awakened by one of the victims, the headmistress of the school called the police, who brought down the madman before he could complete his task.
The police's interjection is regrett
is very unfortunate for
science that n° 5 was not left
his exploits.
The two other patients
diate resumption of
radiation treatme
emselves to be
Jesus Christ
we've
s to shed
-prise
poids
soudain
-puissanc
extraord
patient #5
Hercule

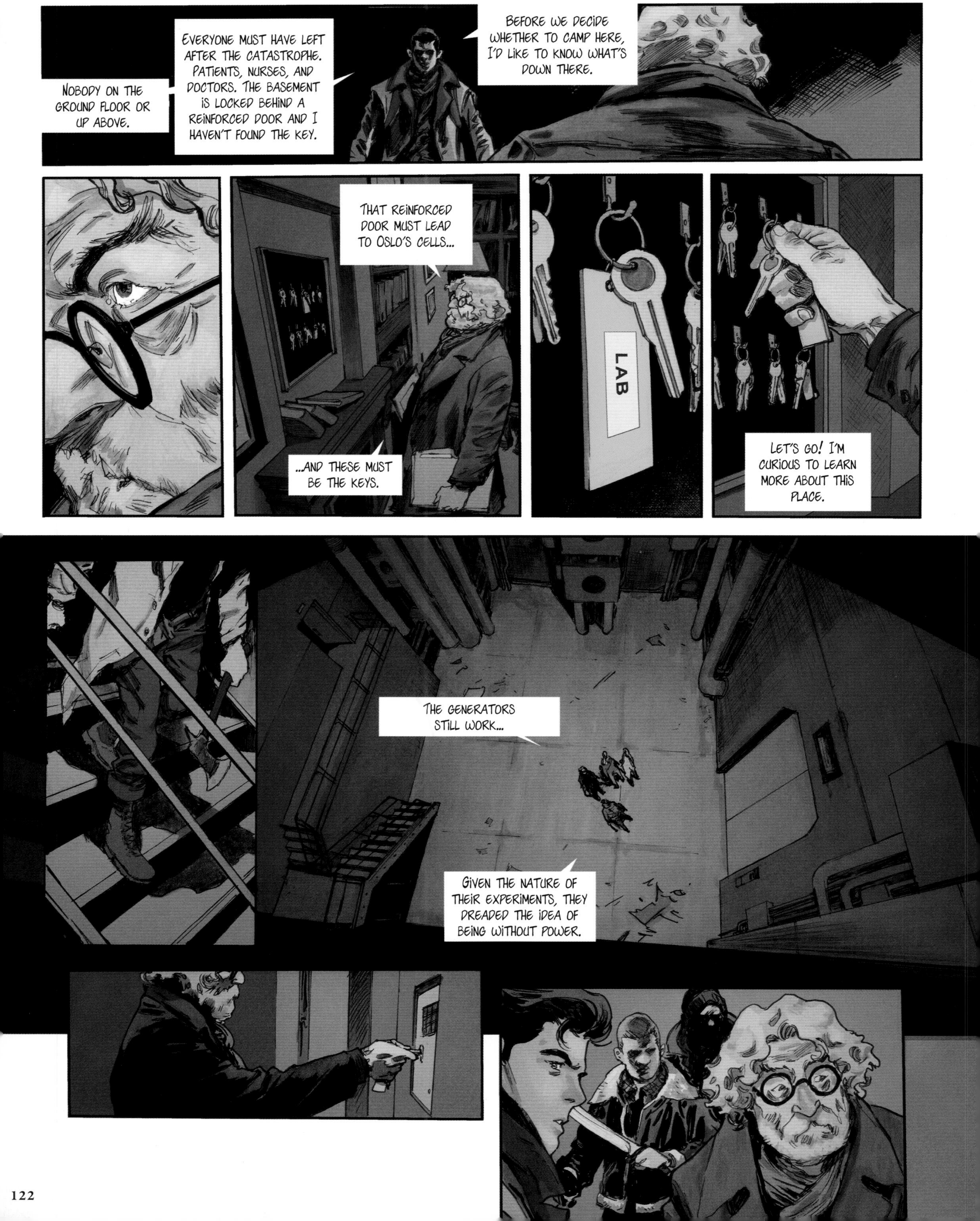
NOBODY ON THE GROUND FLOOR OR UP ABOVE.
EVERYONE MUST HAVE LEFT AFTER THE CATASTROPHE. PATIENTS, NURSES, AND DOCTORS. THE BASEMENT IS LOCKED BEHIND A REINFORCED DOOR AND I HAVEN'T FOUND THE KEY.
BEFORE WE DECIDE WHETHER TO CAMP HERE, I'D LIKE TO KNOW WHAT'S DOWN THERE.
THAT REINFORCED DOOR MUST LEAD TO OSLO'S CELLS...
...AND THESE MUST BE THE KEYS.
LAB
LET'S GO! I'M CURIOUS TO LEARN MORE ABOUT THIS PLACE.
THE GENERATORS STILL WORK...
GIVEN THE NATURE OF THEIR EXPERIMENTS, THEY DREADED THE IDEA OF BEING WITHOUT POWER.

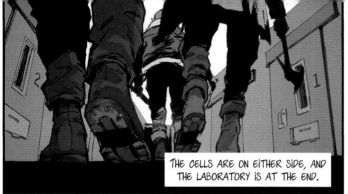

THE CELLS ARE ON EITHER SIDE, AND THE LABORATORY IS AT THE END.

THERE WERE FIVE MEN DOWN HERE WHO UNDERWENT SOME STRANGE TREATMENT THAT LED TO THREE SUPPOSED "MIRACLES"...

BURNED, AS I THOUGHT.

LET'S GO SEE THE "NEW HERCULES" IN CELL 5...

CAN A HUMAN REALLY BE THAT STRONG?

CLEARLY HE WENT AT IT FOR DAYS BEFORE DYING OF THIRST...

WHOA! COME AND LOOK AT THIS!

IS THAT "CHRIST'S" CELL?

...

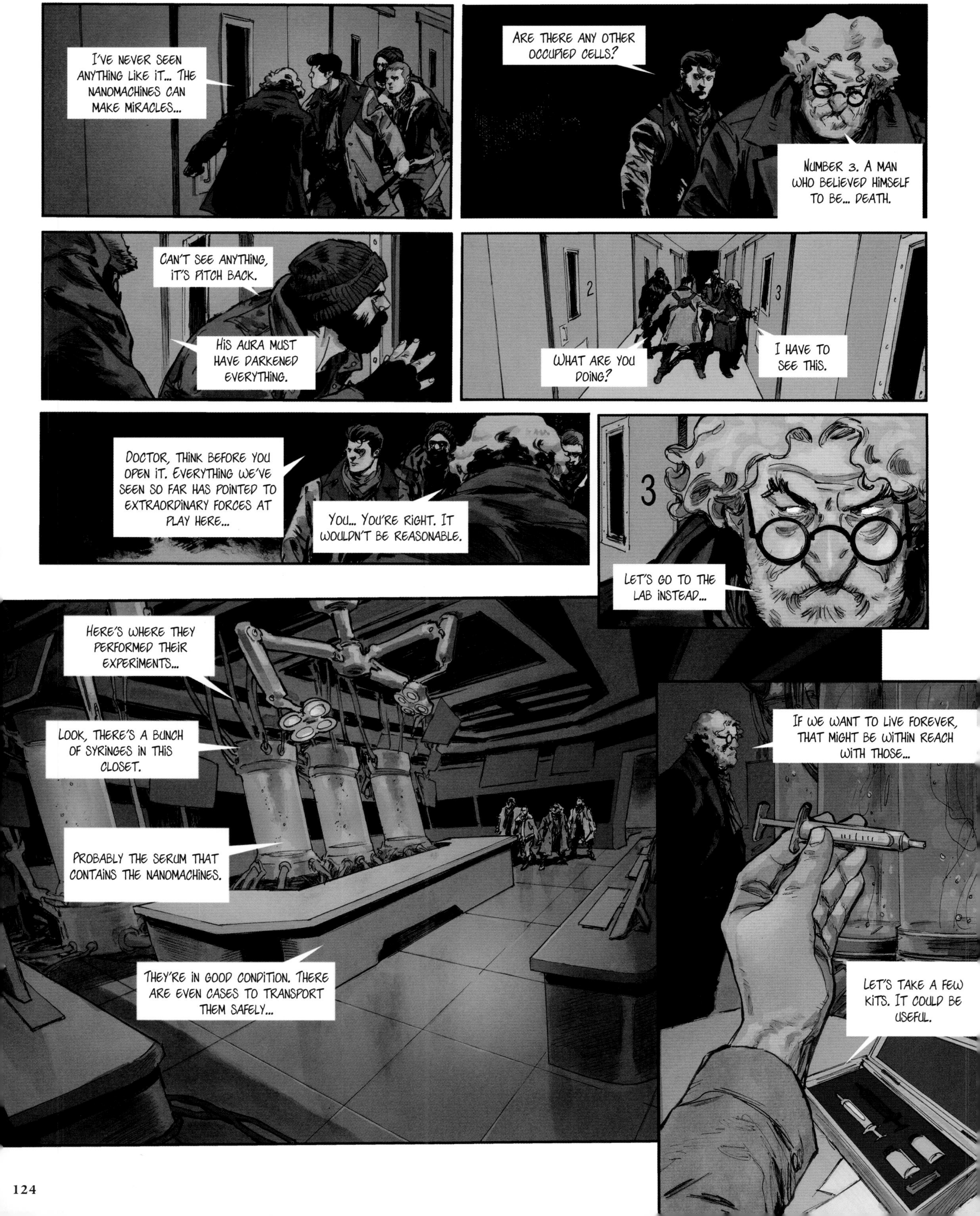
I'VE NEVER SEEN ANYTHING LIKE IT... THE NANOMACHINES CAN MAKE MIRACLES...
ARE THERE ANY OTHER OCCUPIED CELLS?
NUMBER 3. A MAN WHO BELIEVED HIMSELF TO BE... DEATH.
CAN'T SEE ANYTHING, IT'S PITCH BACK.
HIS AURA MUST HAVE DARKENED EVERYTHING.
WHAT ARE YOU DOING?
I HAVE TO SEE THIS.
DOCTOR, THINK BEFORE YOU OPEN IT. EVERYTHING WE'VE SEEN SO FAR HAS POINTED TO EXTRAORDINARY FORCES AT PLAY HERE...
YOU... YOU'RE RIGHT. IT WOULDN'T BE REASONABLE.
3
LET'S GO TO THE LAB INSTEAD...
HERE'S WHERE THEY PERFORMED THEIR EXPERIMENTS...
LOOK, THERE'S A BUNCH OF SYRINGES IN THIS CLOSET.
PROBABLY THE SERUM THAT CONTAINS THE NANOMACHINES.
THEY'RE IN GOOD CONDITION. THERE ARE EVEN CASES TO TRANSPORT THEM SAFELY...
IF WE WANT TO LIVE FOREVER, THAT MIGHT BE WITHIN REACH WITH THOSE...
LET'S TAKE A FEW KITS. IT COULD BE USEFUL.

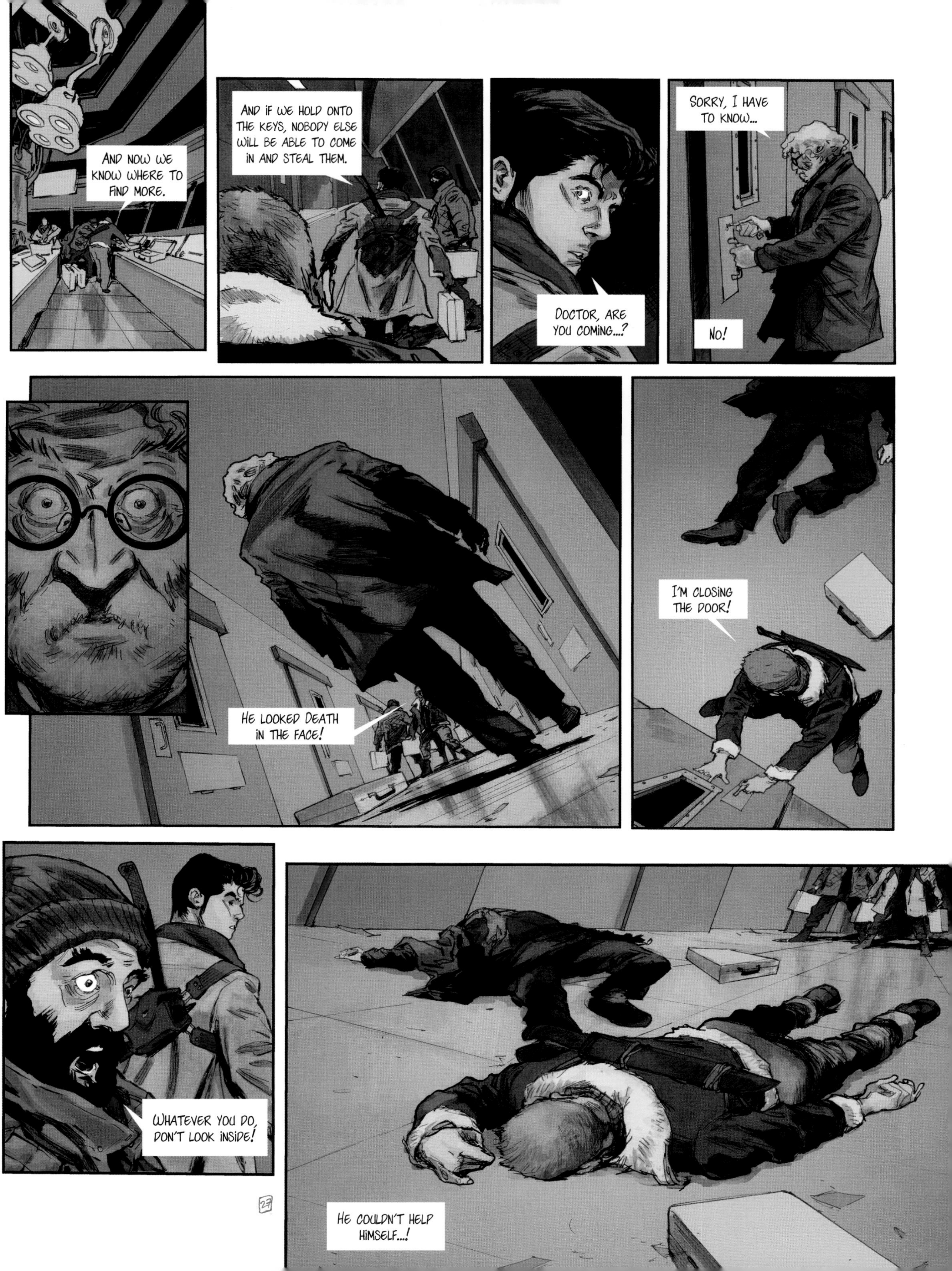
AND NOW WE KNOW WHERE TO FIND MORE.
AND IF WE HOLD ONTO THE KEYS, NOBODY ELSE WILL BE ABLE TO COME IN AND STEAL THEM.
DOCTOR, ARE YOU COMING...?
SORRY, I HAVE TO KNOW...
NO!
HE LOOKED DEATH IN THE FACE!
I'M CLOSING THE DOOR!
WHATEVER YOU DO, DON'T LOOK INSIDE!
HE COULDN'T HELP HIMSELF...!

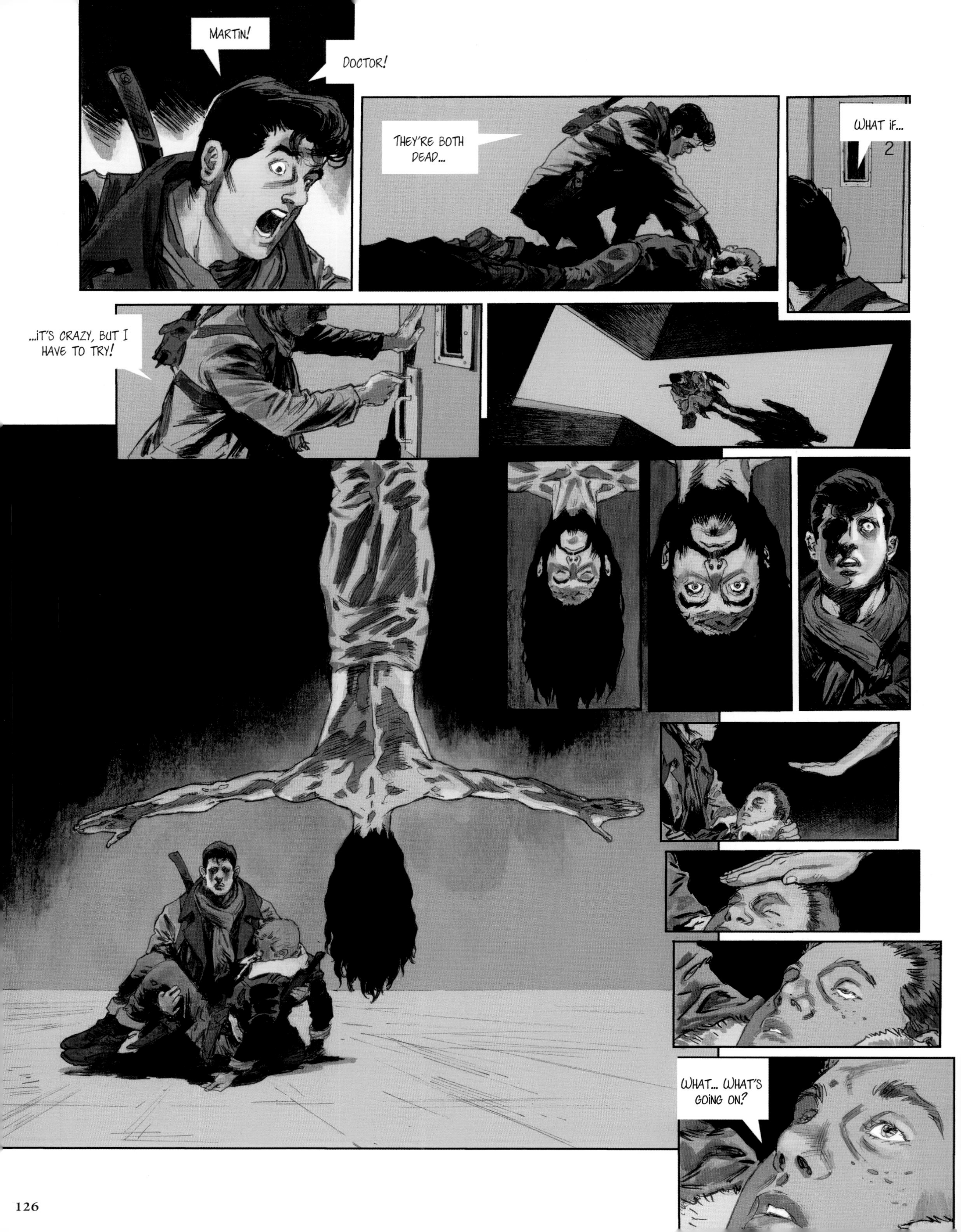
MARTIN!
DOCTOR!
THEY'RE BOTH DEAD...
WHAT IF...
...IT'S CRAZY, BUT I HAVE TO TRY!
WHAT... WHAT'S GOING ON?

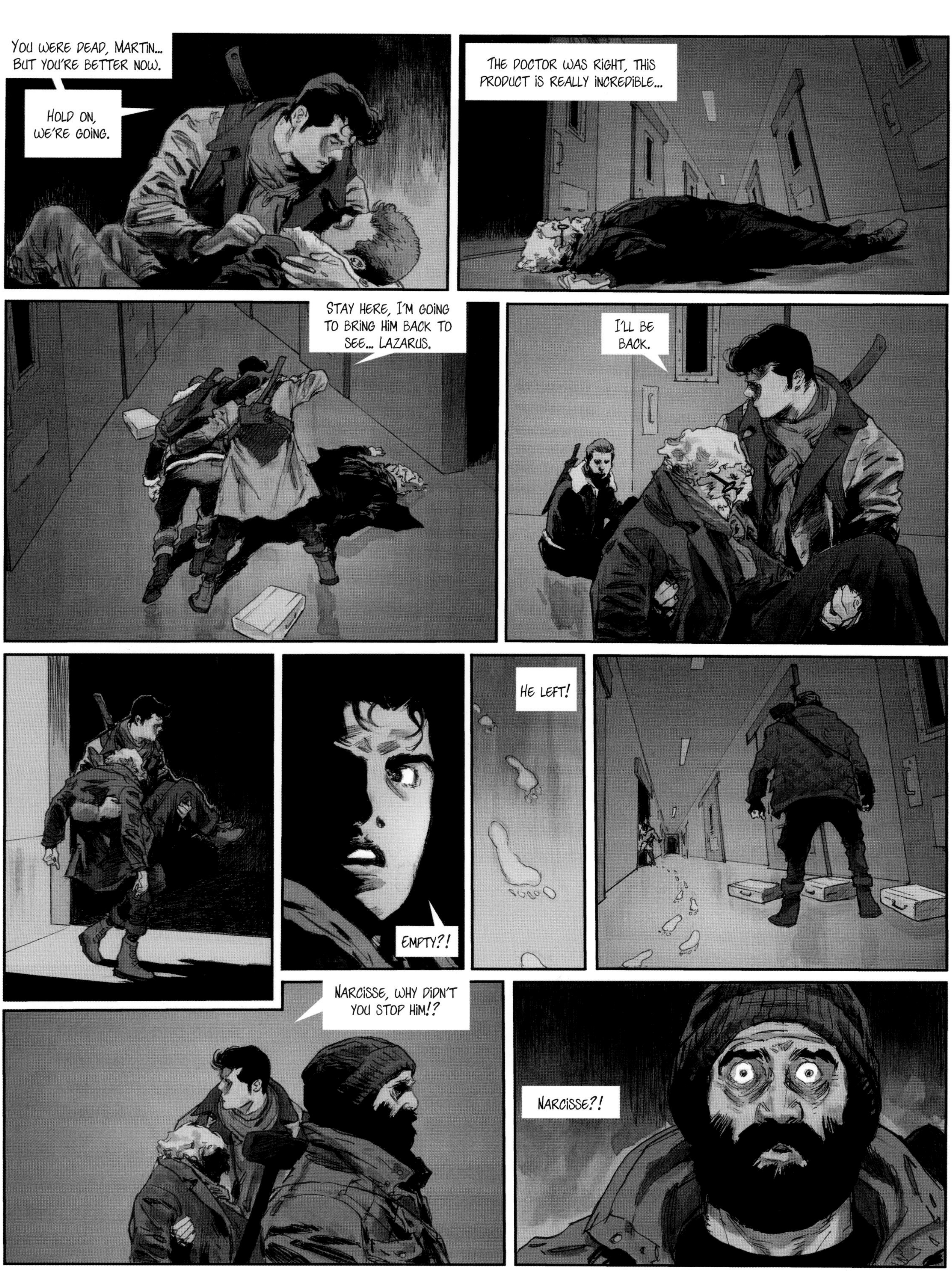
You were dead, Martin... But you're better now.
Hold on, we're going.
The doctor was right, this product is really incredible...
Stay here, I'm going to bring him back to see... Lazarus.
I'll be back.
Empty?!
He left!
Narcisse, why didn't you stop him!?
Narcisse?!

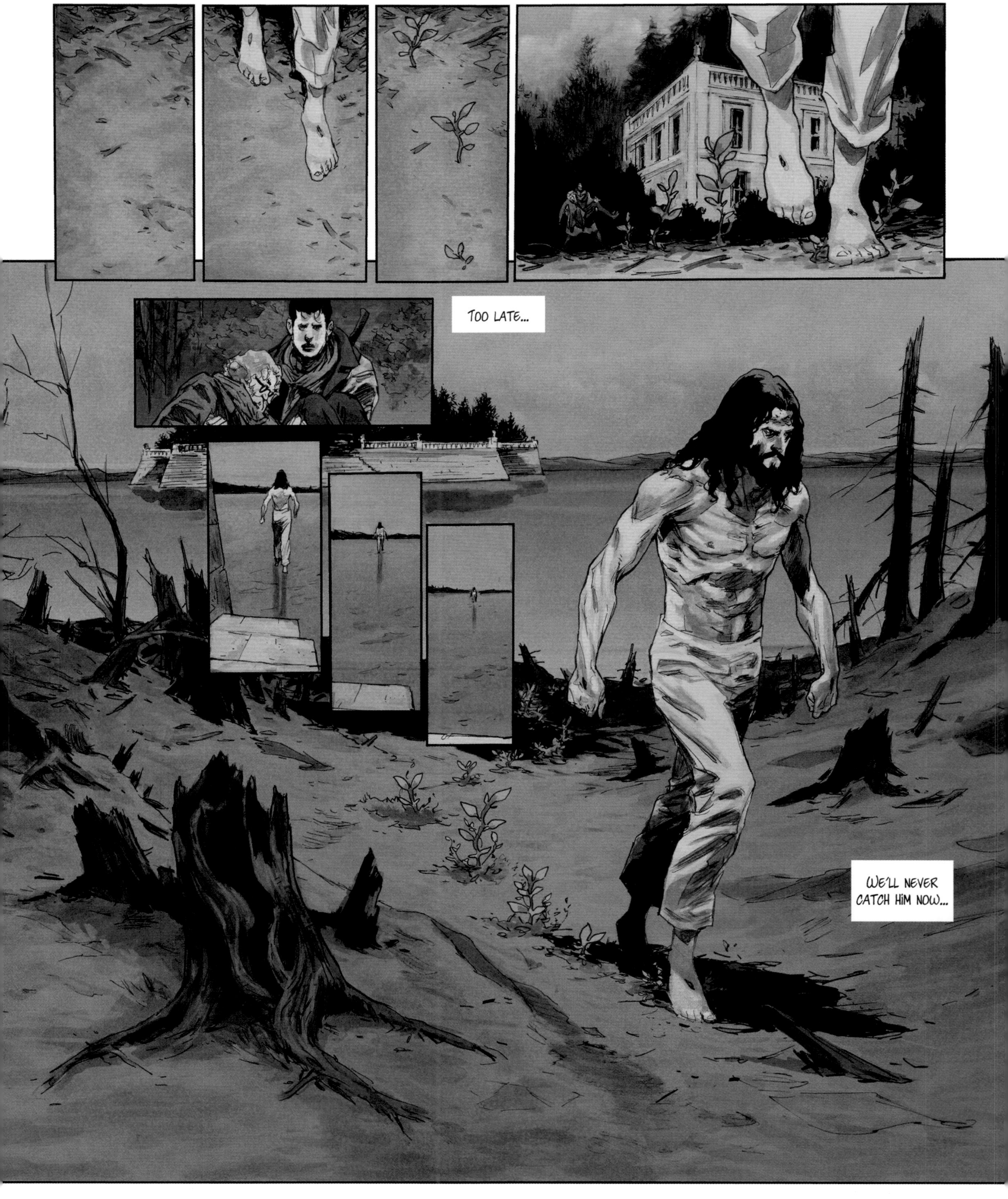
TOO LATE...
WE'LL NEVER CATCH HIM NOW...

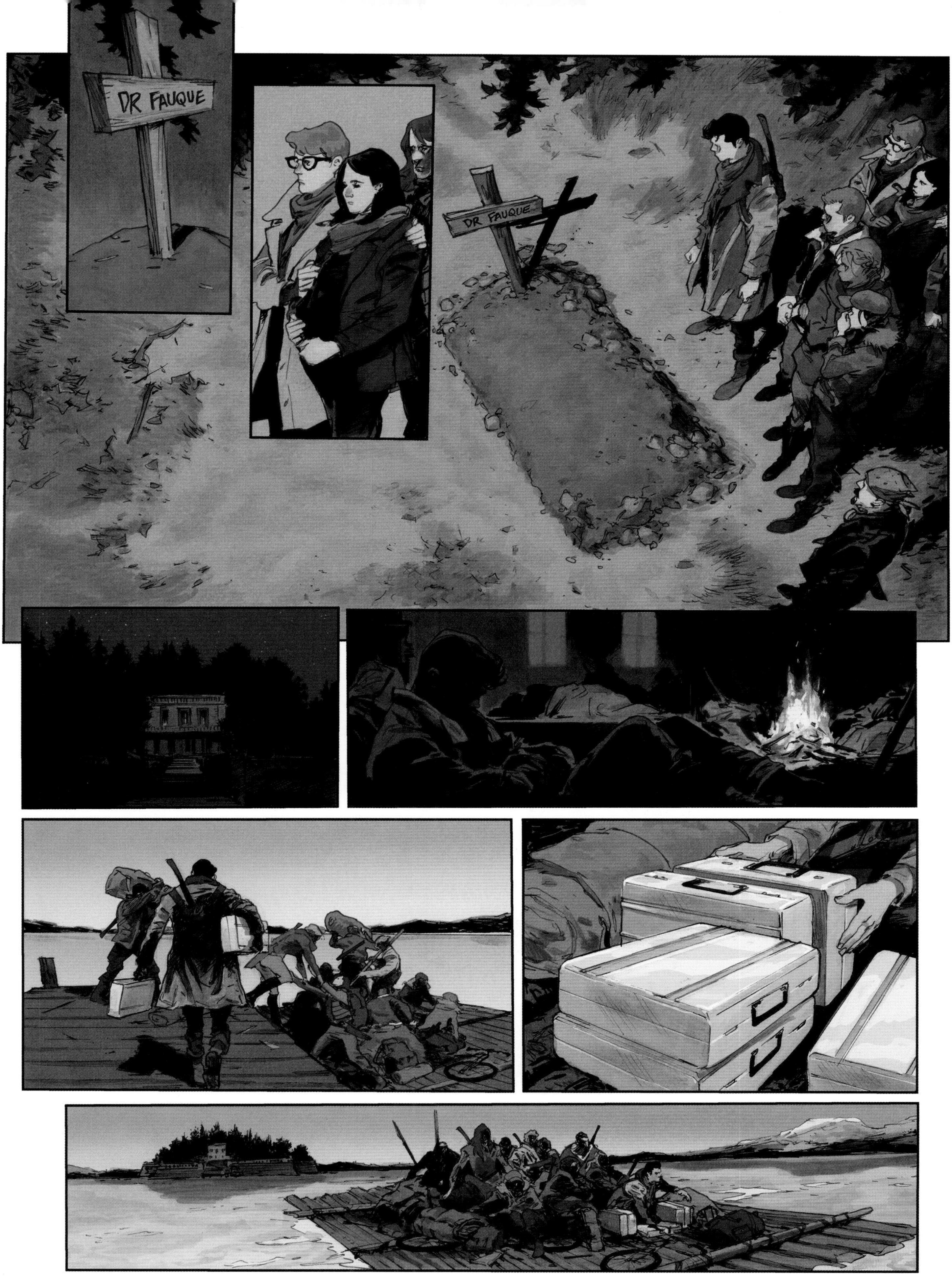
DR FAUQUE
DR FAUQUE

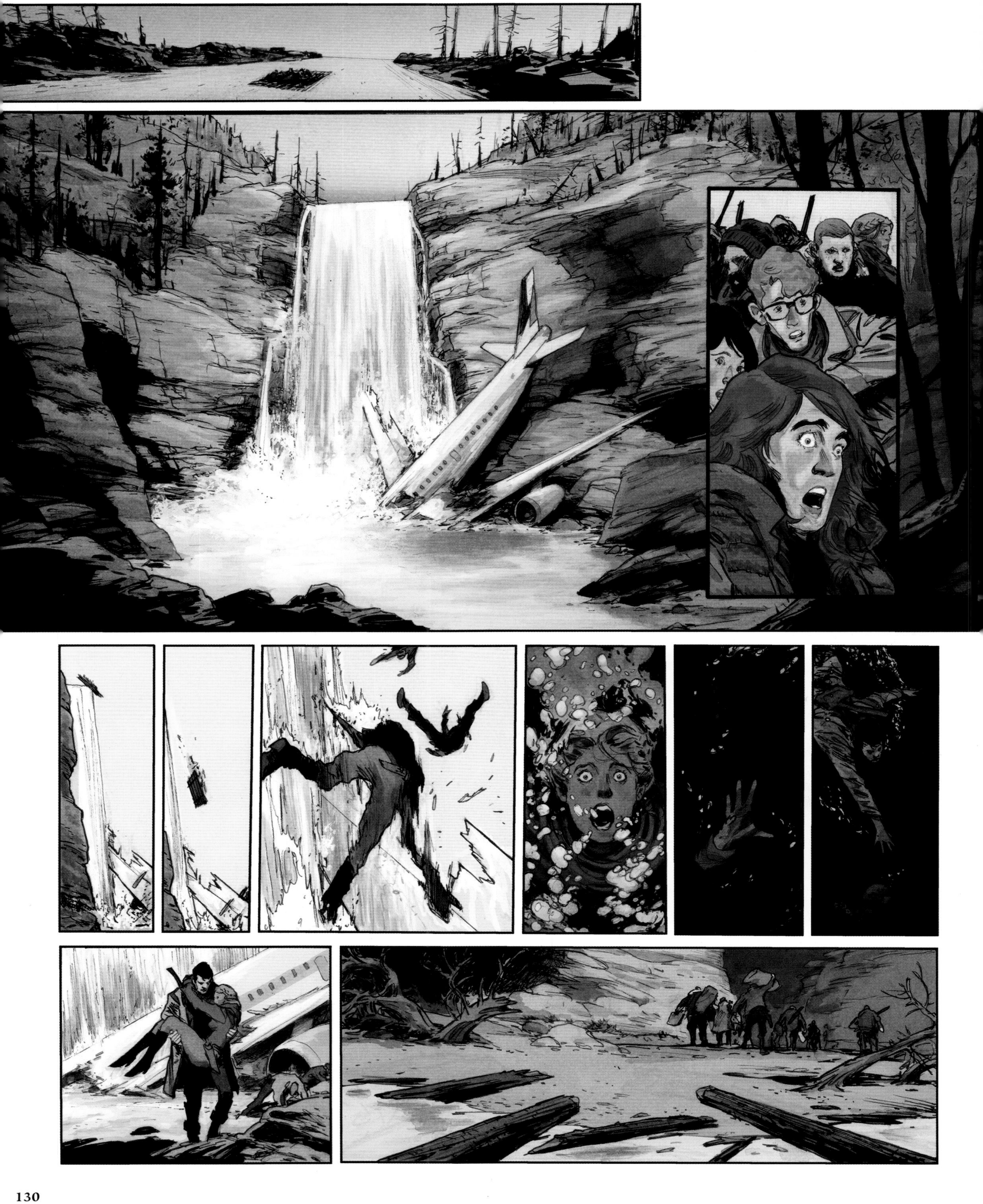

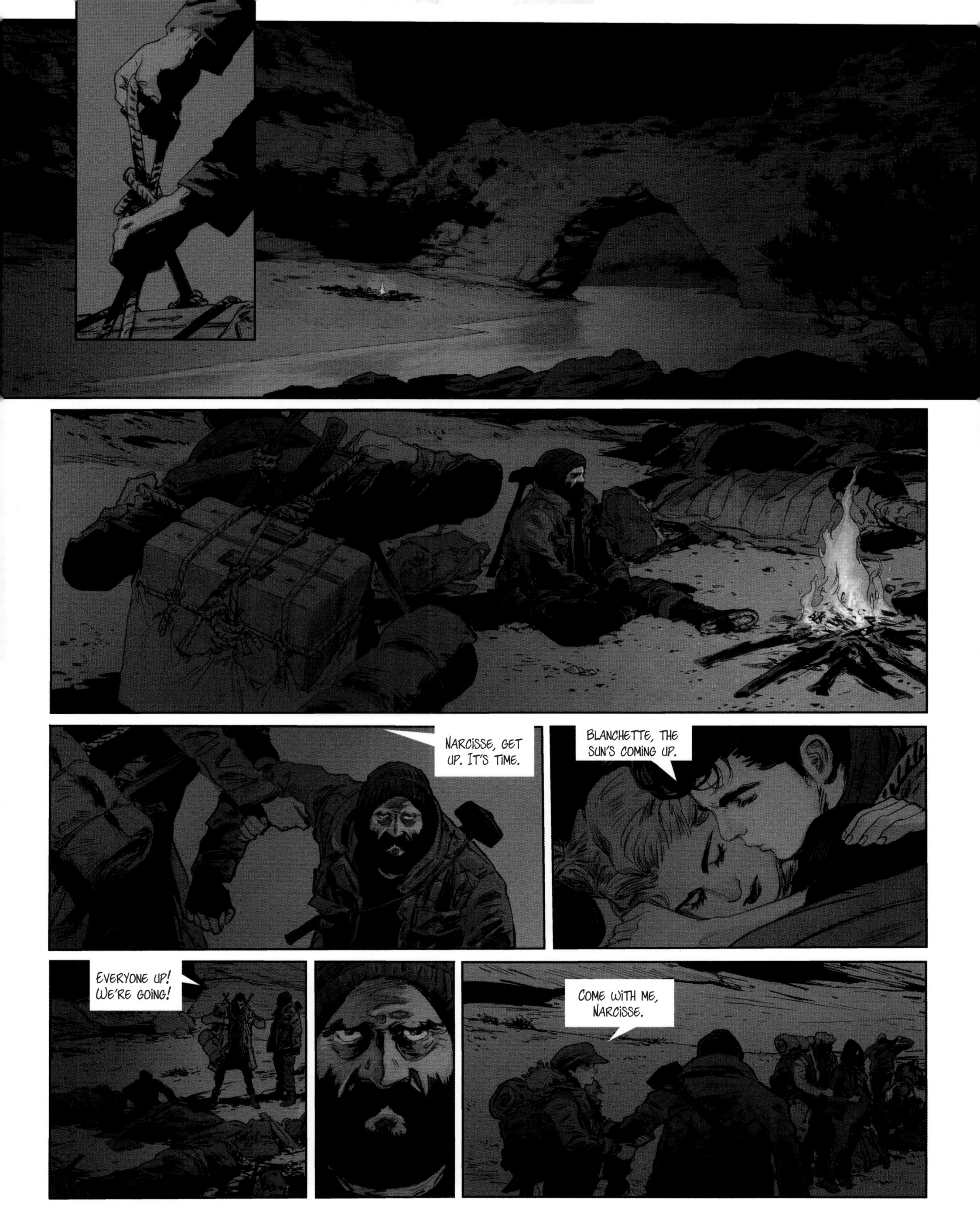
NARCISSE, GET UP. IT'S TIME.
BLANCHETTE, THE SUN'S COMING UP.
EVERYONE UP! WE'RE GOING!
COME WITH ME, NARCISSE.

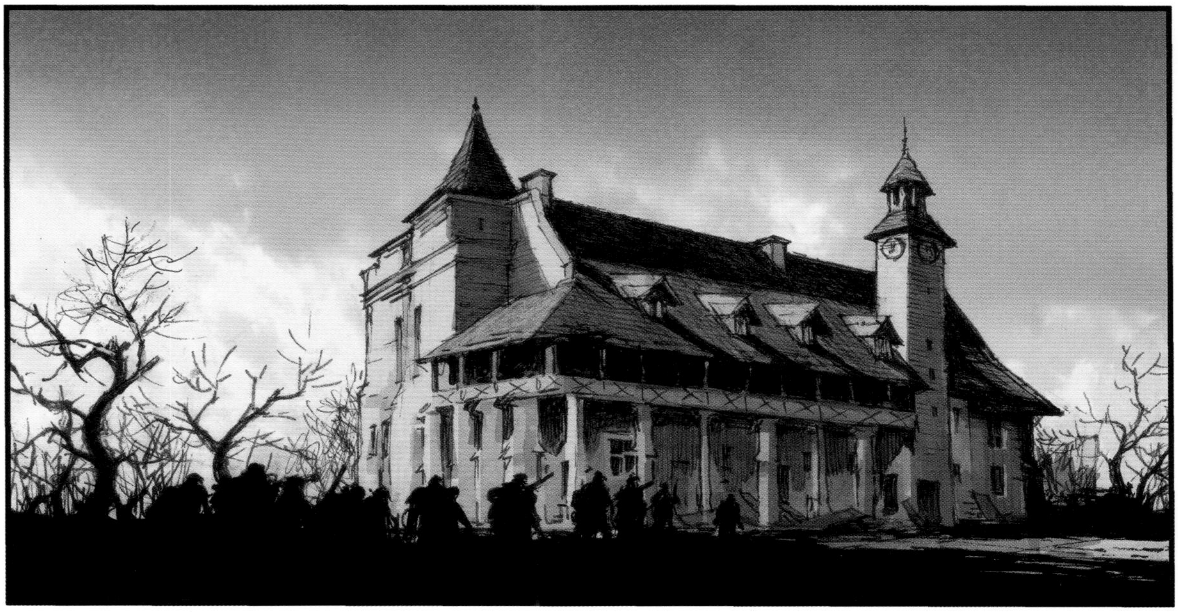

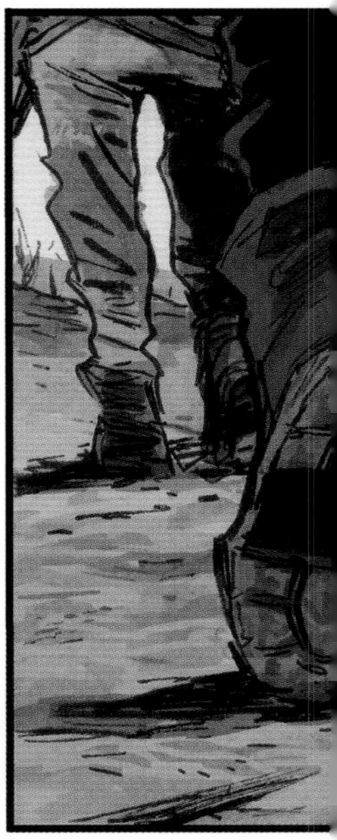

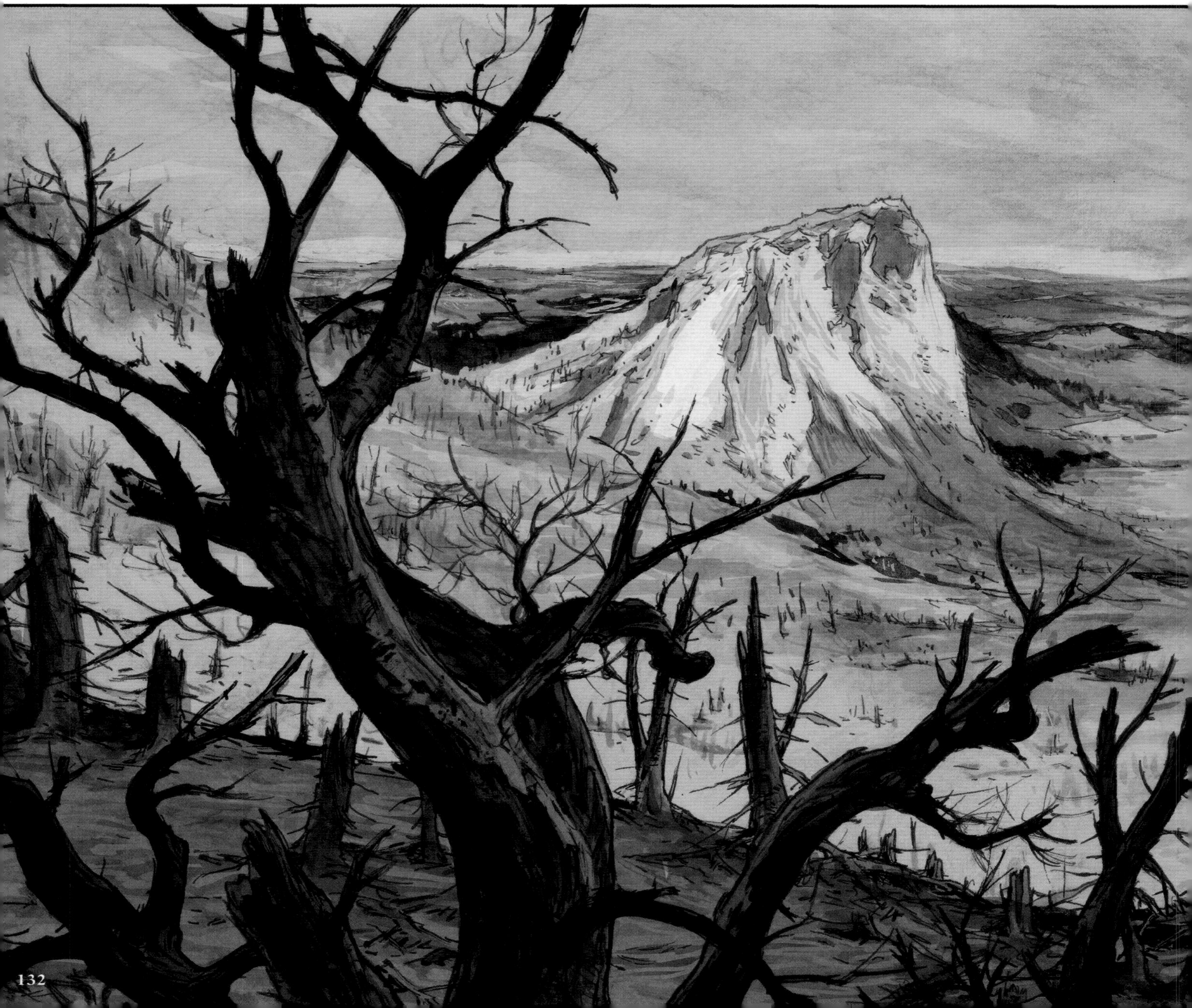

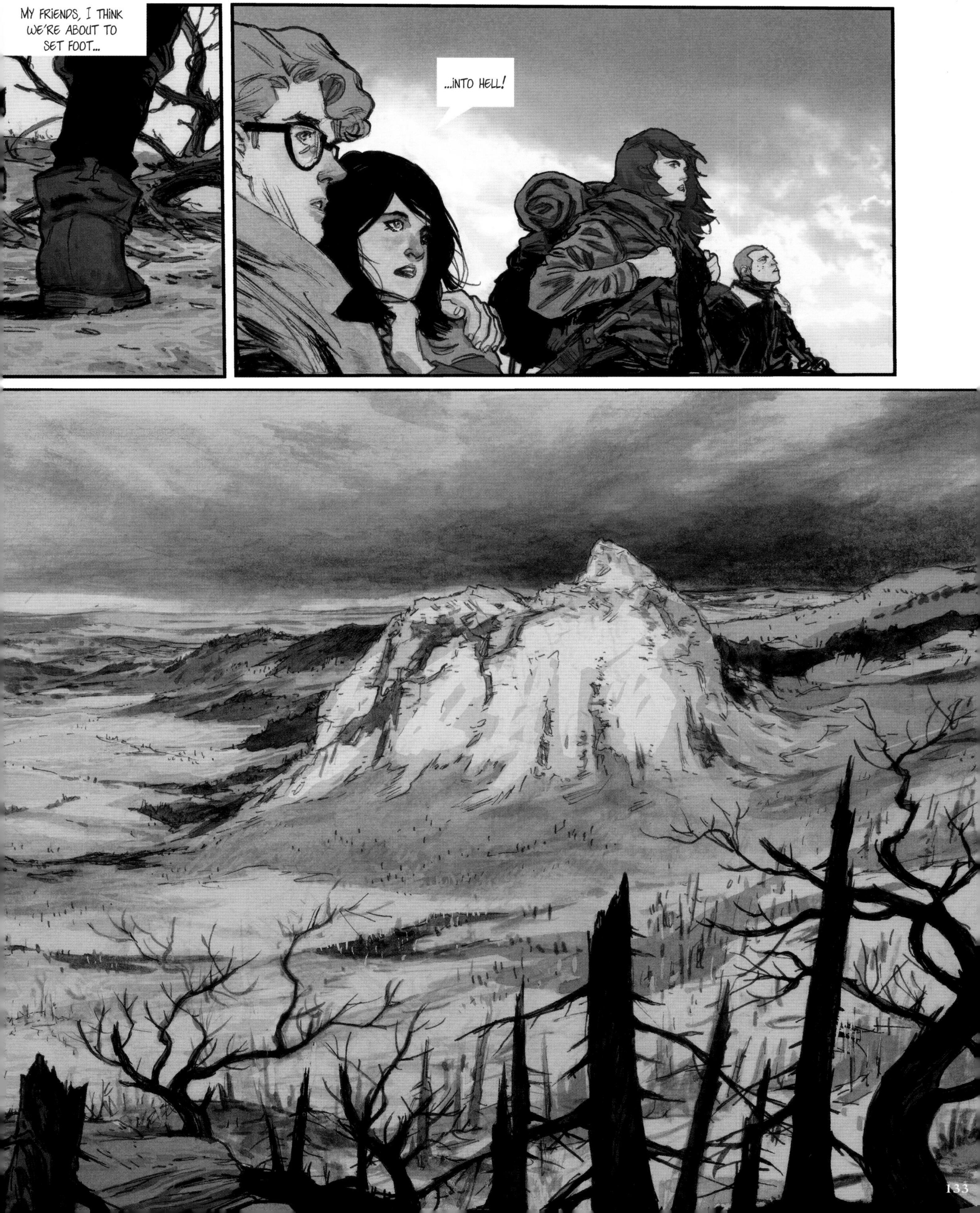
MY FRIENDS, I THINK WE'RE ABOUT TO SET FOOT...
...INTO HELL!

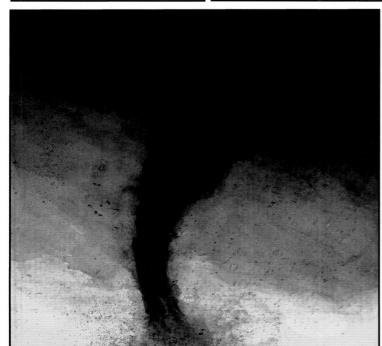

TAKE SHELTER BEHIND THE ROCKS!

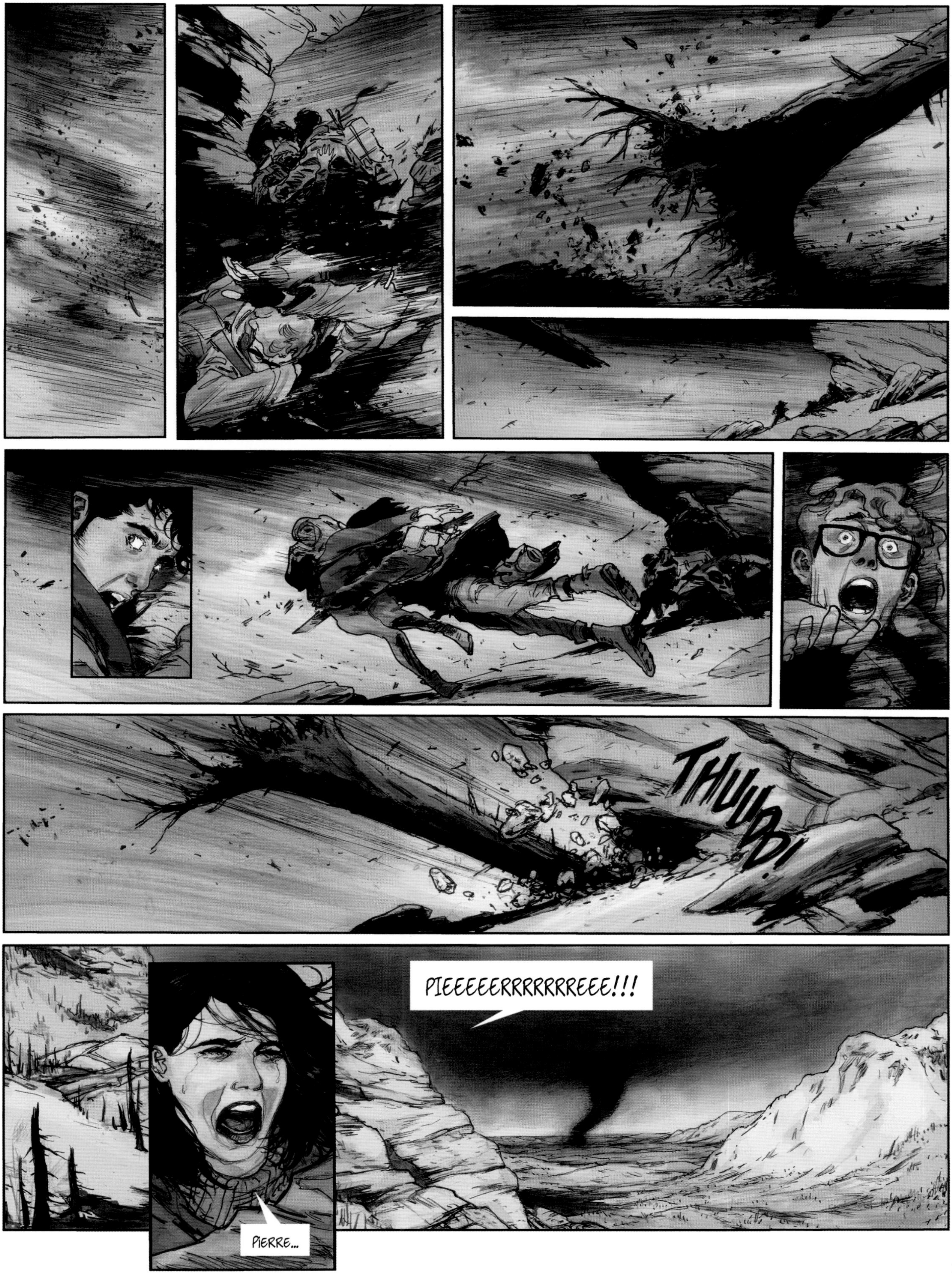
THUUDD!
PIEEEEERRRRRRREEE!!!
PIERRE...

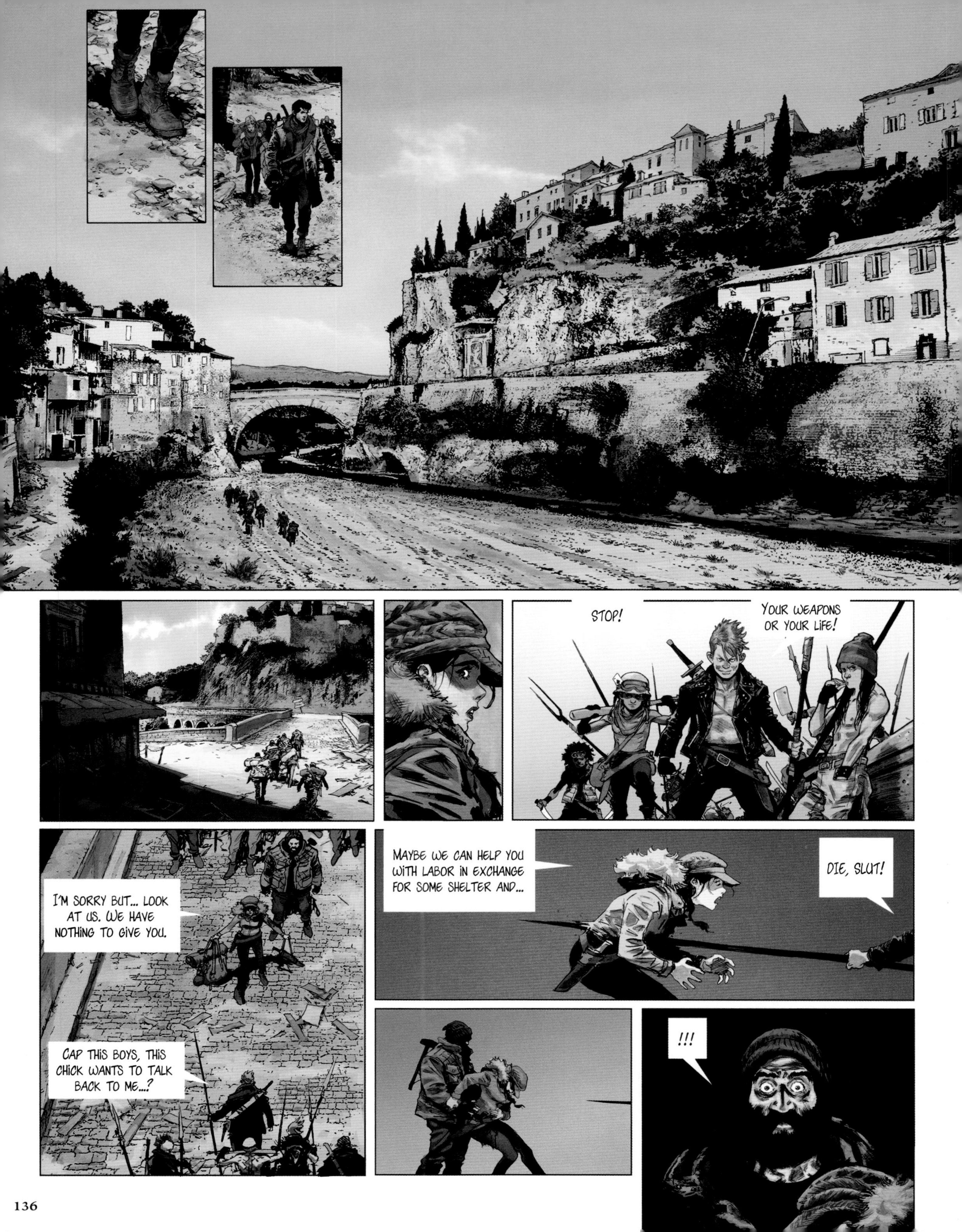
STOP!
YOUR WEAPONS OR YOUR LIFE!
I'M SORRY BUT... LOOK AT US. WE HAVE NOTHING TO GIVE YOU.
CAP THIS BOYS, THIS CHICK WANTS TO TALK BACK TO ME...?
MAYBE WE CAN HELP YOU WITH LABOR IN EXCHANGE FOR SOME SHELTER AND...
DIE, SLUT!
!!!

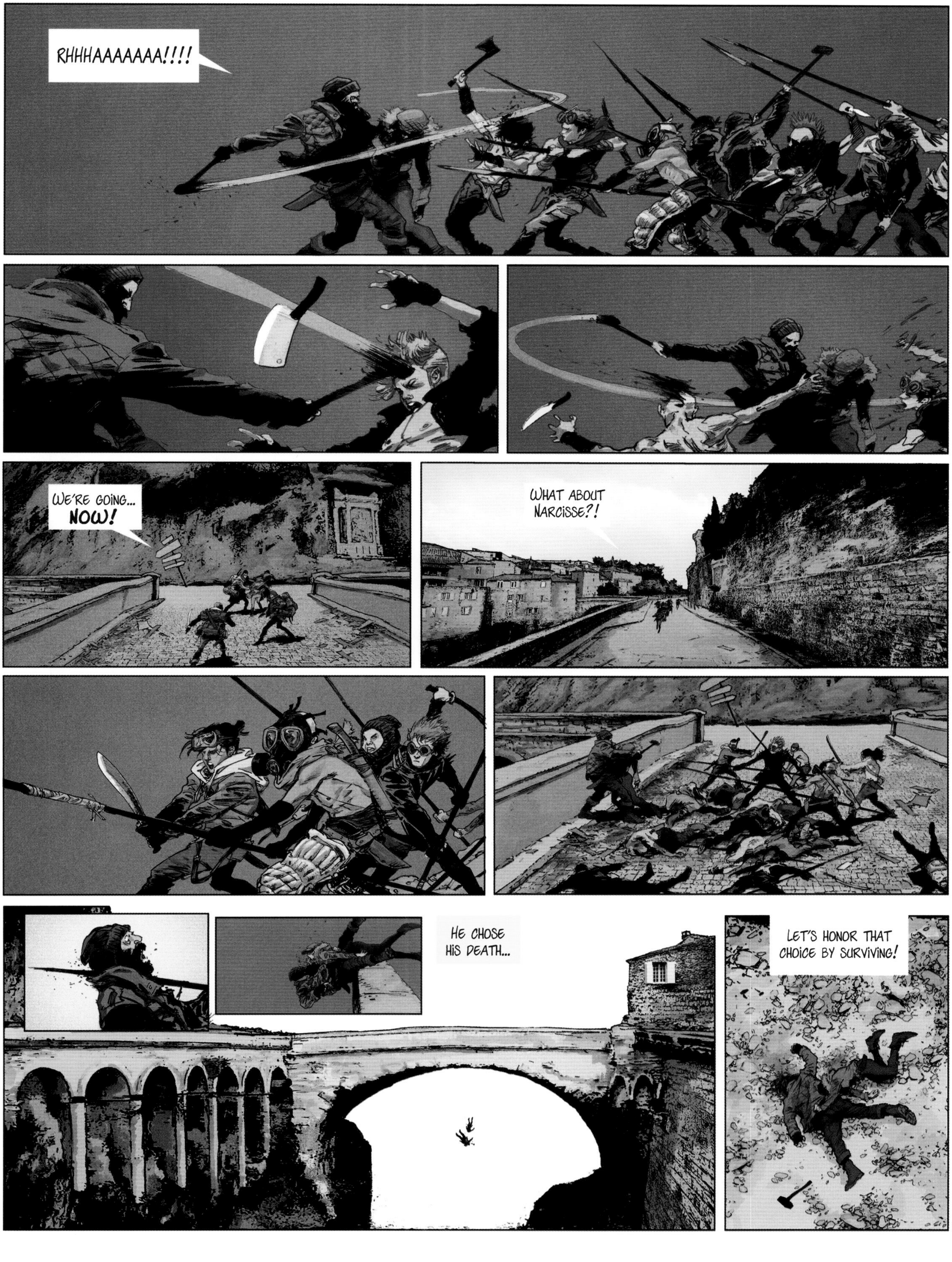
RHHHAAAAAAA!!!!
WE'RE GOING...
NOW!
WHAT ABOUT
NARCISSE?!
HE CHOSE
HIS DEATH...
LET'S HONOR THAT
CHOICE BY SURVIVING!

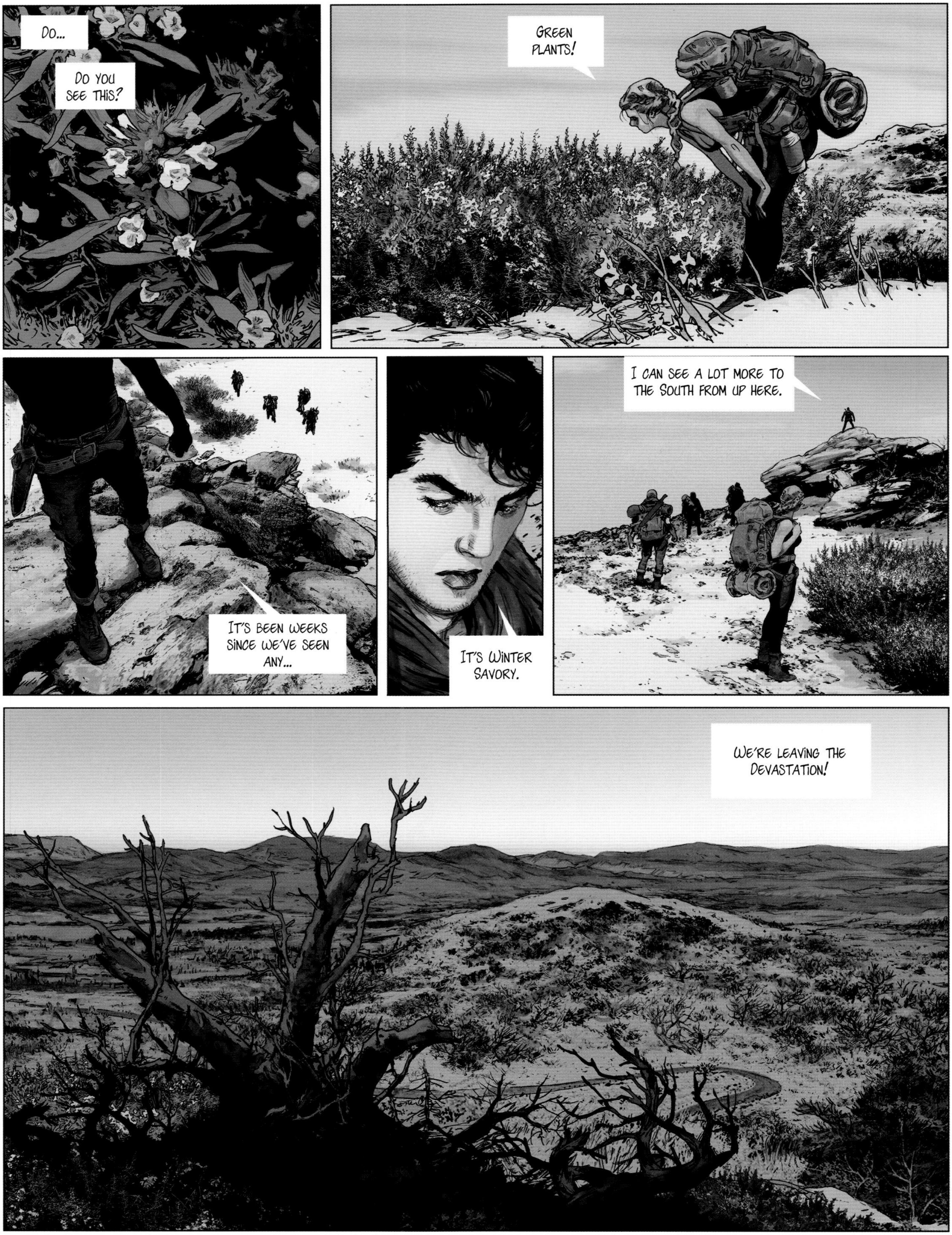
DO...
DO YOU SEE THIS?
GREEN PLANTS!
IT'S BEEN WEEKS SINCE WE'VE SEEN ANY...
IT'S WINTER SAVORY.
I CAN SEE A LOT MORE TO THE SOUTH FROM UP HERE.
WE'RE LEAVING THE DEVASTATION!

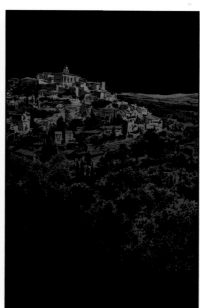

PARADISE...

I FORGOT THAT BEAUTIFUL PLACES LIKE THIS EXISTED...

NOT TO MENTION THE FOOD...!

IT WAS DELICIOUS.

THE RESTAURANT'S CELLARS WERE STILL COOL...

THE CHEF MUST HAVE LIKED TO KEEP THINGS FRESH...

HUH?!

WHAT THE HELL IS THIS?!

RHAAA!!!

?!

139

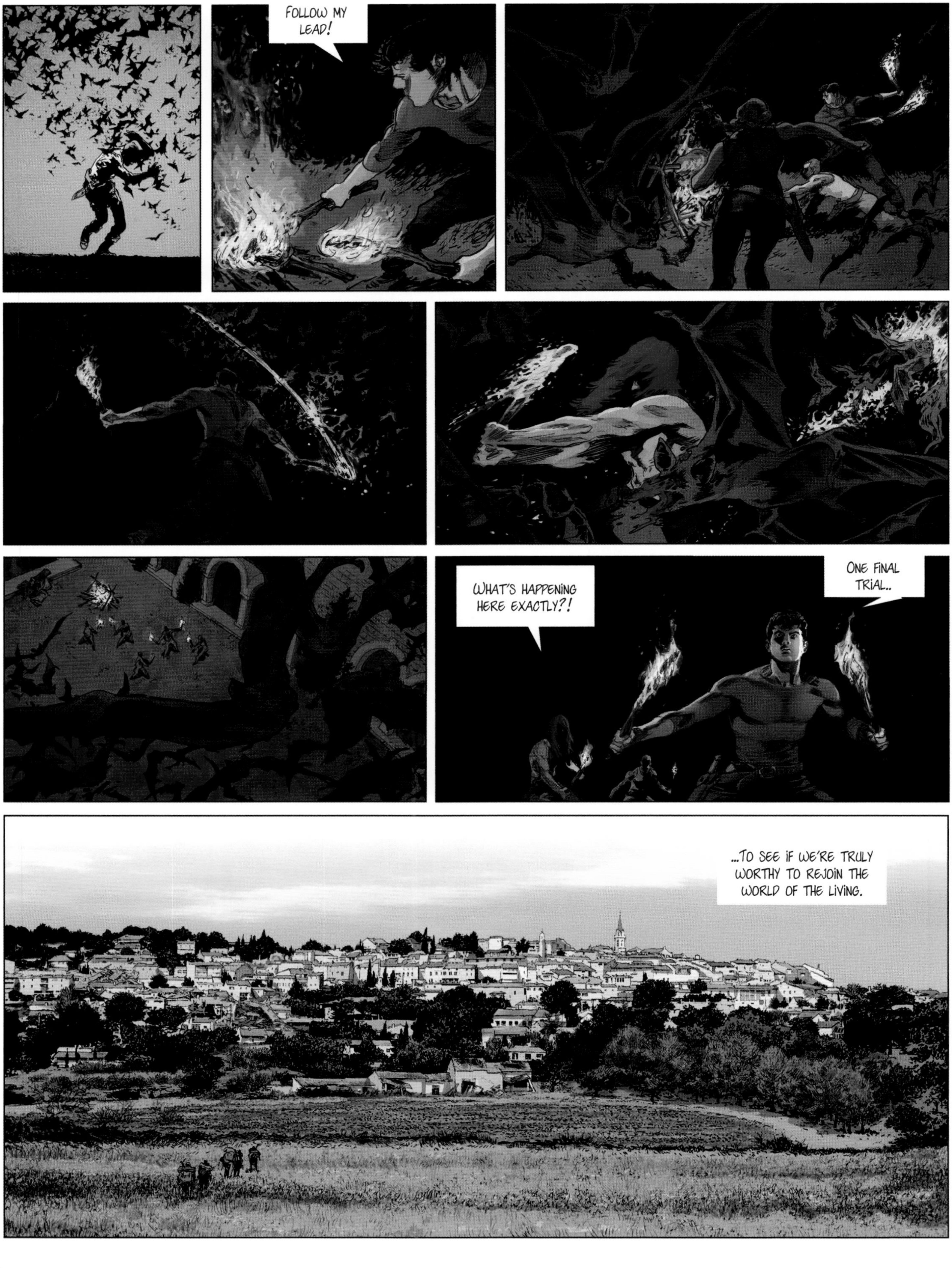
FOLLOW MY LEAD!
WHAT'S HAPPENING HERE EXACTLY?!
ONE FINAL TRIAL..
...TO SEE IF WE'RE TRULY WORTHY TO REJOIN THE WORLD OF THE LIVING.

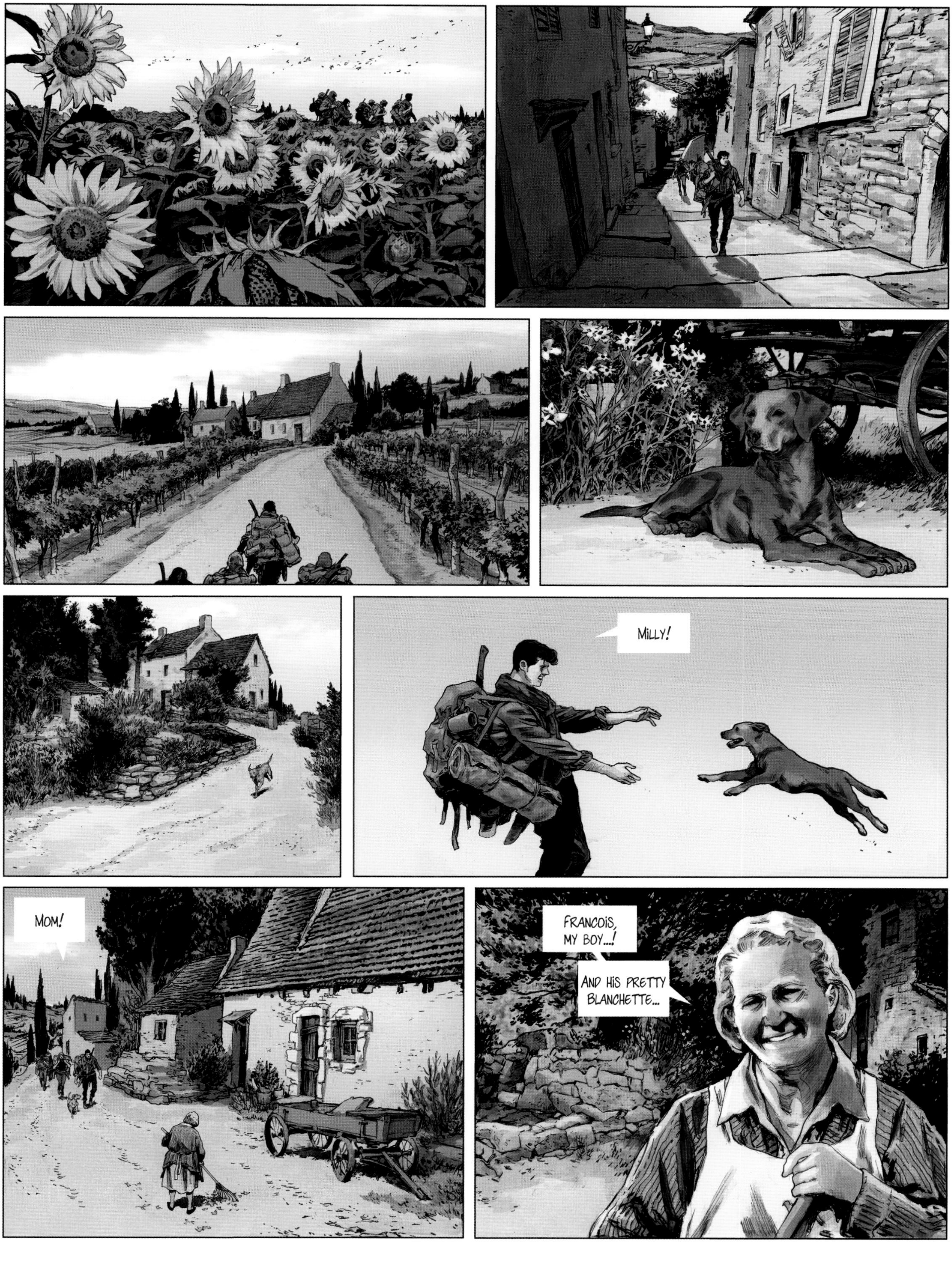
MILLY!
MOM!
FRANCOIS, MY BOY...!
AND HIS PRETTY BLANCHETTE...

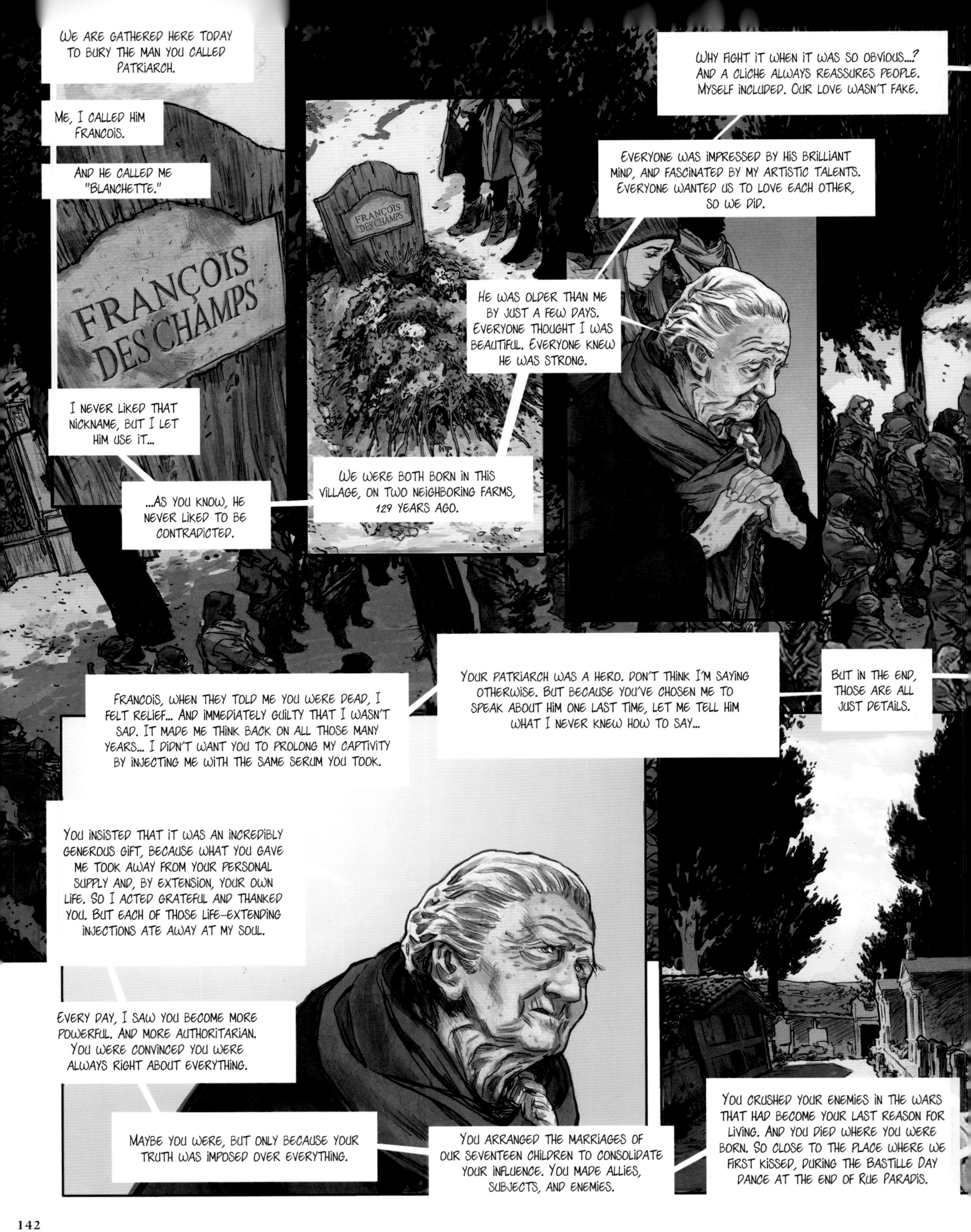
WE ARE GATHERED HERE TODAY TO BURY THE MAN YOU CALLED PATRIARCH.
ME, I CALLED HIM FRANCOIS.
AND HE CALLED ME "BLANCHETTE."
FRANÇOIS DES CHAMPS
I NEVER LIKED THAT NICKNAME, BUT I LET HIM USE IT...
...AS YOU KNOW, HE NEVER LIKED TO BE CONTRADICTED.
FRANÇOIS DES CHAMPS
WE WERE BOTH BORN IN THIS VILLAGE, ON TWO NEIGHBORING FARMS, 129 YEARS AGO.
HE WAS OLDER THAN ME BY JUST A FEW DAYS. EVERYONE THOUGHT I WAS BEAUTIFUL. EVERYONE KNEW HE WAS STRONG.
EVERYONE WAS IMPRESSED BY HIS BRILLIANT MIND, AND FASCINATED BY MY ARTISTIC TALENTS. EVERYONE WANTED US TO LOVE EACH OTHER, SO WE DID.
WHY FIGHT IT WHEN IT WAS SO OBVIOUS...? AND A CLICHE ALWAYS REASSURES PEOPLE. MYSELF INCLUDED. OUR LOVE WASN'T FAKE.
YOUR PATRIARCH WAS A HERO. DON'T THINK I'M SAYING OTHERWISE. BUT BECAUSE YOU'VE CHOSEN ME TO SPEAK ABOUT HIM ONE LAST TIME, LET ME TELL HIM WHAT I NEVER KNEW HOW TO SAY...
BUT IN THE END, THOSE ARE ALL JUST DETAILS.
FRANCOIS, WHEN THEY TOLD ME YOU WERE DEAD, I FELT RELIEF... AND IMMEDIATELY GUILTY THAT I WASN'T SAD. IT MADE ME THINK BACK ON ALL THOSE MANY YEARS... I DIDN'T WANT YOU TO PROLONG MY CAPTIVITY BY INJECTING ME WITH THE SAME SERUM YOU TOOK.
YOU INSISTED THAT IT WAS AN INCREDIBLY GENEROUS GIFT, BECAUSE WHAT YOU GAVE ME TOOK AWAY FROM YOUR PERSONAL SUPPLY AND, BY EXTENSION, YOUR OWN LIFE. SO I ACTED GRATEFUL AND THANKED YOU. BUT EACH OF THOSE LIFE-EXTENDING INJECTIONS ATE AWAY AT MY SOUL.
EVERY DAY, I SAW YOU BECOME MORE POWERFUL. AND MORE AUTHORITARIAN. YOU WERE CONVINCED YOU WERE ALWAYS RIGHT ABOUT EVERYTHING.
MAYBE YOU WERE, BUT ONLY BECAUSE YOUR TRUTH WAS IMPOSED OVER EVERYTHING.
YOU ARRANGED THE MARRIAGES OF OUR SEVENTEEN CHILDREN TO CONSOLIDATE YOUR INFLUENCE. YOU MADE ALLIES, SUBJECTS, AND ENEMIES.
YOU CRUSHED YOUR ENEMIES IN THE WARS THAT HAD BECOME YOUR LAST REASON FOR LIVING. AND YOU DIED WHERE YOU WERE BORN. SO CLOSE TO THE PLACE WHERE WE FIRST KISSED, DURING THE BASTILLE DAY DANCE AT THE END OF RUE PARADIS.

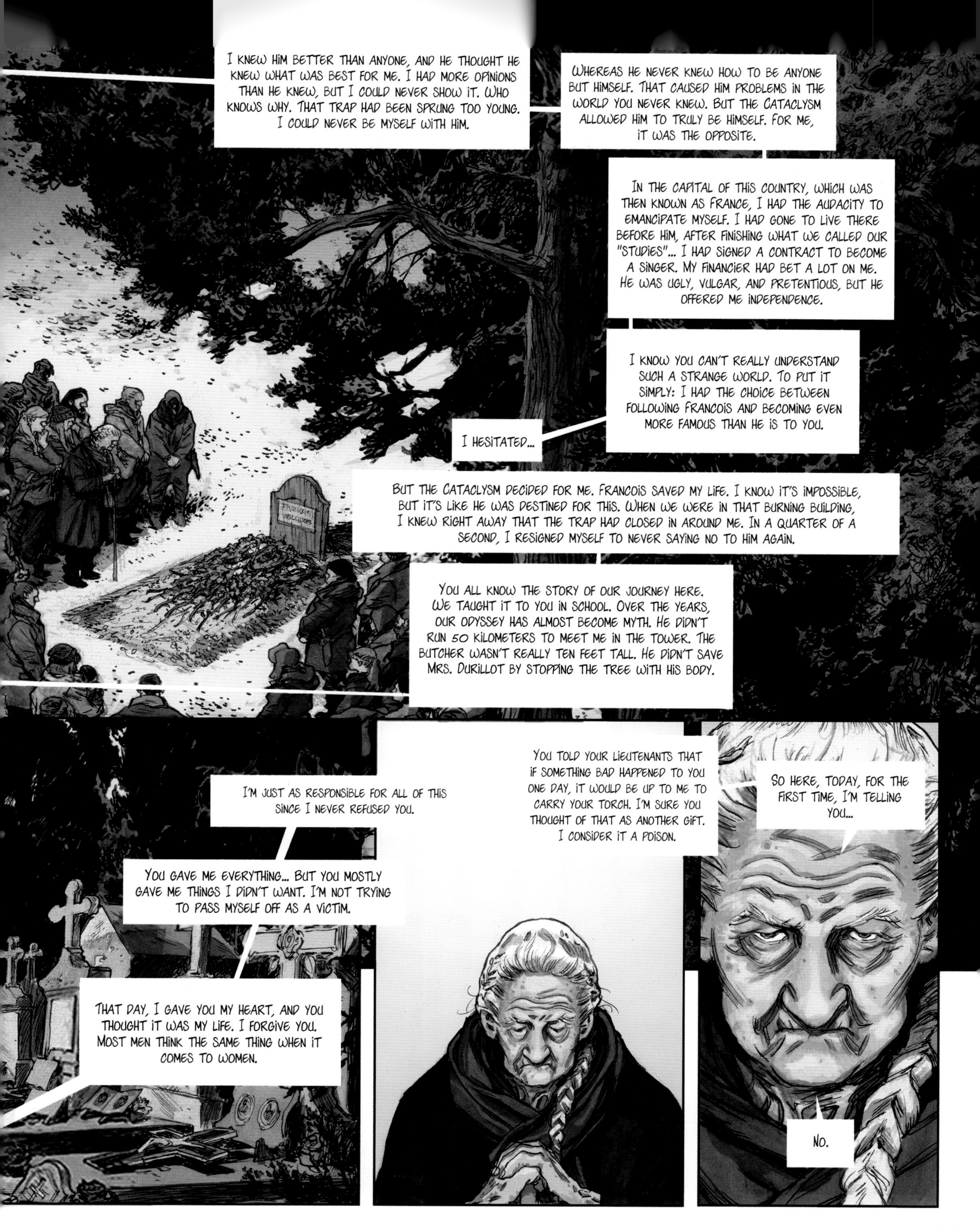
I KNEW HIM BETTER THAN ANYONE, AND HE THOUGHT HE KNEW WHAT WAS BEST FOR ME. I HAD MORE OPINIONS THAN HE KNEW, BUT I COULD NEVER SHOW IT. WHO KNOWS WHY. THAT TRAP HAD BEEN SPRUNG TOO YOUNG. I COULD NEVER BE MYSELF WITH HIM.
WHEREAS HE NEVER KNEW HOW TO BE ANYONE BUT HIMSELF. THAT CAUSED HIM PROBLEMS IN THE WORLD YOU NEVER KNEW. BUT THE CATACLYSM ALLOWED HIM TO TRULY BE HIMSELF. FOR ME, IT WAS THE OPPOSITE.
IN THE CAPITAL OF THIS COUNTRY, WHICH WAS THEN KNOWN AS FRANCE, I HAD THE AUDACITY TO EMANCIPATE MYSELF. I HAD GONE TO LIVE THERE BEFORE HIM, AFTER FINISHING WHAT WE CALLED OUR "STUDIES"... I HAD SIGNED A CONTRACT TO BECOME A SINGER. MY FINANCIER HAD BET A LOT ON ME. HE WAS UGLY, VULGAR, AND PRETENTIOUS, BUT HE OFFERED ME INDEPENDENCE.
I KNOW YOU CAN'T REALLY UNDERSTAND SUCH A STRANGE WORLD. TO PUT IT SIMPLY: I HAD THE CHOICE BETWEEN FOLLOWING FRANCOIS AND BECOMING EVEN MORE FAMOUS THAN HE IS TO YOU.
I HESITATED...
BUT THE CATACLYSM DECIDED FOR ME. FRANCOIS SAVED MY LIFE. I KNOW IT'S IMPOSSIBLE, BUT IT'S LIKE HE WAS DESTINED FOR THIS. WHEN WE WERE IN THAT BURNING BUILDING, I KNEW RIGHT AWAY THAT THE TRAP HAD CLOSED IN AROUND ME. IN A QUARTER OF A SECOND, I RESIGNED MYSELF TO NEVER SAYING NO TO HIM AGAIN.
YOU ALL KNOW THE STORY OF OUR JOURNEY HERE. WE TAUGHT IT TO YOU IN SCHOOL. OVER THE YEARS, OUR ODYSSEY HAS ALMOST BECOME MYTH. HE DIDN'T RUN 50 KILOMETERS TO MEET ME IN THE TOWER. THE BUTCHER WASN'T REALLY TEN FEET TALL. HE DIDN'T SAVE MRS. DURILLOT BY STOPPING THE TREE WITH HIS BODY.
I'M JUST AS RESPONSIBLE FOR ALL OF THIS SINCE I NEVER REFUSED YOU.
YOU GAVE ME EVERYTHING... BUT YOU MOSTLY GAVE ME THINGS I DIDN'T WANT. I'M NOT TRYING TO PASS MYSELF OFF AS A VICTIM.
THAT DAY, I GAVE YOU MY HEART, AND YOU THOUGHT IT WAS MY LIFE. I FORGIVE YOU. MOST MEN THINK THE SAME THING WHEN IT COMES TO WOMEN.
YOU TOLD YOUR LIEUTENANTS THAT IF SOMETHING BAD HAPPENED TO YOU ONE DAY, IT WOULD BE UP TO ME TO CARRY YOUR TORCH. I'M SURE YOU THOUGHT OF THAT AS ANOTHER GIFT. I CONSIDER IT A POISON.
SO HERE, TODAY, FOR THE FIRST TIME, I'M TELLING YOU...
NO.

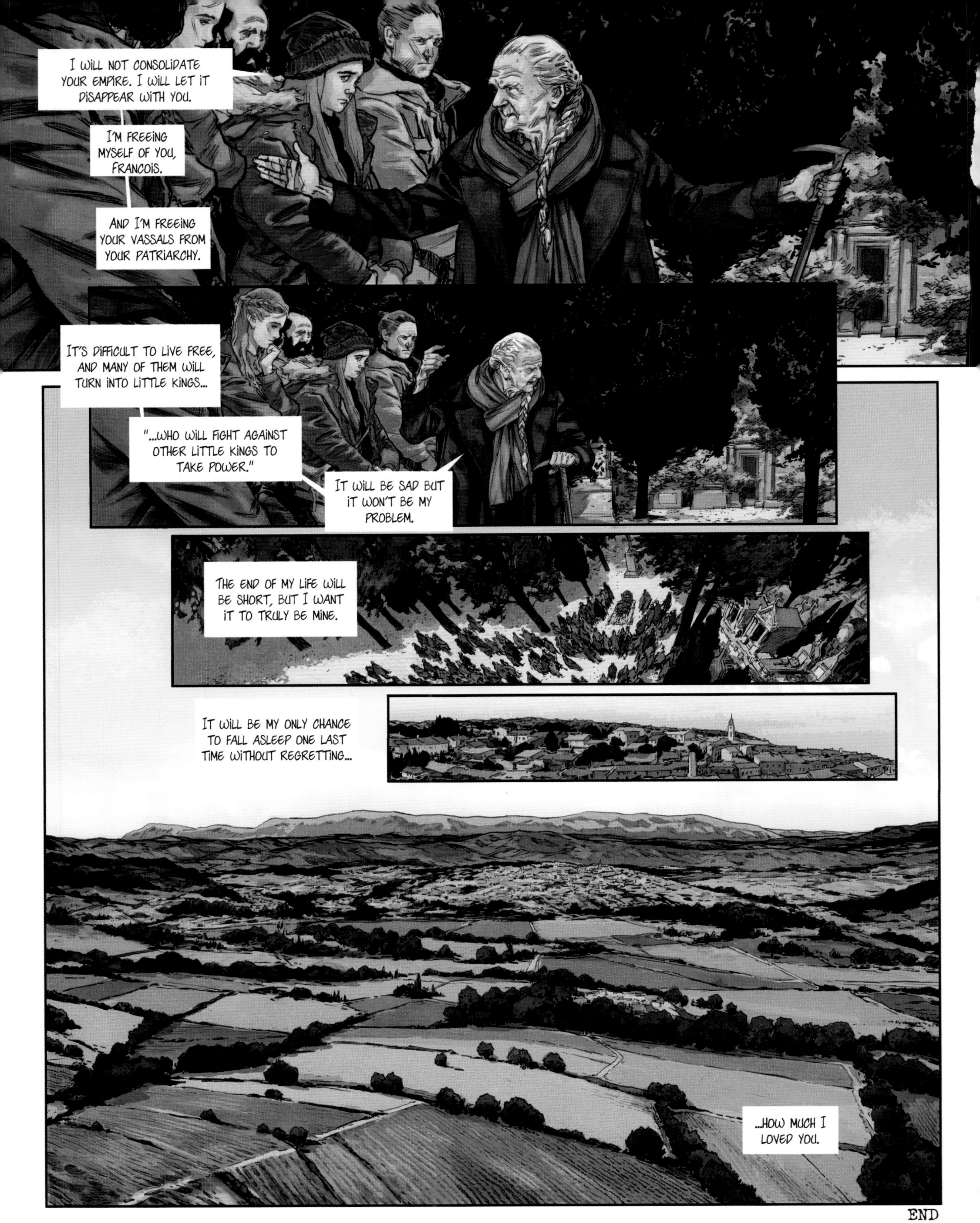
I WILL NOT CONSOLIDATE YOUR EMPIRE. I WILL LET IT DISAPPEAR WITH YOU.
I'M FREEING MYSELF OF YOU, FRANCOIS.
AND I'M FREEING YOUR VASSALS FROM YOUR PATRIARCHY.
IT'S DIFFICULT TO LIVE FREE, AND MANY OF THEM WILL TURN INTO LITTLE KINGS...
"...WHO WILL FIGHT AGAINST OTHER LITTLE KINGS TO TAKE POWER."
IT WILL BE SAD BUT IT WON'T BE MY PROBLEM.
THE END OF MY LIFE WILL BE SHORT, BUT I WANT IT TO TRULY BE MINE.
IT WILL BE MY ONLY CHANCE TO FALL ASLEEP ONE LAST TIME WITHOUT REGRETTING...
...HOW MUCH I LOVED YOU.

END

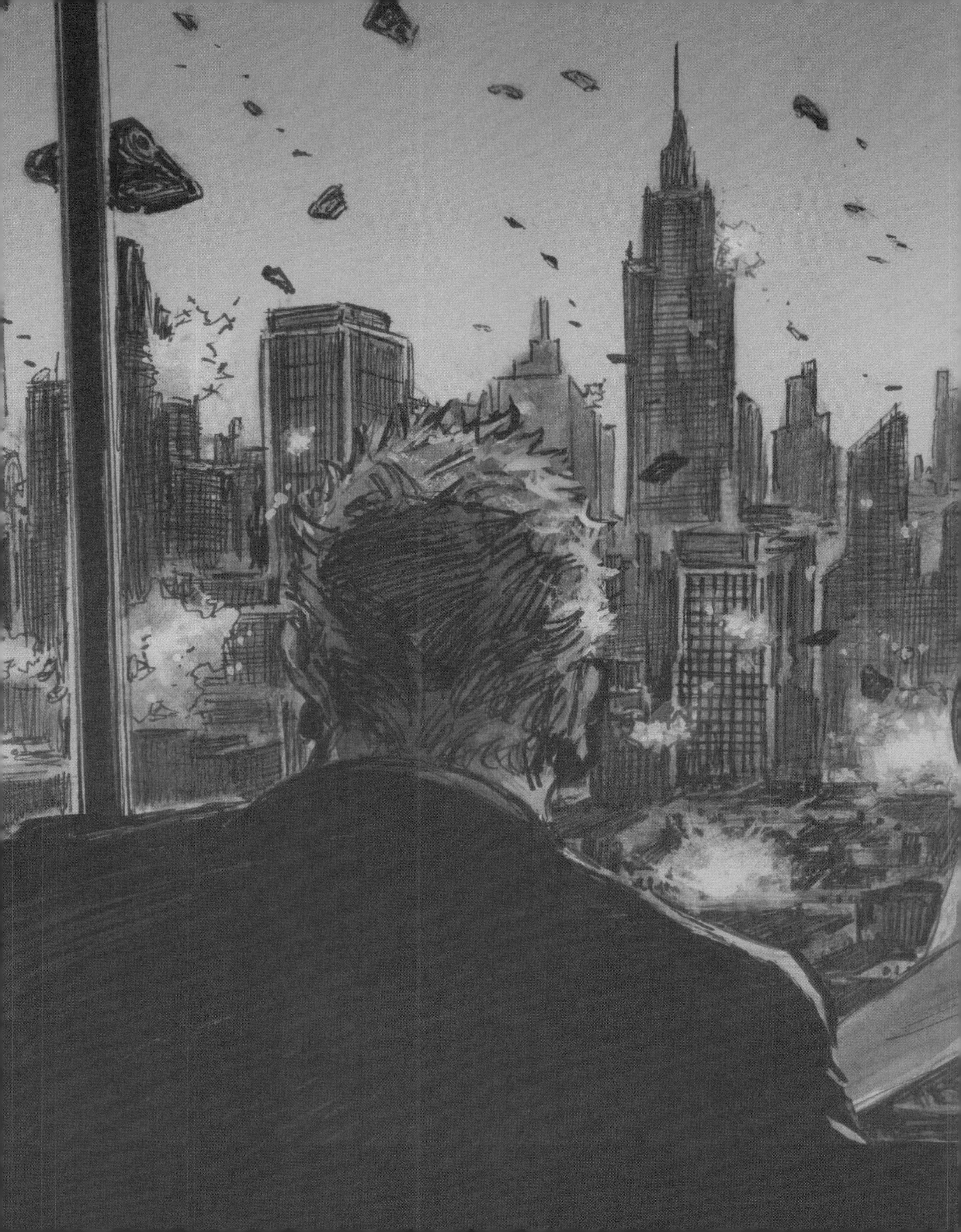